# SPENCER
# CHRISTIAN'S
# ELECTING
# OUR
# GOVERMENT

# ELECTING
# OUR
# GOVERMENT

BY
## SPENCER CHRISTIAN
WITH TOM BIRACREE

ST. MARTIN'S GRIFFIN 🅼 NEW YORK

Published by Thomas Dunne Books
An imprint of St. Martin's Press

ATD Media Book
ELECTING OUR GOVERNMENT Copyright 1996 by Spencer Christian. All rights
reserved. Printed in the United States of America. No part of this book may be
used or reproduced in any manner whatsoever without written permission except
in case of brief quotations embodied in critical articles or reviews. For information,
address St. Martin's Press, 175 Fifth Avenue, New York, N.Y. 10010.

All photographs courtesy of Ida Mae Astute.

Design by FIGURE 5 DESIGN

ISBN 0-312-14324-9

First St. Martin's Griffin Edition: July 1996

10 9 8 7 6 5 4 3 2 1

# DEDICATION

For my wife Diane, and my children, Jason and Jessica, whose patience and inspiration guided through me the completion of this project.
—Spencer Christian

For my son, Ryan, whose compassion for others gives his parents great hope for the future.
—Tom Biracree

# ACKNOWLEDGMENTS

This book was originated by Tom Dunne and Jeremy Katz of St. Martin's Press, whose editorial wisdom and guidance is unparalleled. Tony Seidl piloted this project with his usual skill and tact, and John P. Holms brilliantly handled the multi-faceted tasks involved in getting the book into production. The eye-popping design is the product of the talented team at Figure 5 Design, especially Tim Cooper, Lorenz Skeeter, and Carl Rips Meltzer.

I have admired many great American leaders, but two men in particular fostered my passion for politics and my deep respect for our political system. One is Henry Howell, whose 1969 Virginia gubernatorial campaign was the first in which I volunteered. Although Howell was not elected, I came away with great admiration for the man and for the experience. The other is my personal friend, former Virginia governor Doug Wilder. The grandson of a slave, Wilder's historic achievement in becoming the nation's first elected black governor was a great inspiration to me.

# CONTENTS

# PREFACE

Viewers of ABC's *Good Morning America* know Spencer Christian as an expert weatherman. So it may come as a surprise to learn that he is also an expert on politics and government.

I became aware of this while appearing on *Good Morning America* as the network's political director. Twice every hour, there's a segment of time in which many of the affiliate stations cut away from the network broadcast to present their local news. But some stations stay with the network during the "cutaway" period and that's when Spencer, Charlie Gibson, and Joan Lunden have an informal chat that is totally spontaneous and unrehearsed. I was invited to join them one morning in a free-wheeling discussion of the political campaign and that's when I realized how much Spencer knew and how well he understood the process.

I've also come to admire his skill at explaining it and his ability to focus on what's really important. That's what makes this book so valuable. It can be an introduction to politics and government for those who want to learn more about the system and it can be a reference for those who already have considerable knowledge.

Understanding how the system works is essential for anyone who wants to participate in politics and have an influence on government—whether it's running for office, supporting a candidate or simply trying to be an informed voter.

The idea that there can be an informed and intelligent electorate made up of ordinary citizens is a cornerstone of American democracy. But it was a revolutionary idea when he founding fathers wrote the Declaration of Independence and the Constitution. It was a belief that made the United States different from the rest of the world and, more than 200 years later, it still is a uniquely American concept.

When I served as a foreign correspondent, people in other countries often told me that they didn't like the American government, but did like the American people. In response, I would point out that the American government is the American people, that the government belongs to us and we are responsible for what it does. Some found that difficult to understand and, I'm afraid, too many Americans may have trouble accepting the idea that they are responsible for their government's leadership, actions, and policies.

But it's true at all levels of government—local, state, or national. In every election, so-called "ordinary citizens" determine who their leaders will be and, if we don't like their policies or performance in office, there's always another election. You can't have a democratic government without politics and you can't make good things happen if you don't understand how the system works.

So take a journey through the American political system with my friend and colleague, Spencer Christian. You'll be amazed at how much he knows and how much you're going to learn.

—By Hal Bruno
Political Director
ABC News

# INTRODUCTION

As a youngster growing up in rural central Virginia in the 1950s and 1960s, I considered participation in the political process to be a sacred right. It seemed to me that
there must be something awfully powerful about the right to vote, for example,
because state and local governments in the Old South would often resort to terrible
tactics of intimidation and harassment to keep black citizens from exercising this fundamental freedom. Sometimes more subtle measures were employed, like the imposi-
tion of poll taxes and the administration of literacy tests, to "discourage" voter
participation. These painful experiences left a powerful impression on me—because
freedom fighters had laid down their lives in the struggle for such basic human rights, I
would never take lightly the opportunity to help select my representative government.

In fact, I became so fascinated with the way the electoral process works that I even
fantasized about being a U.S. senator and debating the weighty issues of the day on
the historic Senate floor. I can vividly recall the presidential race of 1960—John
Fitzgerald Kennedy vs. Richard Milhouse Nixon. I was in the 8th grade, and my
English teacher, Miss Bess, chose two students to stage a mock debate. I was Richard
Nixon, and my opponent was John Kennedy. I won the debate—and Nixon lost the
election ( a story I had the pleasure of telling Nixon just a few years before his death).
I couldn't wait until I was old enough to vote.

It was also in the 8th grade that I took my first course in civics. We had a wonderful teacher named Mrs. Coleman, who made the study of government truly interesting. The framers of the Constitution seemed so eloquent; the balance of powers
among the three branches of government seemed so precious; and the right of citizen participation seemed so important. In Mrs. Coleman's class, we learned how a
bill becomes a law, and how to write to our representatives to help shape legislative
decisions. It became so clear to me that government belongs to the people, and it is
up to the people to make government work.

By the time I entered college in the fall of 1965, the historic Civil Rights Bill and
Voting Rights Act had become law. For the first time in my life, I was able to go to the
school of my choice. I could drink from the same water fountains and use the same
restrooms as white citizens. My parents no longer had to go in the back doors of restaurants and order from the kitchen. This had come about because large numbers of citizens (black and white) had mobilized their efforts to make government work. The
great civil rights movement of the 1950s and 1960s had brought pressure to bear on
Congress to pass legislation to insure the basic human rights of all citizens, to make government fairer and more responsive, and to force the private sector to comply with the
new laws. "Amazing," I thought, "it works just like the way Mrs. Coleman taught us."

As I moved through my college years in the late 1960s, I became even more fascinated with the workings of government. This was a time of intense political activity, and the passions ran deep. Great civil disturbances erupted in our cities, as the promise of equal opportunity struck many of our poorest citizens as just empty rhetoric. The Vietnam War produced bitter divisions and violent confrontations all over the country. The assassinations of two popular political figures (Dr. Martin Luther King and Robert Kennedy) left many people disheartened and disillusioned. And, yet, despite the turmoil and tragedy, this was also a time of hope. More young people than ever before had become active in the political process (I worked in a number of political campaigns during my college years). More women and minorities were being elected to public office. And there seemed to be a general disdain for apathy and a general belief that each individual's vote did count. Most people seemed to believe that the system works, but it takes citizen involvement to make it work.

How distant that time seems now! As we approach this election year, there is more dissatisfaction with government and less appetite for involvement than I have seen in my 48 (soon to be 49) years. People are not only unhappy with the workings of government, many seem not to understand how it works, and even more seem to have little interest in fixing it. In the 1994 Congressional election, only 34 percent of eligible American voters actually bothered to cast their ballots. Polls show that many didn't care, and others did not even know that elections were being held. This is appalling! Even in our last presidential race, slightly more than 50 percent of eligible voters voted. Most other democratic nations enjoy far greater voter participation. Why does the world's greatest democracy inspire so little citizen participation?

I don't have all of the answers to that question, but I do believe this book will help address the problem. In *Electing Our Government*, it is my purpose to explain the structure and functions of government (local, state, and federal), how you can make government more responsive by exercising your most fundamental rights, and how you may broaden your role as a citizen from simply registering to vote to joining a political party, to actually running for office. This book will also offer you historical perspectives, insights into the thinking of the Founding Fathers, and little-known facts about some of our best-known political figures.

As we approach the last presidential election of this millennium, I believe it is more important than ever before for Americans to understand how their government works and to participate in its workings. The challenges of life in the 21st century will test our ability to survive as a free society. If we don't learn to exercise the blessings of liberty, we will surely lose them.

—Spencer Christian

# SECTION ONE

## Meet Your Government

### In Congress July 4, 1776, The Unanimous Declaration of The Thirteen United States of America

"WHEN IN THE COURSE OF HUMAN EVENTS, IT BECOMES NECESSARY FOR ONE PEOPLE TO DISSOLVE THE POLITICAL BANDS WHICH HAVE CONNECTED THEM WITH ANOTHER, AND TO ASSUME AMONG THE POWERS OF THE EARTH, THE SEPARATE AND EQUAL STATION TO WHICH THE LAWS OF NATURE AND OF NATURE'S GOD ENTITLE THEM, A DECENT RESPECT TO THE OPINIONS OF MANKIND REQUIRES THAT THEY SHOULD DECLARE THE CAUSES WHICH IMPEL THEM TO THE SEPARATION.

"WE HOLD THESE TRUTHS TO BE SELF-EVIDENT, THAT ALL MEN ARE CREATED EQUAL, THAT THEY ARE ENDOWED BY THEIR CREATOR WITH CERTAIN UNALIENABLE RIGHTS, THAT AMONG THESE ARE LIFE, LIBERTY, AND THE PURSUIT OF HAPPINESS. THAT TO SECURE THESE RIGHTS, GOVERNMENTS ARE INSTITUTED AMONG MEN, DERIVING THEIR JUST POWERS FROM THE CONSENT OF THE GOVERNED. THAT WHENEVER ANY FORM OF GOVERNMENT BECOMES DESTRUCTIVE OF THESE ENDS, IT IS THE RIGHT OF THE PEOPLE TO ALTER OR TO ABOLISH IT, AND TO INSTITUTE NEW GOVERNMENT, HAVING ITS FOUNDATION ON SUCH PRINCIPLES AND ORGANIZING ITS POWERS IN SUCH FORM, AS TO THEM SHALL SEEM MOST LIKELY TO EFFECT THEIR SAFETY AND HAPPINESS."

In the Declaration of Independence, one of the most remarkable documents ever drafted by man, Thomas Jefferson eloquently outlined the reasons for throwing out the British government and instituting a new government. But while the rhetoric was unusual, the concept of armed revolt against a government was not. Over the course of the last two centuries, the world has seen hundreds of revolutions in countries large and small.

So what is so remarkable about the American Revolution? The fact that the new government created by the leaders of the revolution turned out to be the most flexible, durable, and successful governmental system of modern times. Our system has remained in tact through foreign wars, civil wars, territorial expansion, economic depressions, and social turmoil. At a time when the former Soviet Union and several Eastern European countries have disintegrated, the U.S. remains the most stable and powerful nation on earth.

But we can't rest on our laurels. As technology brings the peoples of the world closer together, we face many new challenges. The struggle to meet these challenges has led many people to have an extremely negative attitude towards our government. Even though we have the world's most open democracy, scarcely two out of five eligible Americans voted in the 1994 elections.

That's tragic, because citizen participation is the fundamental strength of our nation. The first step in participating is learning about the remarkable structure of the governmental system that was created by the founders of our country.

# 1788

## GEORGE WASHINGTON

The selection of the brand new United States of America's first chief executive wasn't an election, but a coronation. Although the struggle to ratify the Constitution had been long and contentious, Americans were unanimous in their opinion that it would be unthinkable that George Washington would not be their first leader.

The only problem was convincing Washington, who enjoyed life at Mount Vernon. On the other hand, he approved of the new Constitution and was anxious that the new democracy get off to a good start. In the end, he gave in to the immense public pressure and agreed to participate in the electoral process. That process involved no primaries, no fund raising, no conventions, no speeches, no debates—in fact, there was no campaigning at all. Instead, the 69 electors ( some were chosen by state legislatures and some by popular vote) all cast one vote for General Washington on February 4, 1789. The nation's first leader was hardly elated—he said, "My movements to the chair of government will be accompanied by feelings not unlike those of a culprit, who is going to the place of his execution."

Washington wasn't the only man who was less than thrilled with an honor bestowed upon him that day. The new Constitution gave each elector a second vote, with the runner-up becoming vice-president. The nod went to John Adams, who told his wife Abigail that "my country has in its wisdom contrived for me the most insignificant office that ever the invention of man contrived or his imagination conceived."

The only bit of controversy surrounding Washington's election centered on the matter of his official title. Congress weighed such lofty terms as "His Excellency," "Elective Majesty," "His Serene Highness," "Elective Highness," and "His Highness, the President of the United States and Protector of the Rights of the Same." In the end—after a great deal of humor—Congress chose "Mr. President." Although the selection seems obvious today, it established an important principle—even a president elected unanimously was not going to be treated as a monarch. Washington could be—and, in fact, was—open to political criticism.

And what about John Adams' title? Despite the suggestion of "His Superfluous Excellency," Congress decided he would be the "Vice-President."

Electoral Votes:

Washington.....................................69

Adams..........................................34

# Your Government Is Unique

This morning, as usual, I was leafing through *The New York Times* in my dressing room between my appearances on the set of *Good Morning America*. Probably because I had just started work on this book, I noticed that the first section contained no less than nine stories about the 1996 presidential election and presidential candidates—well over one year before the election! I reflected that anyone who watches TV news or picks up a newspaper could name at least a half dozen of those seeking the Oval Office.

A few hours later, I found myself stuck in one of those endless traffic jams that make traveling in the New York metropolitan area such a nightmare. Suddenly, a thought struck me: As powerful a position as the presidency of the United States is, the politicians who were in charge of maintaining—or failing to maintain—the roads had a lot more dramatic effect on my everyday life. After all, our troops are sent off to war only a handful of times in a century, but all of us head off to work every morning. Although I could rattle off the names of all of the presidential candidates, I had absolutely no idea who was ultimately in charge of most of the highways I traveled over.

That's why I want you to check out the following statistics. They smash the notion that our national government is the only one with which we need to be concerned.

There are about 538,000 elected officials in the United States. Of these:

Two are the President and Vice-President
535 serve in the U.S. Congress
About 7,300 are members of state legislatures
About 400 are governors, lieutenant governors, or other state officials
More than 529,000 serve in local governments!

We have one federal government and fifty state governments. But we also have more than 3,000 counties, 19,000 municipalities, 14,000 school districts, and 27,000 special districts. Each of these governmental units needs, on the average, dozens of elected officials to make crucial decisions about the delivery of a significant and increasing variety of vital services. While the federal government is run by professional politicians, local governments are filled primarily by volunteers. Only 10 percent of those

529,000 local political offices are full-time paid jobs. The other 475,000 are filled by people whose main qualification is their willingness to devote some time to making their communities better places to live.

While these numbers are impressive, they don't reflect the true scope of citizen participation. You see, almost every local and state government—even the federal government—has commissions, boards, and committees to which people are appointed, not elected. In my small town, these appointees supervise parks and recreation programs, economic development efforts, services for youth, seniors, and the disabled, conservation programs, long-range fiscal planning efforts, and a lot more. In my state, citizen volunteers advise the governor and state legislature on child care regulations, school reforms, landmark preservation, the impact of technology, and a multitude of other areas. While no one has ever counted the exact number of these positions, it's estimated between three and four million Americans are involved.

At the federal level, Congress is dramatically influenced by citizens who form together in interest groups. No, I'm not talking about the highly paid lobbyists who pursue corporate interests. I'm talking about groups of people like you and me who band together because we care deeply about issues like toy safety, domes-

---

# WHAT DOES IT MEAN?
## GOVERNMENT

I like this definition of what a government is: Government consists of institutions, agencies, and political officials (elected or appointed) whose purpose is to write, enforce, and interpret laws and public policies. The main goals of government are to maintain public order, provide goods and services that help the lives of citizens, and to protect basic liberties and freedoms.

Some famous people have said:

"Government is not reason, it is not eloquence—it is force."
—GEORGE WASHINGTON

"What is government itself but the greatest of all reflections on human nature? If men were angels, no government would be necessary."
—JAMES MADISON

"The government is us; we are the government, you and I."
—TEDDY ROOSEVELT

"The ways of God and government and girls are all mysterious, and it is not given to mortal man to understand them."
—ROBERT HEINLEIN

"The most terrifying words in the English language are, 'I'm from the government and I'm here to help.'"
—RONALD REAGAN

tic violence, lead poisoning, child support, automobile safety, etc. We've all seen that the dramatic stories of people who were courageous enough to testify before Congress have influenced major legislation.

The governmental system that allows so much citizen participation is called federalism. Let's take a look at how this system came about.

## COLONIAL RULE IN AMERICA

All of us know that our forefathers successfully fought a war to win independence. The main reason that this war was fought was that the residents of the Colonies wanted control over their own affairs. But local control was not a feature of British government. England, and the vast majority of countries in the world, had what is called a unitary government system. In a unitary system, the country has just one government, a strong national government. Local administrative units are agencies of that central government instead of being independent government systems.

---

# WHAT DOES IT MEAN?

## DEMOCRACY

*Democracy* comes from a Greek phrase that means "the people rule," and the concept dates back to the ancient Greek city-state of Athens, where all citizens (except women, slaves, and foreigners) participated in making important decisions. Today, we call this type of government a direct democracy, and it is still practiced in New England town meetings.

However, direct democracy is impractical for larger communities. So our forefathers decided to use representational democracy, in which the people elect representatives to make decisions for them.

Does it work? Here are some opinions:

"Democracy is the worst form of government, except for all those other forms that have been tried from time to time." —WINSTON CHURCHILL

"Were there a people of gods, their government would be a democracy." —JEAN-JACQUES ROUSSEAU

"As I would not be a slave, so I would not be a master. This expresses my idea of democracy." —ABRAHAM LINCOLN

"Democracy is the recurrent suspicion that more than half of the people are right more than half of the time." —E. B. WHITE

"Democracy is the art and science of running the circus from the monkey cage." —H. L. MENCKEN

"Democracy is a process by which people are free to choose the man who will then get the blame." —LAWRENCE J. PETER

In establishing their new government, most colonists were violently opposed to a new unitary system. In fact, they distrusted central government so much that they went to the other extreme and formed a confederation.

## What is a confederation?

A confederation is an alliance or association of several sovereign states that features a weak central government. Immediately after the American Revolution, the thirteen original states got together and signed a document called the Articles of Confederation, which created the Confederation of the United States. If you wonder why it didn't work, pick up a newspaper and read about what's going in the former Yugoslavia and the former Soviet Union. You'll see conflict between new republics that ranges from economic squabbles to full-scale warfare. The Articles of Confederation nearly produced the same level of conflicts on our shores.

What was the problem? The central governing body, the Congress, which was made up of one delegate appointed by every state, couldn't raise money through taxes or borrowing, regulate commerce, or even issue currency. Any legislation required agreement of two-thirds of the states, which was difficult to achieve.

The result was that the states not only waged fierce tariff wars against each other, they even fought battles over disputed borders and claims to western territories. Each state could issue its own currency, and several printed so much money that inflation became rampant and a serious economic depression ensued. Foreign governments, sensing weakness, began to pose a serious threat to the independence of the new land.

## RELUCTANT RHODE ISLAND

Rhode Island may be the smallest state in the Union, but in its early history, it was also the most feisty. In Colonial America, Rhode Island established itself as the leading commercial trading center. The colonists grew to deeply resent British efforts to regulate both legal trade and lucrative smuggling. They were among the earliest and most vociferous proponents of the War of Independence.

When the war was over, Rhode Island strongly opposed the creation of a central government that might dare to pass laws affecting its trade. Alone among the thirteen colonies, Rhode Island refused to send delegates to the Constitutional Convention, then refused to ratify the Constitution or join the new United States even after the Constitution took effect.

Then the patience of the other states grew thin, and an ultimatum was issued: Join the Union or face being declared a foreign government. Faced with isolation from its much bigger neighbors, the feisty little state finally gave in.

In late 1786, a man named Daniel Shays led of force of 2,500 desperate, debt-ridden farmers in an attack on a military arsenal. Although the Shays Rebellion was quelled, it was a clear signal that the confederation system of government had to be changed. The Confederation Congress authorized the formation of a convention to be held in Philadelphia to "devise such further provisions as shall appear to them necessary to render the constitution of the federal government adequate to the exigencies of the Union." However, the fifty-five delegates from twelve states (Rhode Island refused to attend) who convened in Philadelphia on May 25, 1787, realized that it was the confederation system that was the problem. They would end up writing a Constitution that would create a new governmental system which would create a strong central government and still allow significant autonomy to the states. That system was called federalism.

## WHAT DOES IT MEAN?
# CONSTITUTION

The word *constitution* comes from the Latin word *constituere*, which means "to set up." That word in turn comes from the root of the word *statutum*, which means "law or regulation." So our word *constitution*, when talking about government, means an established body of rules and laws that defines the relationship between the government and the people.

Not all nations have constitutions, including many nations that were monarchies, such as Great Britain. However, the founders of our country wanted a constitution that served as protection against shifts in public opinion or power grabs by any individual or group.

Here's what some of our most
famous leaders had to say about the Constitution:

"In questions of power, let no more be heard of
confidence in man, but bind him down from mischief
by the chains of the Constitution." —THOMAS JEFFERSON

"It is, sir, the people's Constitution, the
people's government, made for the people, made by the
people, and answerable to the people." —DANIEL WEBSTER

"The American Constitution is the most
wonderful work ever struck off at a certain time by
the brain and purpose of man." —WILLIAM GLADSTONE

"Our Constitution is in actual operation; everything appears
to promise that it will last; but in this world nothing can be
said to be certain, except death and taxes." —BENJAMIN FRANKLIN

## What is federalism?

Federal government, or federalism, is a form of government where political power is shared between a central or national authority and smaller, locally autonomous units such as provinces or states, generally under the terms of a constitution. The concept goes all the way back to ancient Greece, where the Delian League and the Achaean League are generally considered among the earliest political attempts to achieve united or national strength without the sacrifice of local independence. Elements of federalism existed in the Roman Empire. During the Middle Ages many leagues of states were formed for specific purposes, one of the best known being the Hanseatic League. During the Renaissance, the Union of Utrecht, an alliance formed in 1579 by seven provinces of the Netherlands, was in the nature of a federation and was the strongest Protestant force in Europe for about two centuries. Modern nations with federalist governments include Canada, Mexico, Australia, India, Switzerland, and Germany.

## HOW WAS OUR CONSTITUTION WRITTEN?

The fifty-five framers of our Constitution, led by Alexander Hamilton, James Madison, and eighty-one-year-old Benjamin Franklin, spent sixteen long weeks in debates that featured some of the most eloquent rhetoric in American history. Shortly after the convention began, a critical struggle developed between the large states and the small states over the structure of the Congress of the new government. A plan proposed by Virginia, a large state, called for both a House of Representatives and a Senate with representation based on the size of each state's population. Under this plan, the House would be elected by popular vote and it in turn would select senators from nominations submitted by state legislatures. The Congress would elect the chief executive of the government and the Supreme Court. The executive and selected judges could veto both federal and state laws, giving great power to the central government.

In response, the small states offered the New Jersey plan, which called for a single (unicameral) legislature with one delegate selected by each state legislature. This legislature would elect a chief executive, who would appoint a Supreme Court. The power of the central government would be much more limited than under the Virginia plans.

Debate over these two different visions of government stymied the convention until a compromise was offered by two delegates from Connecticut. The Connecticut or Great Compromise proposed a bicameral Congress. The House of Representatives would have popularly elected members apportioned according to the population of each state. The Senate would consist of two members from each state who would be selected by the state legislature. The chief executive or President would be elected by popular vote, and the President would nominate members of the Supreme Court.

After many other compromises, the convention finished its work on September 12, 1787, and thirty-nine delegates (the others were away or were opposed to the

final draft) signed the historic document. Before it could take effect, however, the Constitution had to be ratified by nine of the thirteen states.

## STATE RATIFICATION DATES

| State | Date Ratified | For | Against |
|-------|---------------|-----|---------|
| 1. Delaware | December 7, 1787 | 30 | 0 |
| 2. Pennsylvania | December 12, 1787 | 46 | 23 |
| 3. New Jersey | December 18, 1787 | 31 | 0 |
| 4. Georgia | January 2, 1788 | 26 | 0 |
| 5. Connecticut | January 9, 1788 | 128 | 40 |
| 6. Massachusetts | February 6, 1788 | 187 | 168 |
| 7. Maryland | April 28, 1788 | 63 | 11 |
| 8. South Carolina | May 23, 1788 | 149 | 73 |
| 9. New Hampshire | June 21, 1788 | 57 | 46 |
| 10. Virginia | June 25, 1788 | 89 | 79 |
| 11. New York | July 26, 1788 | 39 | 27 |
| 12. North Carolina | November 21, 1789 | 195 | 77 |
| 13. Rhode Island | May 29, 1790 | 34 | 32 |

## The struggle for ratification

The new Constitution pleased those who wanted a strong federal government. But many opponents, who included Thomas Jefferson, had strong concerns.

The top three were:

- The strong central government would be dominated by the rich.
- The Constitution didn't go far enough in spelling out states rights.
- The Constitution didn't contain provisions protecting the personal freedoms ("life, liberty, and the pursuit of happiness") outlined in the Declaration of Independence.

The prospects for ratification in several states were not good. But a series of essays called *The Federalist Papers* which were written by Alexander Hamilton, James Madison, and John Jay played a critical role in persuading many people who were sitting on the fence. These essays argued that:

- A large federal government with many factions competing for power would make it impossible for one faction to seize power.
- Dividing the central government into three branches with overlapping power would insure liberty.
- Language would be added to the Constitution to "reserve" the rights of states.
- A Bill of Rights would be added to the Constitution after ratification.

On June 21, 1788, New Hampshire (by a margin of 9 votes) became the ninth state to ratify the Constitution, and the United States was born. When the first Congress convened in 1789, it was presented with more than 145 proposed amendments to the

PRESIDENTIAL ELECTION 2

# 1792

## GEORGE WASHINGTON

It wasn't surprising that the office of the presidency seemed to fit George Washington—after all, it was designed with the assumption that he would be the first to hold the office. And even after he had spent four years in office, his fellow countrymen were nearly unanimous in urging him to accept a second term. Washington, however, wanted to retire, for two reasons. Although he was only 60 years old, his health was poor, and he longed to return to Mount Vernon, where he could live a more tranquil life. Secondly, he was bitterly disappointed that despite his urgings, the "spirit of party" had arisen, dividing the country into two distinct political camps.

The men who headed the two fledgling political parties had been brought into government by President Washington because they were the two most brilliant and capable American political figures—Alexander Hamilton and Thomas Jefferson. Hamilton, the secretary of the treasury, headed the Federalists, who believed in a strong central government, favored wealthy commercial interests, and were strongly pro-British. Jefferson, leader of the emerging Democratic-Republicans, was passionate about defending farmers and small businessmen, was a champion of states' rights, and was strongly pro-French.

Although George Washington was anxious to prove to the world that the new American democracy could survive the passing of leadership to a new president, he finally decided that factionalism could split the new nation apart if he stepped down. He was endorsed by both the Federalists and the Democratic-Republicans, and was once again the unanimous choice of the Electoral College. John Adams finished second with 77 votes, but he was not happy that he bested New York Governor George Clinton, who received 50 votes. Adams' response: "Damn 'em, damn 'em, damn 'em!" However, he did reluctantly agree to serve a second term as Vice President.

Electoral Votes:

| | |
|---|---|
| Washington | 132 |
| Adams | 77 |
| Clinton | 50 |

Constitution. It ended up approving twelve, of which ten were ratified by the states. These ten, which are known as the Bill of Rights, protect personal liberties and contain language reserving all powers to the state which are not given to the federal government in the Constitution.

The U.S. Constitution served as the model for state constitutions, which called for a sharing of power with local government. Our country had implemented a unique form of government that was "of the people, by the people, for the people." In America, the doors to positions of influence aren't closed, but are wide open. The only thing that holds most people back is that they don't know enough about the federal, state, and local governments. So before we talk about how you can become more involved, we'll take some time to introduce you to the three levels of government and who does what at each level.

---

## WHAT DOES IT MEAN?
### CITIZEN

In the free republics of classical antiquity, the term *citizen* signified not merely a resident of a town but a free, governing member of the state. In the Greek idea of citizenship, as expressed by Aristotle, citizens had the right to participate in both the legislative and judicial functions of their political community. This right was carefully guarded and was rarely conferred on anyone of foreign birth. In ancient Rome two classes of citizens were recognized. The first possessed the rights of citizenship, including the privilege of voting in the public assembly; the other possessed these rights and the additional right of holding offices of state. As in the United States and other modern states, citizenship in Rome, although usually acquired by birth, could also be attained by naturalization, or by special grant of the state.

In the United States, the word *citizen* is used in its broadest sense to mean an individual who, by birth or by naturalization, is a member of the United States. By extension, a citizen owes allegiance to and may lawfully demand protection from our government. However, I would like to see all of us adopt the Greek concept of the term—in other words, I think a fundamental part of citizenship is exercising the right of voting and other participation in political activity.

PRESIDENTIAL ELECTION 3

# 1796

## JOHN ADAMS

George Washington was adamant about stepping down from the presidency in 1796, He was bone tired, in poor health, and he thought it unwise for one man to hold power so long. By refusing a third term he established a tradition which lasted (except for President Franklin D. Roosevelt's four terms) until it was made into law by the 22nd Amendment, ratified in 1951.

If he had decided to run, he would more than likely have faced opposition. Britain and France had gone to war in 1793, and Washington's efforts to appease the British outraged the Democratic-Republicans. Said Benjamin Franklin Bache, Ben's grandson, "If ever a nation was debauched by a man, the American nation has been debauched by Washington." Although the first president warned that "excessive partiality for one foreign nation and excessive dislike of another" was a recipe for disaster, his advice was ignored as America experienced its first true presidential campaign.

Although the real leader of the pro-British Federalist party was Alexander Hamilton, he had a great many enemies. So the party's chose John Adams, who had served patiently as vice-president for eight years, as its candidate for the highest office, and named as his running mate Thomas Pinckney of South Carolina. The pro-French Democratic-Republicans, on the other hand, supported their leader, Thomas Jefferson. To attract northern votes, they added to the ticket Aaron Burr of New York.

Neither Adams nor Jefferson campaigned for office, but their supporters gleefully traded vicious insults and slanders. The turning point in this close contest may have come when the French minister to the United States publicly attacked the Federalists and made his country's preference for Jefferson well known. Despite attempts at damage control by the Democratic-Republicans, many Americans were dismayed by the attempt of a foreign power to influence the election.

Still, Adams was elected by just three electoral votes—71 to 68. Jefferson was gracious in defeat and quickly accepted the office of Vice President. Despite the venomous rhetoric of the campaign, the seat of power had been peacefully passed on. This was the first successful test of the American democracy.

Electoral votes:

| | |
|---|---|
| Adams | 71 |
| Jefferson | 68 |
| Pinckney | 59 |
| Burr | 30 |

# WHO WAS ALEXANDER HAMILTON?

Alexander Hamilton, one of the greatest American statesman, was born on January 11, 1755, on the West Indian island of Nevis, the illegitimate son of James Hamilton, a Scottish trader, and of Rachel Fawcett (Faucette) Levine. He came to public attention when he wrote two pamphlets, *A Full Vindication of the Measures of Congress from the Calumnies of Their Enemies* (1774) and *The Farmer Refuted* (1775). During the Revolutionary War, Hamilton became aide-de-camp and confidential secretary to George Washington. At the close of the Revolution Hamilton left the army and studied law at Albany, New York. He served in Congress in 1782–83 and then returned to the practice of law, becoming one of the most eminent lawyers in New York City.

In 1786 Hamilton drafted the resolution that led to the assembling of the Constitutional Convention at Philadelphia in the following year. At the Constitutional Convention, Hamilton presented his plan of a strongly centralized federal government, which involved representation based on wealth and property and absolute veto power vested in the executive. Although the aristocratic principles of the plan were rejected, the Constitution did outline a powerful federal government with a chief executive with limited veto power. Even though he didn't get his way, Hamilton turned his energy and ability to securing ratification of the Constitution adopted by the convention. He conceived and started the series of essays written to refute arguments put forward by people who opposed ratification. These essays, which were published first in the *New York Independent Journal*, were subsequently collected and published under the title of *The Federalist*. Of the eighty-five essays, fifty-five were written by Hamilton and constitute the works for which he is best known.

Shortly after the establishment of the new government in 1789 with Washington as President, Hamilton was appointed secretary of the treasury and he instituted a series of reforms and wrote reports that have strongly influenced the administration of the national government since that time. In 1795 Hamilton returned to practice law in New York City. In the election of 1800, which was thrown into the House of Representatives because Thomas Jefferson and Aaron Burr had received equal numbers of electoral votes, Hamilton exerted his great influence in favor of Jefferson, who had always been his chief political opponent, rather than Burr, whom he considered a man of dangerous ambitions. In 1804 Hamilton was instrumental in the defeat of Burr as candidate for governor of New York State. After his defeat Burr forced a quarrel with Hamilton and challenged him to a duel. Although he strongly disapproved of dueling, Hamilton felt obliged to accept the challenge, and they met on July 11, 1804, at Weehawken, New Jersey, on the spot where Hamilton's eldest son had been killed in a duel three years before. Hamilton was mortally wounded and died the next day.

## PRESIDENTIAL ELECTION 4

# 1800

# THOMAS JEFFERSON

If you think the rhetoric of Newt Gingrich is inflammatory, check out a typical Federalist version of what life in American would be like if Democratic-Republican candidate Thomas Jefferson were elected in 1800: "Murder, robbery, rape, adultery, and incest will be openly taught and practiced, the air will be rent with the cries of the distressed, the soil will be soaked with blood, and the nation black with crimes."

Not to be outdone, Jefferson's supporters described John Adams, running for reelection as a Federalist, as a fool, hypocrite, tyrant and criminal whose presidency had been "one continued tempest of malignant passions." They accused Adams of conniving to marry his daughter into British royalty and of using the U.S. Navy to fetch mistresses for him. All in all, the level of the political debate in the campaign that pitted John Adams and his running mate Charles Cotesworth Pinckney against Thomas Jefferson and his running mate Aaron Burr may have been the lowest of any presidential election in history.

By the time the electors cast their votes, a split in Federalist ranks made a Democratic-Republic party victory a certainty. But the election was far from over. The 73 Democratic-Republican electors had each cast one vote for Thomas Jefferson and one vote for Aaron Burr. Although Jefferson had been the party's nominee for the top spot, he and Burr were tied, which through the election into the House of Representatives

It so happened that the defeated Federalists controlled the House of Representatives, and that caused turmoil when it convened on February 11, 1801. Some of the Federalists preferred Burr to the hated Jefferson. Others hatched a scheme to keep the House deadlocked past March 4, the date on which the Constitution required that a new president be sworn in. With no new president, they argued, the Federalist President Pro Temp of the Senate could be the chief executive.

As a result, the House voted 35 times over seven days without Jefferson receiving the support of the required nine states. Finally, some Congressmen tired of sleeping on the House floor or in their chairs, abstained or changed their votes so that Jefferson was named president on the 36th ballot. For the first time in U.S. history, a new political party peacefully assumed control of the nation's highest office.

The nation had, however, learned that the Constitutional requirements for electing a president could have bizarre and grueling effects. That same year, the Congress approved the 12th Amendment to the Constitution, which required that the Electoral College vote separately for president and vice-president, and the states ratified the Amendment by 1804.

Electoral Votes:

Jefferson . . . . . . . . . . . . . . . . . . . . . . . . . 73
Burr . . . . . . . . . . . . . . . . . . . . . . . . . . . . 73
Adams . . . . . . . . . . . . . . . . . . . . . . . . . . 65
Pinckney . . . . . . . . . . . . . . . . . . . . . . . . 64

# Meet Your Federal Government

Make no mistake about it—the federal government is huge. The folks in Washington, D.C. direct a work force of about three million employees who supervise the spending of about $1.4 trillion, or about $5,600 per man, woman, and child—a lot of money, by any standard. When you consider that the federal government has run up a debt of about $4.3 trillion (or $16,600 per person) by spending more than it has taken in, it's easy to understand why some people mutter that they wish the federal government didn't exist at all.

In Chapter One, we learned that there was a time when the federal government in fact didn't exist, nearly destroying the new nation. So the framers of the Constitution came up with a new system that featured a strong central government that consisted of three co-equal branches of government: the Congress, which consisted of a House of Representatives and a Senate, an executive branch headed by an elected President, and a judicial branch headed by a Supreme Court nominated by the President and confirmed by the Senate. Each branch has its own area of authority. These areas overlap, making it necessary for the three branches to share in, and compete for, the power to govern effectively. Each branch has some constitutional authority that it can use to impede the functioning of the other branches, creating a system of "checks and balances." The purpose of this somewhat cumbersome machinery of government, as intended by the framers of the Constitution, is to prevent the concentration of power in a small group of politicians, which could lead to tyranny. To prevent one branch from becoming dominant, the Constitution created a system of "checks and balances" by giving the branches overlapping powers.

This system was one of the world's first true democracies. Let's take a look at its parts.

## THE LEGISLATIVE BRANCH

"All legislative powers herein granted shall be vested in a Congress of the United States, which shall consist of a Senate and a House of Representatives."—CONSTITUTION OF THE UNITED STATES, ARTICLE I, SECTION I

"I have reached the conclusion that one useless man is called a disgrace, two useless men are called a law firm, and that three or more become a Congress."—JOHN ADAMS

As we've just discussed, the fiercest debate concerning the structure of our government involved what kind of legislative body our fledgling nation would adopt. And the first elected representatives barely had time to take their seats before President Adams helped initiate a tradition of biting jokes at the expense of Congress that's nearly as old as our country. But I'm going to resist the temptation to share my favorites to make an important point:

You and I and our fellow voters are responsible for making the decisions about who is elected to represent us in Washington.

The only way to get a Congress that's more responsive to the people is for more people to get involved in the process by which congressional candidates are nominated and elected. The crony system that made it difficult for anyone who wasn't a party insider to run for Congress is long gone. The proof is an amazing fact: More than half of the new representatives elected in 1994 had never held any political office before!

The first step in becoming more involved is to learn more about what Congress does and how it's organized.

## WHO IS CONGRESS

Congress consists of 435 members of the House of Representatives and 100 members of the Senate.

The first Congress seated seventy-four members of the House, but as states joined the Union, that number gradually increased until it was fixed at its current level. The Constitution requires that each congressman represent about the same number of people (each member of the first Congress represented about 30,000 people, while every member today represents about 500,000 constituents). Every ten years, the Census Department counts the population, and when the results are in, the number of representatives from each state is re-apportioned to give more seats to the fastest growing states and take seats from states that are losing population or growing less swiftly. That means that Sunbelt states such as Florida, California, and Texas have been gaining seats, while northern states such as New York and Pennsylvania have been losing them. Every state is required to have at least one representative.

The voters in each state, regardless of size, elect two senators. That means that Wyoming's 453,000 residents choose two senators who have the same voting power as the two senators elected by 29,000,000 Californians. The Constitution originally required that senators be elected by the legislatures of each state. The Seventeenth Amendment, which was ratified in 1913, gave the power directly to the voters.

# NUMBER OF MEMBERS OF THE HOUSE OF REPRESENTATIVES ELECTED FOR EACH STATE

| State | Number of Representatives | State | Number of Representatives |
|---|---|---|---|
| Alabama | 7 | Montana | 1 |
| Alaska | 1 | Nebraska | 3 |
| Arizona | 6 | Nevada | 2 |
| Arkansas | 4 | New Hampshire | 2 |
| California | 52 | New Jersey | 13 |
| Colorado | 6 | New Mexico | 3 |
| Connecticut | 6 | New York | 31 |
| Delaware | 1 | North Carolina | 12 |
| District of Columbia | 1 | North Dakota | 1 |
| Florida | 23 | Ohio | 19 |
| Georgia | 11 | Oklahoma | 6 |
| Hawaii | 2 | Oregon | 5 |
| Idaho | 2 | Pennsylvania | 21 |
| Illinois | 20 | Rhode Island | 2 |
| Indiana | 10 | South Carolina | 6 |
| Iowa | 5 | South Dakota | 1 |
| Kansas | 4 | Tennessee | 9 |
| Kentucky | 6 | Texas | 30 |
| Louisiana | 7 | Utah | 3 |
| Maine | 2 | Vermont | 1 |
| Maryland | 8 | Virginia | 11 |
| Massachusetts | 10 | Washington | 9 |
| Michigan | 16 | West Virginia | 3 |
| Minnesota | 8 | Wisconsin | 9 |
| Mississippi | 5 | Wyoming | 1 |
| Missouri | 9 | | |

## What are the responsibilities of Congress?

Congress can only exercise the responsibilities that are expressly defined or implied by the Constitution. Among these are the power to lay and collect taxes, borrow money on the credit of the United States, regulate commerce with foreign nations and among the several States, coin money, establish post offices, declare war, raise and support armies, and make all laws necessary for the execution of its own powers and all other powers vested by this Constitution in the government of the United States. Congress also acts like a giant city council to administer the District of Columbia.

## WHAT DOES IT MEAN?
## CONGRESS

The word *congress* comes from the Latin verb *congressus*, which means to come together. In the United States, we use the word in two ways. Congress is the legislative body consisting of the House of Representatives and the Senate (some linguistic purists insist on using the phrase "the Congress" to indicate that august body). When we put a number in front of the word, as in 104th Congress, it means a specific two-year period of history from one election to the next—in this case, from 1994 to 1996.

In addition to making laws, Congress has also had the responsibility to conduct investigations to make sure its laws are being properly administered. From the McCarthy hearings to the Watergate hearings to the Iran-Contra hearings, this investigative function has produced some of the most dramatic political episodes of the last half century.

Finally, Congress approves the President's appointment of a Vice-President if that position is vacant because the Vice-President resigns, dies, or assumes the presidency—for example, when Gerald Ford was selected by President Nixon after Spiro Agnew resigned.

### Who has the power to amend the Constitution?

Congress shares this power with the states. Any constitutional amendment must be passed by a two-thirds majority of both houses, then must be approved (ratified) by two-thirds of the states. When the first Congress met, it was faced with voting on no less than 142 proposed amendments to the Constitution—only twelve, including the ten in the Bill of Rights, made it through the long process.

### Do the House and the Senate each have special responsibilities?

The answer is yes. Because the entire House of Representatives must answer to the voters every two years, the framers of the Constitution required that all revenue bills (those that involve taxation, borrowing money, or spending money) must be considered in the House first.

The House of Representatives also:

- Chooses a President if no candidate gets a majority of the electoral votes (that's only happened once, in 1800, when Thomas Jefferson and Aaron Burr tied).
- Acts like a grand jury in bringing charges of impeachment against a President, Vice-President, or certain other officials. For example, the House brought charges against Richard Nixon, but he resigned before he was tried by the Senate.

Perhaps because six-year terms make senators a bit more resistant to political pressure, the Constitution gave the Senate the power to "advise and consent" to the President's nominees for Cabinet positions, Supreme Court seats, ambassadorships, and other important jobs, as well as to all treaties with other nations. The Senate also sits as a giant jury when impeachment charges are brought by the House (only seven people, all federal judges, have ever been impeached). The Senate selects the Vice-President if the House is forced to select a President.

PRESIDENTIAL ELECTION 5

# 1804

## THOMAS JEFFERSON

The election of 1804 established a political maxim that has held true to the present day—when a president's first term is tranquil, so is the reelection campaign. A number of factors made Jefferson's first term much less contentious than the presidency of John Adams. Among them were a lull in the conflict between Britain and France, economic prosperity, and the overwhelming national pride in the massive Louisiana Purchase. Politically, the Federalists lost their leader when Alexander Hamilton was killed in a duel by Aaron Burr.

Jefferson was selected to run for reelection in his party's first official national nominating caucus, which also chose George Clinton of New York as his running mate. In contrast, the Federalists held no caucus at all, but informally agreed to support Charles Pinckney of South Carolina for the presidency and New York Senator Rufus King for the vice presidency.

With no major controversies capturing national attention, the Federalists resorted a campaign based largely on personal slander—attacks on Jefferson's religious beliefs, his ties to France, and his rumored affair with a mulatto slave named Sally Hemings. However, the public had heard all of this before, and the election was a yawner. Jefferson got 162 electoral votes and Pinckney garnered just 14. Reflecting on his landslide victory, Jefferson concluded that the vicious partisanship that had marred his first election was a thing of the past. He wrote "the two parties which prevailed with so much violence when you were here are almost wholly melted into one." But as it turned out, his obituary for the two party system was very premature.

Electoral votes:

Jefferson . . . . . . . . . . . . . . . . . . . . . . . . 162

Pinckney . . . . . . . . . . . . . . . . . . . . . . . 14

## What checks and balances limit the power of Congress?

There are two main restraints to congressional power. The first is the presidential veto. The Constitution gives the chief executive ten days to veto any piece of legislation passed by Congress, and the only way that veto can be overridden is by a vote of two-thirds of the members of both houses. The only exception is any bill passed less than ten days before Congress adjourns. If the President doesn't sign the bill before Congress goes home, the bill is automatically killed—this is known as a "pocket veto."

The second restraint is the right of the Supreme Court to nullify any legislation by declaring that it is unconstitutional. This right of judicial review was established in 1803 in *Marbury* v. *Madison*, the first famous Supreme Court decision. When a law is declared unconstitutional, Congress either has to revise the law or try to pass a constitutional amendment.

# WHY IS CONGRESS MADE UP OF TWO LEGISLATIVE BODIES?

Congress, as well as forty-nine of the fifty state legislatures, is bicameral (from the Latin *camera* meaning "chamber"), which means it has two houses. The structure resembles those of European countries such as Great Britain, which traditionally had one legislative body that represented the common people and one that represented the aristocracy. A bicameral legislature was essential to the compromise between two different classes—big states and small states. Big states were comforted by having larger representation in the House of Representatives, while all states had the same number of representatives in the Senate.

## How is Congress organized?

About 20,000 bills are introduced in each two-year session of Congress, a number far, far too large to be reviewed or debated by the entire membership. That's why each chamber has established a system of committees and sub-committees to determine which few should be brought to the entire membership for a vote. Each chamber has a number of standing committees (nineteen for the House, sixteen for the Senate) that cover such major areas agriculture, foreign affairs, commerce, the judiciary, etc. Each standing committee has several sub-committees, and special committees are often formed to deal with specific problems or legislation.

The majority party in each chamber selects the committee chairmen and has a major-

ity on every committee. The majority party also selects the leader of each house, the Speaker of the House of Representatives and the President Pro Temp of the Senate (the Vice-President is the President of the Senate, but he is allowed to vote only in case of a tie).

## What are the responsibilities of an individual representative or senator?

Hearings and other related committee work occupy a considerable portion of the time of the typical congressman or senator. Because of the difference in the size of the two bodies, a congressman normally sits on just one committee, while a senator sits on several. The leadership of each party makes committee assignments, and all members lobby vigorously for the most important and prestigious ones. For a congressman, the best assignment is on a committee that has a major impact on his or her district—for example, the Agriculture Committee for a representative from a farm district.

Members also spend a considerable amount of time considering and voting on legislation that is approved by committees for consideration by the entire House or Senate. The voting record is one of the yardsticks by which interest groups and individual voters judge candidates for re-election.

The last, but by no means the least, important responsibility of members of Congress is serving constituents—in other words, we voters. Congressmen and senators act as liaisons between the public and the government, providing information, answering questions, and helping to solve problems by cutting red tape. We'll discuss how you can take advantage of the services offered by your representatives later in this book.

# WOMEN IN CONGRESS

In 1916, twenty-eight-year-old Jeanette Rankin became the first woman elected to Congress when she captured Montana's sole seat in the House of Representatives. At the time, Montana was one of only a handful of states in which women had the right to vote. It wasn't until 1981 that the number of females in the 435-member House reached twenty. The greatest increase occurred in the 1992 elections, when the number of women jumped from twenty-nine to forty-seven.

On October 3, 1922, Rebecca Felton of Georgia became the first woman senator when she was appointed to fill a vacant seat for a period of exactly one day. It wasn't until 1948 when Republican Margaret Chase Smith of Maine became the first elected woman senator. No more than two women served in the Senate at any one time until 1992, when the number of females jumped from two to seven.

## Who's eligible to run for Congress?

The Constitution set forth slightly different requirements for individuals who wanted to run for the House and Senate.

### To serve in the House, a person must:

- Be at least twenty-five years old
- Have been a U.S. citizen for seven years
- Be a resident of the state, but not necessarily the congressional district which he or she wants to represent.

# CONGRESSIONAL PAY

Both senators and congressmen earn $133,600 per year. The Speaker of the House pulls down $171,500, while the Senate President Pro Temp and the majority and minority leaders of both houses each get $148,400.

Serving in Congress wasn't always so lucrative. Members of the first Congress were paid just $6 per day. Believe it or not, congressional salaries have gone down rather than up—in the middle of the Great Depression, Congress cut the annual pay from $10,000 to $9,000 in 1932, and took another $500 hit the next year before going back up to $10,000 in 1935.

As late as 1975, congressmen and senators earned just $42,500 per year. However, maintaining residences both in Washington and back in their districts has proved to be increasingly difficult for members who weren't independently wealthy. Salaries have tripled in the last two decades so that serving the public wouldn't be a financial sacrifice for so many people.

### To serve in the Senate, a person must:

- Be at least thirty years old
- Have been a U.S. citizen for nine years
- Be a resident of the state which he or she wants to represent.

The House and the Senate have the ultimate power to determine who should be seated and what standards of conduct their members should meet. The majority party has played politics to seat the popular vote-loser rather than the winner in very close elections, and several representatives and senators have been expelled for illegal or unethical conduct.

## THE EXECUTIVE BRANCH

"The executive Power shall be vested in a President of the United States of America. He shall hold his Office during the Term of four Years, and, together with the Vice-President, chosen for the same term."—Constitution of the United States, Article II, Section 1

In Great Britain, and in many other countries of the world, the leader of the government (in this case, the prime minister) is a member of Parliament and is chosen by his peers. The men who drafted the Constitution believed that a strong nation required a strong leader who was elected independently and who could serve to check the power of Congress. Although the founders of our nation conceived of the executive branch as co-equal with Congress and the judiciary, strong presidential leadership has in fact dominated government. It is this trend that the new Republican leadership seeks to counter.

---

## WHAT DOES IT MEAN?
## SENATE

In Latin, the word *senex*, meaning "old" and "old man," gave rise to the noun *senatus*, which denoted "a council of elders" in ancient Rome. In the Middle Ages *senatus* was used for the council of a monarch or of a city. By the middle of the sixteenth century, however, senate was being used to denote the governing body of a nation, and in the eighteenth century it was applied to the upper and smaller branches of a bicameral legislature in various countries and in the various states that made up those countries. Also in the eighteenth century the term began to be used for a governing body at a university or college. In some American colleges, the senate is composed of both faculty and student representatives, to whom are referred matters of discipline and of general concern.

---

### What are the responsibilities of the President?

The Constitution gives the President a number of specific responsibilities. Over the last two centuries, our nation's elected leaders have stretched the limits of their responsibilities to assume powers that the founders of our government didn't imagine. Among the major roles and powers of the President are the following:

- Chief of State: The President serves as the symbol of the nation, presiding over important ceremonies, greeting foreign leaders, and representing the nation at appropriate gatherings and ceremonies throughout the world.

• Leader of foreign policy: The Constitution gives the President the power to appoint ambassadors and negotiate treaties with other nations. The check on this power comes from the Senate's right to "advise and consent" to nominations and treaties, and that body has in fact rejected twenty treaties (the most famous is the Treaty of Versailles, which established the League of Nations after World War I). However, Presidents have also successfully asserted the right to negotiate "executive agreements" with other nations that have the same force as treaties but don't need Senate approval. The United States has entered into

## WHO WAS JAMES MADISON?

James Madison (1751-1836), fourth President of the United States (1809-17) who was known as the father of the Constitution, was born in Westmoreland County, Virginia, on March 16, 1751, the son of a wealthy planter. In 1780 he was elected to the Continental Congress. Although he was the youngest member, Madison quickly rose to a position of leadership. In 1787, working with other proponents of a strong central government, Madison was largely instrumental in persuading Congress to summon a convention to revise the Articles of Confederation, or federal constitution. At the convention, which met in Philadelphia in May 1787, Madison played a leading role, drafting the Virginia Plan that became the basis for the structure of the new government. His argument that liberty would be more secure in a large unit than in small ones because no group would be able to form an absolute majority has been confirmed by subsequent experience.

Elected to the U.S. House of Representatives in 1789, Madison sponsored the first ten amendments to the Constitution (known as the Bill of Rights). He also joined Thomas Jefferson and James Monroe in founding the Democratic-Republican party to counteract the centralizing and aristocratic tendencies of the Federalists then in power. In 1794 he married Dolley Payne Todd (1768-1849), a widow, who is especially remembered for her charm as a hostess during his presidency.

Madison retired from Congress in 1797, but returned to Washington in 1800 to serve as secretary of state under newly elected President Thomas Jefferson. After Jefferson served two terms, Madison became the Democratic-Republican party candidate and was elected President in 1809 with 122 electoral votes to 47 for the Federalist candidate Charles Pinckney. His first term was marked by escalating tension with the British. This led to Congress to declaring war against Great Britain in 1812. Although the war went badly for the United States at first, Madison won re-election with ease. A British invasion force captured Washington in 1814, but in December of that year the war was ended by the Treaty of Ghent.

In January, 1817, Madison retired to his estate, Montpelier in Orange County, Virginia. He helped Thomas Jefferson found the University of Virginia and became its rector in 1826. Madison died at Montpelier on June 28, 1836.

some 9,000 executive agreements, as compared with 1,300 treaties. Unlike treaties, executive agreements are not binding on a President's successors.

- Commander-in-Chief: The President has direct authority over all the nation's military forces, and that authority includes the right to call out the National Guard and declare martial law. Although Congress has the constitutional right to declare war, it has only done so five times in our entire history. Presidents have taken upon themselves the power to use military force in "limited" actions, and Congress has generally gone along. Korea, Vietnam, and the Persian Gulf were all "undeclared" wars.

- National Economic Manager: Presidents are expected to submit annual budgets to Congress and take other actions to bring about economic prosperity. This is often the President's most frustrating responsibility, because the health of the economy is determined by a myriad of factors, including the attitude of the public, the actions of private companies and foreign nations, acts of nature, and political events. Although the President appoints the members of such influential economic organizations as the Federal Reserve Board (which controls the money supply and sets interest rates), he has no direct control over their actions.

- Chief Legislator: The vast majority of bills considered by Congress are developed by the executive branch and submitted by the President. These bills determine public policy and establish programs in a wide variety of areas from agriculture to consumer safety. The President spends an enormous amount of time trying to mobilize public opinion to obtain support for the legislation his administration has introduced into Congress.

  The President also has wide authority in many areas to make policy by issuing binding executive orders, which have the same force as laws. The use of this power has given rise to many serious disputes between the President and Congress.

- Chief Executive: The executive branch of the government comprises fourteen departments: the departments of State, Treasury, Defense, Justice, Interior, Agriculture, Commerce, Labor, Health and Human Services, Education, Housing and Urban Development, Transportation, Energy, and Veterans Affairs. The President appoints the secretary and other top administrators of each of these departments. The executive branch also includes a number of independent agencies. Some of these, such as the Central Intelligence Agency (CIA), the Environmental Protection Agency, and the Federal Emergency Management Agency, are directly controlled by the President. Others are not directly supervised by the President, such as the Interstate Commerce Commission, the Federal Communications Commission, and the Federal Reserve System.

  In order to manage this massive bureaucracy, the President needs a substantial staff of advisers. The executive organization of the President includes the White House Office (the chief of staff, press secretary, appointments secre-

tary, legal counsel, etc.), the Office of Management and Budget, the National Security Council, and the Council of Economic Advisors. The President has sole authority to appoint and remove members of the executive organization.

## What are the limits on Presidential power?

Both other branches of governments act as checks to the power of the President. Congress can limit power by:

- Refusing to enact legislation
- Overriding presidential vetoes
- Investigating departments and agencies of the government
- Amending the Constitution to limit presidential discretion.

---

### WHAT DOES IT MEAN?
## CABINET

*Cabinet* is the name for a body of advisors to the chief executive of a parliamentary government. The term originated in England in the fifteenth century. The Privy Council, the king's most important group of advisers, met in the royal chamber or cabinet and was therefore called the cabinet council. In the eighteenth century, however, when the center of governmental power shifted from monarch to Parliament, the cabinet became the council of the most important minister in the government, the prime minister. Members of the cabinet of the British government constitute the supreme executive authority of the government, and are the sole advisers to the Crown. They are members of Parliament, usually of the same political party as the prime minister, and thus combine executive and legislative duties.

In the United States, the cabinet is made up of the administrative heads of the executive departments of the federal government, under the President. The Vice-President also participates, and the President may accord cabinet rank to other executive-branch officials, such as his national security advisor and the director of the CIA.

The cabinet as a governmental institution is not provided for in the U.S. Constitution. It developed as an advisory body out of the President's need to consult the heads of the executive departments on matters of federal policy and on problems of administration. Aside from its role as a consultative and advisory body, the cabinet has no function and wields no executive authority. The President may or may not consult the Cabinet and is not bound by the advice of the cabinet. Furthermore, the President may seek advice outside the cabinet; a group of such informal advisers is known in American history as a "Kitchen Cabinet."

# 1808

## JAMES MADISON

When a foreign nation victimizes American citizens, the American president can be in political hot water—for example, Jimmy Carter's failure to win release of the hostages held by Iran was a major factor in his defeat in his reelection campaign. In Thomas Jefferson's second term, the British resumed seizing American ships and impressing American sailors into service with the British Navy. Jefferson ignored cries for military action and instead imposed an embargo on trade with both Britain and France.

This embargo turned out to be a major political problem, but not for Jefferson, who followed Washington's example and retired after two terms. Instead, it became the major issue in the campaign of his Secretary of State, James Madison, whose stature as one of the master builders of the Constitution insured his selection as the Democratic-Republican candidate for the presidency. Although the Federalist ticket of Charles Pinckney and Rufus King had failed to excite the voters in 1804, they pounded away at the injustice of what was called the "Dambargo" with such fury that the outcome of the election in several large states was thought to be in doubt.

In the end, however, the Federalists were done in by a demographic trend that was progressively weakening the party—the wealthy commercial interests they represented were becoming an increasingly smaller percentage of American voters. Only in New England, which was becoming the last bastion of the Federalist Party, were there enough people hurt by the embargo to overcome the popularity that Jefferson had handed over to Madison. The electors in the seventeen states cast their ballots on December 7, and Madison outpolled Pinckney by more than two-to-one. On the eve of Madison's inauguration, Thomas Jefferson signed a bill repealing the embargo.

Electoral votes:

Madison . . . . . . . . . . . . . . . . . . . . . . 122

Pinckney . . . . . . . . . . . . . . . . . . . . . . 47

The Supreme Court has the power to review executive orders, executive agreements, and other presidential actions to determine if they are unconstitutional. Two examples are the Court's refusal to allow President Truman to seize the nation's steel mills during the Korean War and its rejection of President Nixon's claim of executive privilege in refusing to turn over the Watergate tapes to Congress.

A third check on presidential power is the Twenty-second Amendment to the Constitution, which limits a President to serving no more than two terms, or eight years. Finally, Presidents are very dependent on public opinion. Congress is far more reluctant to confront popular Presidents than Presidents whose approval ratings are low.

## What are the responsibilities of the Vice-President?

Thomas Marshall, Vice-President under Woodrow Wilson, was fond of telling a story about two brothers: "One ran away to sea. The other became Vice-President of the United States. Neither were ever heard from again." Marshall was expressing a frustration at the fact that the only constitutional responsibility given to the only other nationally elected political figure is to preside over the Senate and cast the deciding vote in case of a tie. Under many Presidents, the Vice-President's job has consisted largely of standing in for the chief executive at ceremonies such as the funerals of foreign leaders.

However, the nation's first Vice-President, John Adams, placed the real importance of the office in perspective when he said, "I am nothing, but I may become everything." In other words, the Vice-President's most important function is to be ready to assume the presidency. That's happened no less than eight times in our history—seven because of the death of the President and once because of resignation.

Recognizing the importance of preparing the number-two person to take the top job, recent Presidents have delegated a great deal of administrative responsibility to their Vice-Presidents.

## Who can run for the Presidency?

The Constitution requires that the President and Vice-President be at least thirty-five years old, be a natural born citizen, and have resided in the United States for at least the last fourteen years.

If you take a look at who has held the nation's top office, you might think that the Constitution also requires that the President be a male white Anglo-Saxon Protestant. We've never had a black, Hispanic, Jewish, or female President, and John F. Kennedy, Jr. was the lone Catholic. One thing the major parties don't look for in a candidate is diversity.

What do they look for? We'll explain every element of the race for the presidency, the Super Bowl of politics, in the later sections of this book.

## THE JUDICIAL BRANCH

"The judicial Power of the United States, shall be vested in one supreme Court, and in such inferior Courts as the Congress may from time to time ordain and establish."—CONSTITUTION OF THE UNITED STATES, ARTICLE III, SECTION 1

The framers of the Constitution created an independent judicial system to guard against political excesses of the elected Congress and the President. They also believed that this system would serve to protect people without political influence or economic power. Although federal judges are appointed by the President and confirmed by the Senate, they serve for life and may not be removed unless they are impeached.

# WHO WAS JOHN MARSHALL?

John Marshall, the fourth chief justice of the United States, was principally responsible for developing the power of the United States Supreme Court and formulating constitutional law in the nation. He was born in Germantown, Virginia, on September 24, 1755, the eldest of fifteen children. He briefly studied law at the College of William and Mary before being admitted to the bar in 1780. He was elected to the U.S. House of Representatives in 1799, and in 1800 he became secretary of state in the Cabinet of President John Adams. A year later Adams appointed him chief justice of the United States. Marshall held this office for thirty-four years until his death.

The most important judicial figure in United States history, Marshall is justly famed as the "Great Chief Justice." Before his appointment to the bench, the Supreme Court was regarded as ineffectual. By the force of his personality and the wisdom of his decisions, Marshall raised the Court to a position of great power in the federal government. He succeeded in making it the ultimate authority in constitutional matters.

The first and perhaps most important of Marshall's great cases was *Marbury* v. *Madison* (1803), which established once and for all the right of judicial review. The decision upheld the Court's power to review legislation and to overrule acts of Congress and of state legislatures that it considered unconstitutional. The power of judicial review was fundamental to Marshall's interpretation of constitutional doctrine. Marshall and the Court followed this with decisions that made sure federal law would be exercised under a unified judicial system. In *Fletcher* v. *Peck* (1810) the Court ruled that a state could not arbitrarily interfere with an individual's property rights. *Dartmouth College* v. *Woodward* (1819) reaffirmed the inviolability of a state's contract.

One of the most famous cases to come before the Court during Marshall's tenure was *McCulloch* v. *Maryland* (1819), which established the principle that the Constitution granted certain implied powers to Congress, in this case, the power to create a United States bank. The importance of this decision was in its affirmation of a broad interpretation of the Constitution, thus making it a flexible instrument to support the federal government.

Although Marshall's decisions were controversial, his personal integrity, wit, and charm made him much admired even among his enemies. His legal opinions were characterized by a precise and lucid style, literary skill, and thorough, logical analysis. He was the author of *Life of George Washington* (5 volumes, 1804–7). Marshall died in Philadelphia on July 6, 1835.

## What is the structure of the federal judiciary?

The federal judicial system is organized in three levels:

- Ninety-four district courts, which includes at least one for each state, make up the lowest level of the federal system. These courts, which have one to twenty-seven judges, hear approximately 250,000 cases per year, about 80 percent of the total federal caseload.

PRESIDENTIAL ELECTION 7

# 1812

## JAMES MADISON

No war-time president has ever been defeated for reelection. But the very first to run, James Madison, had to serve a unique challenge that was made possible only by the poor communication system in America in the early nineteenth century.

British attacks on American shipping finally persuaded a reluctant President Madison to ask for a declaration of war in June, 1812. This war, like all others in our history, had its critics—both those who wanted peace and those who wanted a more vigorous war effort. An ambitious member of Madison's own party, New York Mayor DeWittt Clinton, decided to make an effort to snag the presidency from the incumbent by seeking the support of both of these factions.

How could someone get away with agreeing with the hawks and doves? It's inconceivable to us at a time when every word a presidential candidate utters is replayed and analyzed on the evening news. But communication was much more difficult in 1812. The message Clinton delivered to pro-British Federalists in New England didn't reach the rest of the country, where his supporters were spreading a vehemently pro-war stance. With this mixed message, Clinton managed to win support from the New York State Democratic-Republican Party as well as a reluctant endorsement from Federalists who couldn't come up with a candidate of their own.

Some political figures who knew what was going on were disgusted. Former president John Adams, a staunch Federalist, was so upset he agreed to head the Madison campaign in his Massachusetts district. But the tactic made the race between Madison and his running mate, Elbridge Gerry of Massachusetts and Clinton and vice-presidential candidate Jared Ingersoll of Philadelphia, much closer than anyone could have predicted. It was only Madison's sweep of southern states that gave him a second term.

### Electoral votes:

Madison . . . . . . . . . . . . . . . . . . . . . . 128

Clinton . . . . . . . . . . . . . . . . . . . . . . . 89

• Thirteen courts of appeal handle appeals of decisions made in the district courts. About 10 percent to 15 percent of all lower court decisions, or about 35,000 cases, are appealed each year. This intermediate level of the court system was created by Congress in 1891 to ease the burden of the Supreme Court. Normally, appeals are heard by three judge panels formed from the three to twenty-four judges in each district.

• The Supreme Court, which is made up of a chief justice and eight associate justices, is the highest court in the country. The Constitution gives the Supreme

PRESIDENTIAL ELECTION 8

# 1816

## JAMES MONROE

Following what had a become a tradition, James Madison announced he would step down as president after two terms and pass the torch of his party's leadership to James Monroe. Another distinguished Virginian, Monroe was a revolutionary war hero who had served as governor of Virginia, ambassador to France, secretary of state, and finally, secretary of war in 1814. Although the U.S. didn't win the war, the conflict ended with Andrew Jackson's stirring defeat of the British in the Battle of New Orleans, which generated a wave of national pride. The candidacy of Monroe, a man of little charisma, didn't generate any significant excitement, but peace and relative prosperity gave voters enough reasons to support the Democratic-Republican nominee and his running mate, Governor Daniel Tompkins of New York.

On the other side of the political spectrum, the Federalists' opposition to the war dealt a final death blow to the party. The party had little support outside of its traditional strongholds such as Massachusetts, Connecticut, and Delaware. The Federalists held no nominating caucuses or conventions, but informally supported Rufus King, who had been the party's vice-presidential nominee in 1808 and 1812.

The results were a forgone conclusion even to King, who remarked, "Federalists of our age must be content with the past." Monroe received nearly six times as many electoral votes as the last Federalist presidential candidate.

Electoral votes:

Monroe . . . . . . . . . . . . . . . . . . . . . . . . 183
King . . . . . . . . . . . . . . . . . . . . . . . . . . . 34

---

Court the responsibility to try cases involving ambassadors, other diplomatic personnel, and those in which one of the fifty states is a party, but the Court only handles an average of four or five such cases a year. The overwhelming bulk of its work is as a last court of appeal of lower court rulings. About 4,000 cases a year are appealed to the Supreme Court, but the justices decide to review only about 300. The justices are appointed for life to guarantee that they are beyond the reach of political influence.

## What kinds of cases are decided in federal courts?

We have a dual court system in the United States—a state court system and a federal court system. The state court systems try the vast majority of cases—criminal cases, divorces, custody cases, civil cases, etc. The federal court system basically hears three types of cases:

- Cases involving violations of federal law, from kidnapping to terrorism to tax fraud.
- Cases involving interpretation of the Constitution, federal laws, or treaties. These include deciding the constitutionality of state laws, federal laws, and executive orders.
- Cases involving citizens from two different states. In most cases, the defendant in a civil matter has the option of having the case heard in state or federal court.

## Who serves on the Supreme Court?

Of the 113 justices who have served on the Supreme Court, only two have been women, and both serve on the Court now. Sandra Day O'Connor became the first female justice in 1981, and Ruth Bader Ginsburg joined her in 1994. Thurgood Marshall was appointed as the first black justice in 1967, and Clarence Thomas became the second in 1991, the year Marshall retired.

## What are the limits on the power of the Supreme Court?

The founders of our country wanted the court system to be isolated from political trends, so Supreme Court justices can't be fired nor can their decisions be vetoed. The only direct affect Congress can have is to amend the Constitution, rewrite a law to meet the courts objects, or, in some cases, write new laws limiting the jurisdiction of the district courts and the kinds of cases eligible for appeal.

Presidents can and do try to influence the long-term philosophy of the courts by selecting federal judges who more closely mirror their own opinions. All nominations are subject to the advice and consent of the Senate.

---

## WHAT DOES IT MEAN?
### VETO

The word *veto* is Latin for "I forbid." Through 1992, Presidents had exercised their right to veto 1,492 times, and just 104 of these vetoes were later overridden by Congress. Chief executives had also used the pocket veto (which can't be overridden because Congress isn't in session) to kill 1,066 pieces of legislation.

The all-time veto champ was Franklin D. Roosevelt, who kayoed 372 bills and was overridden just nine times. The worst victory record was chalked up by Andrew Johnson, who had fifteen of his twenty-one vetoes overturned. The most famous recent wielder of the veto was George Bush, who used the power thirty-seven times and was only overridden once. Said Senator Howard Metzenbaum of Bush, "He sleeps the veto and dreams the veto. He breathes the veto. The veto is his constant companion."

# Meet Your State Government

As goodwill ambassador to the nation for *Good Morning America*, I've had the good fortune to visit all fifty states, and it's the part of my job I love most. This travel has given me a profound appreciation of what I believe is one of our nation's greatest strengths—our physical, cultural, and economic diversity. You can find almost every type of landform that exists on earth within our borders, from snowcapped mountains and glaciers to rock-strewn deserts to fertile plains to vast forests to sandy beaches. Our natural resources include magnificent deep water ports, a vast navigable river system, rich mineral deposits, and more top-quality farmland than any other nation. The staggering breadth of our economy, the world's strongest, ranges from leadership in finance and high technology to abundant agricultural production to the creative forces that drive our entertainment community. If it sounds as if I'm totally captivated by the majesty of this land, that's because I am—I have even written *Spencer Christian's Geography Book* (St. Martin's Press, 1995) so that I can introduce others to the wonders of America.

What does American geography have to do with politics, you might ask? The answer is that the great physical, economic, and cultural diversity between the states requires diverse approaches to government. The people of an agricultural state like Kansas have different problems and needs than the people of Alaska or an industrial state like Rhode Island.

The founders of our country recognized the wisdom of having strong state governments within a strong federal government. That's why our Constitution calls for a kind of sharing of power between state and federal governments that set an example for other countries. Let's take a look at what responsibilities our states have and how their governments are structured.

## STATES AND THE CONSTITUTION

The Tenth Amendment, the last in the Bill of Rights, reserves to the states all powers that are not given to the federal government by the Constitution. That Constitution does spell out a number of things state governments can't do, including:

• Having anything other than a democratic state government

# WHAT DOES IT MEAN?
# STATES' RIGHTS

States' Rights is a political doctrine advocating the strict limitation of the federal government to those powers explicitly assigned to it in the Constitution of the United States, and reserving to the several states all other powers not explicitly forbidden them. The ratification of the U.S. Constitution still left many prominent Americans dissatisfied, including Thomas Jefferson, who believed that the federal government was only a voluntary compact of the states, and that the latter could legally refuse to carry out federal enactments they regarded as unconstitutional encroachments on their sovereignty. In 1798, Jefferson put forth this argument in a document called the Kentucky Resolution. It condemned federal passage of the Alien and Sedition Acts which gave the government the power to limit immigration, deport undesirable foreign residents, and severely restrict public criticism of the government. However, the issue never came to a head because Jefferson was elected President in 1800 and the much-hated Alien and Sedition Acts expired.

In the early 1800s, several states or groups of states who were unhappy with certain federal laws or policies put forth the Doctrine of Nullification. This doctrine stated that a state had the right to nullify any federal law that harmed its interests. The New England states, unhappy with the War of 1812, attempted to nullify federal trade embargo laws, but the war ended shortly afterwards. Nine years later, the Georgia legislature nullified a federal law granting land to American Indians, but a compromise was soon reached. A more serious crisis came about in 1832, when Sen. John C. Calhoun, infuriated by federal tariffs, got the South Carolina legislature to nullify those laws. Some Northern politicians called for the use of armed force to bring South Carolina into line, but President Andrew Jackson kept a cool head and negotiated a compromise. However, U.S. Senator Daniel Webster, in his most famous speech before the U.S. Senate, warned Senator Robert Young Hayne of South Carolina in 1830 that nullification would cause the Union to fall apart and that the American flag, "stained with the blood of fratricidal war, would wave over the dismembered fragments of our once glorious empire."

Webster proved to be a prophet. After the election of the staunch abolitionist Abraham Lincoln in 1860, the Southern states took nullification to the most extreme level—they tried to secede from the United States. After the bloodiest of all American conflicts, both the Confederacy and the concept of nullification were finished.

However, states' rights proponents continued to argue that the federal government's powers should be strictly limited to those expressly stated in the Constitution. Once again, a schism emerged over the rights of black Americans in 1948, when the Democrats included an extensive civil rights program into its platform. Some outraged Southerners withdrew from the Democratic party to form the "States'-Rights Democrats," and they nominated Strom Thurmond, the governor of South Carolina, to run for President. Thurmond collected about 1 million popular votes and 38 electoral votes.

Opposition to civil rights drove many Southern Democrats into the Republican party in the 1950s and 1960s, and in 1968, Georgia Governor George Wallace formed the American Independent party and ran for President on a states' rights platform. He won five Southern states.

The election of Ronald Reagan in 1980 rekindled the issue of states' rights once again. This time, states' rights advocates have argued that the federal government should pass along more funds and more control over government programs to the states. This movement is gaining strength in the 1990s.

PRESIDENTIAL ELECTION 9

# 1820

## JAMES MONROE

The presidential election of 1820 holds the distinction of being the dullest in U.S. history. George Washington ran unopposed for two terms because everyone in the country believed he was the perfect man for the job; James Monroe ran unopposed in 1820 because no one else cared to run.

Monroe and his running mate Daniel Tompkins were the unanimous choice of what had become, temporarily, America's only major political party. Federalist support had dwindled to the point at which the party could neither nominate or informally support a candidate. With no opponent on the horizon, one newspaper wrote, "The unanimous re-election of Mr. Monroe is morally certain, as certain as almost any contingent event can be." Public interest was so low that in Richmond, Virginia, only seventeen people turned out to vote.

But as it turned out, the election proved the old saw that nothing is certain but death and taxes. Monroe was denied sharing the distinction of a unanimous election with George Washington when a lone elector, William Plumer, a former New Hampshire governor and senator, cast a ballot for John Quincy Adams.

Electoral vote:

Monroe . . . . . . . . . . . . . . . . . . . . . . 231

Adams . . . . . . . . . . . . . . . . . . . . . . . 1

- Making a treaty with a foreign nation
- Granting titles of nobility
- Passing any laws abridging the right to a fair trial
- Passing any retroactive laws that make a noncriminal act into a criminal act
- Issuing currency
- Levying taxes on imports or exports
- Impairing the "obligation of contract"
- Keeping military forces in peacetime.

States are also prohibited from passing any laws that conflict with the Constitution or federal laws. For example, no state today could pass a law making slavery legal again or restricting the right to vote.

Finally, the Constitution governs relationships between the states. All states are required to honor each other's legal records, documents, and civil court rulings (for example, if you're married in New York, you're married in the other forty-nine states).

## State Revenues and Expenditures

### (fiscal year 1992)

Source: Census Bureau, U.S. Dept. of Commerce

| State | Revenue (millions) | Expenditures (millions) | State | Revenue (millions) | Expenditures (millions) |
|---|---|---|---|---|---|
| Alabama | 10,536 | 9,651 | Nebraska | 3,751 | 3,624 |
| Alaska | 6,227 | 6,255 | Nevada | 3,948 | 3,826 |
| Arizona | 9,551 | 9,096 | New Hampshire | 2,727 | 2,871 |
| Arkansas | 5,864 | 5,478 | New Jersey | 28,922 | 29,316 |
| California | 100,154 | 97,079 | New Mexico | 5,582 | 4,972 |
| Colorado | 9,079 | 7,492 | New York | 74,931 | 72,153 |
| Connecticut | 11,764 | 11,627 | North Carolina | 17,664 | 16,046 |
| Delaware | 2,848 | 2,504 | North Dakota | 2,072 | 2,001 |
| Florida | 28,311 | 27,089 | Ohio | 35,590 | 30,425 |
| Georgia | 14,761 | 14,054 | Oklahoma | 8,379 | 8,183 |
| Hawaii | 5,299 | 5,301 | Oregon | 10,025 | 7,979 |
| Idaho | 2,902 | 2,604 | Pennsylvania | 36,699 | 33,622 |
| Illinois | 27,665 | 26,832 | Rhode Island | 3,609 | 3,968 |
| Indiana | 13,490 | 12,341 | South Carolina | 9,897 | 9,428 |
| Iowa | 7,520 | 7,227 | South Dakota | 1,756 | 1,565 |
| Kansas | 5,794 | 5,464 | Tennessee | 11,126 | 10,406 |
| Kentucky | 10,640 | 10,154 | Texas | 36,763 | 33,894 |
| Louisiana | 11,842 | 11,750 | Utah | 4,917 | 4,481 |
| Maine | 3,755 | 3,722 | Vermont | 1,898 | 1,841 |
| Maryland | 13,730 | 13,004 | Virginia | 15,292 | 13,921 |
| Massachusetts | 20,456 | 20,368 | Washington | 17,366 | 17,316 |
| Michigan | 26,298 | 25,509 | West Virginia | 5,452 | 5,262 |
| Minnesota | 15,090 | 13,526 | Wisconsin | 17,131 | 13,596 |
| Mississippi | 6,177 | 5,762 | Wyoming | 2,007 | 1,925 |
| Missouri | 11,619 | 10,446 | | | |
| Montana | 2,661 | 2,460 | United States | 741,857 | 699,432 |

United States citizens have a right to all privileges offered in all states—for example, a New York resident has the right to file suit in a New Jersey court. The states must honor each other's criminal indictments and judgments. Finally, the states can't enter into interstate agreements without federal approval.

## What responsibilities are reserved to the states?

Despite the preeminence of the federal government in many areas, the states still have enormous responsibilities. Traditionally, states have nearly complete power in three areas:

# 1824

## JOHN QUINCY ADAMS

The 1820 presidential election was a one-man race; the 1824 election was a street brawl featuring, at one time, as many as 17 presidential candidates. The fierce contest to succeed Monroe began in 1822, and by the time 1824 came around, the field had been whittled to five major contenders, all from the same party: John Quincy Adams, son of the second president; Kentucky's Henry Clay, Speaker of the House of Representatives, South Carolina Senator John Calhoun; William Crawford, Monroe's secretary of the treasury, and War of 1812 hero Andrew Jackson.

Crawford was Monroe's choice, and with the support of the President, he was nominated by the Democratic-Republican caucus. That nomination, however, did him far more harm than good. Rank-and-file party members across the country had come to bitterly resent the fact that a handful of Washington officials got together and decided among themselves who the presidential and vice-presidential candidates could be. "Caucus" became a dirty word, and the demise of the old system of politics would soon give birth to a new system based on the nominating convention.

John Calhoun dropped out, but the four other contenders went to the wire in a raucous campaign that featured vicious personal attacks. One politician said that if all the attacks were taken seriously, one would have to conclude that "our Presidents, Secretaries, Senators, and Representatives, are all traitors and pirates, and the government of this people had been committed to the hands of public robbers."

As the selection of the electors began, it became clear that the real race was a close contest between Adams and Jackson. When the results were tallied, Jackson received the most electoral and popular votes, with Adams a close second. Because Jackson didn't receive a majority of electoral votes, the election (for the second time in U.S. history) was thrown into the House of Representatives.

The Constitution required the House to choose between the top three vote getters, which eliminated Henry Clay. Clay, as Speaker of the House, instantly became the power broker. Jackson and Adams supporters lobbied vigorously for Clay's support, but the Speaker was convinced that Adams' long experience made him by far the most qualified candidate. With Clay's support, Adams received the support of 13 states, enough to give him the presidency.

After Adams took office, he appointed Henry Clay as Secretary of State. Jackson's supports immediately charged that the appointment was the result of a secret deal that had robbed the "public's choice" of the office he deserved. Although Adams emerged from the election as the President, Jackson came out with an enhanced reputation that encouraged him to immediately begin campaigning for 1828.

| Electoral votes: | | Popular vote: | |
|---|---|---|---|
| Jackson | 99 | Jackson | 155,872 |
| Adams | 84 | Adams | 105,321 |
| Crawford | 41 | Clay | 46,587 |
| Clay | 37 | Crawford | 44,282 |

- Law enforcement
- Education
- Land use (zoning, housing development, etc.).

Over time, the relationship between state and federal governments has evolved into a "cooperative federalism." That means that in many areas from highways to welfare, the federal government provides funds or block grants which are administered and distributed by the states. Traditionally, the federal government has often provided strict guidelines on how the states may use these funds. In recent years, however, the trend is for Congress to give more and more discretion to the states. That has increased the already significant responsibilities of state government.

You can get an idea of the scope of state government by glancing at these figures: The states spent $700 billion in fiscal 1992 ($2,748 per person), which is about $180 billion more than the federal government spent on everything except national defense, social

## Size of State Legislatures

| State | House members | Senate members | | House members | Senate members |
|---|---|---|---|---|---|
| Alabama | 105 | 35 | Montana | 100 | 50 |
| Alaska | 40 | 20 | Nebraska | 49 Unicameral | |
| Arizona | 60 | 30 | Nevada | 42 | 21 |
| Arkansas | 100 | 35 | New Hampshire | 400 | 24 |
| California | 80 | 40 | New Jersey | 80 | 40 |
| Colorado | 65 | 35 | New Mexico | 70 | 42 |
| Connecticut | 151 | 36 | New York | 150 | 61 |
| Delaware | 41 | 21 | North Carolina | 120 | 50 |
| Florida | 120 | 40 | North Dakota | 98 | 49 |
| Georgia | 180 | 56 | Ohio | 99 | 33 |
| Hawaii | 51 | 25 | Oklahoma | 101 | 48 |
| Idaho | 70 | 35 | Oregon | 60 | 30 |
| Illinois | 118 | 59 | Pennsylvania | 203 | 50 |
| Indiana | 100 | 50 | Rhode Island | 100 | 50 |
| Iowa | 100 | 50 | South Carolina | 124 | 46 |
| Kansas | 125 | 40 | South Dakota | 70 | 35 |
| Kentucky | 100 | 38 | Tennessee | 99 | 33 |
| Louisiana | 105 | 39 | Texas | 150 | 31 |
| Maine | 151 | 35 | Utah | 75 | 29 |
| Maryland | 141 | 47 | Vermont | 150 | 30 |
| Massachusetts | 160 | 40 | Virginia | 100 | 40 |
| Michigan | 110 | 38 | Washington | 98 | 49 |
| Minnesota | 134 | 67 | West Virginia | 100 | 34 |
| Mississippi | 122 | 52 | Wisconsin | 99 | 33 |
| Missouri | 163 | 34 | Wyoming | 60 | 30 |

security, and interest on the national debt! That's why state governments control the scope and structure of local governments, and decisions by the state legislatures have dramatic effects on local schools, highways, crime, housing, welfare, and health programs, among others.

## What is the relationship between state government and local government?

There is no mention of local government in the Constitution, which means that theoretically, a state could abolish local government. But fortunately, every state in the union has incorporated the same spirit of federalism in the U.S. Constitution to their own constitutions, which means that all states share authority with local governments within their borders.

## What is the structure of state governments?

Like the federal government, state governments have three branches, legislative, executive, and judicial.

- State legislatures: Forty-nine of the fifty states have bicameral legislatures, consisting of a General Assembly and a Senate. The sole exception is Nebraska, which went to a unicameral (single house) legislature in 1938. Assembly members and senators normally earn the same salary and meet at the same time, but they are elected from different districts and sometimes to different term lengths.

The compensation, workload, and size of state legislatures varies widely. Some meet as few as sixty days per year, while others are in session virtually year around. Compensation ranges from $200 per year in New Hampshire to an annual salary of $57,500 in New York. The number of legislators range from just forty-nine in unicameral Nebraska to 424 in New Hampshire.

Because state legislatures meet only part time, the executive branch of state government tends to have relatively more power than does the executive branch of the federal government. State legislatures do have the power to override governors' vetoes, but they normally do not have the time, the money, or the staff members to conduct as many in-depth investigations of the executive branch as does the U.S. Congress. Also, in many states, such officials as the Attorney General, Treasurer, and Secretary of State are elected by popular vote, not confirmed by the legislature. In some states, the members of the judiciary, including the state supreme court justices, are also elected.

On the other hand, state legislatures have an extremely wide scope of responsibilities. State governments establish election districts, including the districts of members of the U.S. House of Representatives. They establish and administer all election laws. They determine the structure and scope of all local governments. Finally, they allocate the funds that make up, on the average, about two-thirds of all local government revenues.

# WHO WAS THOMAS JEFFERSON?

Thomas Jefferson (1743-1826) was born on April 13, 1743, at Shadwell in Albemarle County, Virginia. His father was a plantation owner, and his mother belonged to the Randolph family, which was prominent in colonial Virginia. After attending the College of William and Mary, he was admitted to the bar in 1767 and first elected to the Virginia House of Burgesses in 1769. He did not seriously consider marriage until 1770, when he met Martha Wayles Skelton (1747-82), a wealthy widow of twenty-three. They were married in 1772.

Jefferson's long bachelorhood gave him the time during his twenties for voracious reading in Enlightenment philosophy, seventeenth-century English history, political theory, and law. Drawing on this learning, he drafted in 1774 *A Summary View of the Rights of British America*. In the pamplet, Jefferson argued that the original settlers of the Colonies came as individuals rather than as agents of the British government. The Colonial governments they formed therefore embodied the natural right of expatriates from one country to select the terms of their subjection to a new ruler. Colonial legislatures and the British Parliament, he asserted, shared power, and both were responsible for "protecting the liberties and rights" of the people.

The Declaration of Independence, drafted principally by Jefferson in late June 1776 for the Second Continental Congress, drew the implications of this historical view to their logical conclusion, proclaiming that the tyrannical acts of the British government gave the colonists the right to dissolve the political bands that had connected them with the mother country.

Jefferson served as governor of Virginia from 1779 to 1781. He served as secretary of state in George Washington's first administration (1790–94). In 1796, he reluctantly allowed his name to be put forward as a candidate for the presidency by the opposition Republican party. He received the second largest number of votes among four candidates and therefore, according to the electoral system then in use, became Vice-President under the Federalist President John Adams in 1797.

During his term in that office he watched with growing indignation as the Federalists capitalized on anti-French feeling to create a standing army under the control of his enemy, Alexander Hamilton, and to pass the Alien Acts, restricting the liberty of supposedly pro-Republican foreigners, and the Sedition Act, which allowed the prosecution of anyone who printed false statements critical of government officials. In resolutions drafted for the Virginia and Kentucky legislatures, Jefferson and James Madison denounced the constitutionality of these laws and assigned to the states the role of bulwark against infringements on individual liberties.

In the election of 1800, Jefferson and his fellow Republican Aaron Burr received an equal number of electoral votes, thus creating a tie and throwing the presidential election into the House of Representatives. After 36 ballots, the House declared Jefferson elected. (The Constitution was then amended to require a single electoral vote for President and Vice-President.) As President, he steered a steady course between two extremes—those who wanted the bulk of power vested in the states and those who wanted a more powerful federal government. He opposed any assault on the independence of the Federalist-dominated judiciary; Jefferson's three appointments to the Supreme Court, made between 1804 and 1807, were all strong nationalists and upholders of judicial independence. Perhaps his major presidential achievement was the purchase from France of Louisiana, all the western land drained by the Missouri and Mississippi rivers, and the organization of a scientific expedition by William Clark and Meriwether Lewis to explore this territory.

After leaving office in 1809 he retired to Monticello, where he lived until his death on July 4, 1826.

# 1828

## ANDREW JACKSON

1828 represented one of the most dramatic turning points in U.S. political history. This presidential election was not just a rematch between the main contenders of 1824, but a conflict between the old and the new in American politics in many ways:

• Adams was the last of the patrician presidents, all of whom were members of what could be called the American aristocracy. All six were from Massachusetts or Virginia, the two oldest colonies. Jackson would become the first president from humble origins, born to Scotch-Irish immigrants in a small settlement in western South Carolina and orphaned at age 14.

• Adams shared with all of his predecessors, including George Washington, a disdain for party politics. Jackson believed that parties were the only way the common man could gain political power, and he built the first modern party organization.

• Adams held to the custom of staying aloof from campaigning, stating that, "If my country wants my services, she should ask for them." Jackson, a charismatic leader, took a vigorous and active role in managing his campaign.

• Adams believed that politics should be based on reason instead of emotion, and so he made his stand on issues known. Jackson was vague on specific issues, preferring instead to hammer home the theme that a vote for him would put power into the hands of the common man.

Jackson's popularity split the Democratic-Republican party in two. Jackson's faction began calling themselves Democrats, and his supporters included Adam's vice-president, John Calhoun, who agreed to take the second spot on Jackson's ticket. Adams' supporters called themselves the National Republicans, and they selected Treasury Secretary Richard Rush to run for vice-president. Because caucuses had been discredited in the election of 1824, Adams was nominated by state legislatures and conventions, while Jackson was named by conventions and mass meetings.

Given the immense contrasts between the two candidates, it isn't surprising that the campaign was brutal and vicious. Adams was portrayed as an immoral aristocrat who plotted to establish a monarchy while squandering tax dollars to maintain a lavish lifestyle. Jackson, on the other hand, was painted as an ignorant and reckless scoundrel whose past sins included adultery and murder.

The key to the election, however, wasn't rhetoric but rather the cumulative effect of a change in the procedure for selecting presidential electors. By 1828, electors were chosen by popular vote in 22 of the 24 states instead of being chosen by state legislatures. This change resulted in three times as many Americans voting in 1828 compared with 1824. So it's no surprise that Jackson's appeal to the common man won the day. He received 56 percent of the popular vote and 70 percent of the votes in the electoral college. Jackson took the oath of office in March, 1829, and he proceeded to change the institution of the presidency as dramatically as he changed the process of presidential campaigning.

| Electoral votes: | | Popular vote: | |
|---|---|---|---|
| Jackson | 178 | Jackson | 647,231 |
| Adams | 83 | Adams | 509,097 |

- The State Executive Branch: The chief executive of all fifty states is a popularly elected governor who serves a term of four years (except in New
Hampshire and Vermont, where the term is two years). Some states limit a
governor to one or two consecutive terms, while in others the governor can
serve as long as he or she can get reelected. The annual salaries of governors
ranges from $55,000 in Montana to $130,000 per year in New York.

Governors tend to have relatively more leverage over state legislatures than the
President does over Congress. For example, in forty-three states, governors have the
power of "line item" veto, which means that they can veto a specific item in the budget
rather than have to accept or reject the budget as a whole. This power is crucial, because
the majority of states are required by law to have a balanced budget. As the federal government increases the amount of money passed along to the states for distribution,
control over the budget puts additional power in the hands of the governors.

On the other hand, many governors have less control over the executive branch,
because key officials such as the Secretary of State, Treasurer, and Attorney General
are popularly elected instead of appointed. In some states, the lieutenant governor is
elected separately, which means that the governor and the lieutenant governor can
be from different parties. Electing key administrative officials serves as an effective
check on the power of the governor.

## What is an Attorney General?

An Attorney General is the chief law officer of state government whose duties are to
advise and represent the government in important legal matters, to supervise the
state law enforcement system, and to initiate and supervise legal proceedings that
affect the welfare of the state. The office of Attorney General dates from the reign
(1272-1307) of King Edward I. It developed gradually until the seventeenth century, when the attorney general became chief legal counsel to the Crown and all
departments of state and represented them in court cases.

In the United States the federal post of Attorney General was created by the
Judiciary Act of 1789. Each of the states established an official with duties similar to
those of the U.S. Attorney General. In some, the state official is appointed by the governor and in others the official is popularly elected.

## What are the duties of a State Treasurer?

The treasurer of a state normally supervises revenue collection (including taxes),
cash management, state borrowing, and state spending. The treasurer may also have
the responsibility of auditing state agencies and programs, although that responsibility is sometimes handled by a separately elected or appointed state comptroller.

PRESIDENTIAL ELECTION 12

# 1832

## ANDREW JACKSON

Jackson had campaigned in 1828 as the candidate of the common man, and right after the general's inauguration, his supporters returned to the White House and proceeded to get, in the language of the day, "liquored up." Then they smashed the china and crystal and trashed the furniture. The more sober guests, including the new President, escaped through the windows. After the mess was cleaned up, Jackson moved in—and proceeded to take advantage of the privileges of power, such as retaining his elitist predecessor's French chef, steward, and butler. When the next election came around, however, the shrewd Jackson's strategy was to once again position himself as the candidate of the people. To accomplish this, he decided that his main target in the campaign would not be the nominee from the other party, but a man named Nicholas Biddle.

And who was this Biddle? No less than the president of the nation's largest and most powerful financial institution, the Bank of the United States. In July, 1832, Jackson stunned the nation's financial community by vetoing a bill renewing the charter of the Bank, proclaiming that the bank only benefited rich and powerful at the expense of "the humble members of society—the farmers, merchants, and laborers." His outraged opponents charged that his veto was a "manifesto for anarchy" that would bring the nation to financial ruin so that Jackson could get the vote of the "great unwashed." Biddle and his bank became practically the sole issue of the campaign.

The election of 1832 was distinctive for two other reasons. For the first time in history, a third political party, the Anti-Masonic party, entered the race for the presidency. Secondly, for the first time in American history, presidential candidates were selected by national nominating conventions. The Anti-Masonic party had the honor of holding the first convention, selecting former U.S. Attorney General William Wirt. Next came the National Republicans, who selected Henry Clay, a fervent bank supporter, for President and a friend of Biddle's, John Sergeant of Pennsylvania, for Vice-President. The Democratic-Republicans renominated Andrew Jackson and picked Martin Van Buren of New York as his running mate. South Carolina's Nullification Party supported John Lloyd.

Biddle and other bank supporters spent an unprecedented amount of money to defeat Jackson, and they even encouraged business owners to threaten to fire employees who voted for the President. But the superb party organization Jackson had built in 1828 more than compensated for his opponent's spending spree. Jackson cruised to victory by a more comfortable margin than he had enjoyed in 1828, capturing 55 percent of the popular vote.

| Electoral votes: | |
|---|---|
| Jackson | 219 |
| Clay | 49 |
| Lloyd | 14 |
| Wirt | 7 |

| Popular vote: | |
|---|---|
| Jackson | 687,502 |
| Clay | 530,189 |

## What are the duties of a Secretary of State?

In the United States, all corporations are registered and regulated by state governments, and this function is normally vested in the Secretary of State. The Secretary of State may also regulate elections, maintain state records, oversee state personnel programs, and administer licensing programs for certain professions or occupations.

## How is the State Judiciary organized?

The judiciary in most states consists of superior courts, which are divided into districts, and a state supreme court. In many areas, there are also county and municipal court systems. Judges are either elected or appointed, but unlike the federal judiciary, the appointments are normally for a specific term. State court systems are not as well insulated from public opinion and political pressure as are federal courts.

## How to get information on your state government

Almost every library has copies of state constitutions, statutes, and other publications. In addition, every state maintains an information office that can answer questions, provide publications, and direct callers to the appropriate agencies.

---

### STATE GOVERNMENT INFORMATION TELEPHONE NUMBERS

| | | | |
|---|---|---|---|
| Alabama | Indiana | Nebraska | South Carolina |
| (334) 261-2500 | (317) 232-1000 | (402) 471-2311 | (803) 734-1000 |
| Alaska | Iowa | Nevada | South Dakota |
| (907) 465-2111 | (515) 281-5011 | (702) 885-5000 | (605) 773-3011 |
| Arizona | Kansas | New Hampshire | Tennessee |
| (520) 542-4900 | (913) 296-0111 | (603) 271-1110 | (615) 741-3011 |
| Arkansas | Kentucky | New Jersey | Texas |
| (501) 371-3000 | (502) 564-2500 | (609) 292-2121 | (512) 463-4630 |
| California | Louisiana | New Mexico | Utah |
| (916) 332-9900 | (504) 342-6600 | (505) 827-4011 | (801) 538-3000 |
| Colorado | Maine | New York | Vermont |
| (303) 866-5000 | (207) 289-1110 | (518) 474-2121 | (802) 828-1110 |
| Connecticut | Maryland | North Carolina | Virginia |
| (203) 566-2750 | (401) 974-3431 | (919) 733-1110 | (804) 786-0000 |
| Delaware | Massachusetts | North Dakota | Washington |
| (302) 739-4000 | (617) 727-7030 | (701) 224-2000 | (360) 753-5000 |
| Florida | Michigan | Ohio | West Virginia |
| (904) 488-1234 | (517) 373-1837 | (614) 466-2000 | (304) 348-3456 |
| Georgia | Minnesota | Oklahoma | Wisconsin |
| (404) 656-2000 | (612) 296-6013 | (405) 521-1601 | (608) 266-2211 |
| Hawaii | Mississippi | Oregon | Wyoming |
| (808) 548-2211 | (601) 359-1000 | (503) 378-3131 | (307) 777-7220 |
| Idaho | Missouri | Pennsylvania | |
| (208) 334-2411 | (314) 751-2000 | (717) 787-2121 | |
| Illinois | Montana | Rhode Island | |
| (217) 782-2000 | (406) 444-2511 | (401) 277-2000 | |

# Meet Your Local Government

4

"ALL POLITICS ARE LOCAL."

—TIP O'NEILL

The above quote from the former Speaker of the House seems dead on when you consider that there are about 80,000 local governments in the United States. But even though these governments are closest to home, we tend to know a lot less about them than we do about the federal and state governments. We'll begin to remedy that by describing the structure of local governments and the positions available.

## A SHORT HISTORY OF LOCAL GOVERNMENT IN AMERICA

The original thirteen colonies were governed by England, so it was natural that the first settlers adopted the British model when establishing the first local governments. Because most people were widely dispersed on small farms or plantations, most of the colonies were divided into large counties. As America spread westward, new states and territories were divided into counties even before settlers moved in.

There were, of course, urban areas that sprang up around ports or other transportation hubs. To provide the higher level of services needed for a denser population, governments outside of New England were modeled on the English boroughs, which were granted a charter, or contract to conduct certain activities and collect certain taxes, from the king. These boroughs were governed by aldermen or councilmen elected by the people and a mayor appointed by the governor. There were twenty-four chartered boroughs when the United States won its freedom from Great Britain, and they developed into the modern municipality.

New England was an exception to both trends. Settlements were more compact, so counties weren't necessary. More important, the settlers were fiercely democratic. They refused to seek charters from the king or accept appointed officials. So their communities were organized as towns, in which all important decisions were made by all of the residents who gathered together for town meetings.

PRESIDENTIAL ELECTION 13

# 1836

## MARTIN VAN BUREN

Despite the urgings of his supporters, Andrew Jackson decided not to run for a third term. As his successor, he made sure his party nominated his Vice-President, Martin Van Buren, a wily politician who had been largely responsible for creating the efficient party organization that had given Jackson two easy victories. Many Democrats grumbled that Van Buren was far from a "man of the people," and even more disliked Jackson's choice for Vice-President, Col. Richard M. Johnson of Kentucky, who openly lived with a black woman and had two children by her. But the party organization worked vigorously for the ticket's election.

Hard work was needed, for Jackson had alienated many Southerners by threatening force to quell opposition to a tariff enacted in 1832. In 1834, significant number of Southerners joined together with the Anti-Masons and the national bank supporters to form a new party. The coalition called themselves the Whigs, after the English Whigs who had fought against royal despotism, because they wanted to bring down the party of the autocratic President they called "King Andrew the First." The Whigs weren't organized enough to hold a national convention in 1836, so they decided on a novel strategy—to run three different candidates, each of whom had strong appeal in different areas of the country.

Candidate number one was the famed orator, statesman, and senator Daniel Webster, who was extremely popular in New England. To get the Southern vote, they selected Tennessee Senator Hugh L. White. And to appeal to Westerners, they chose William Henry Harrison of Ohio, who during the War of 1812 had led a force that defeated the famous Indian chief Tecumseh at the Battle of Tippicanoe. To make things more complicated, an Anti-Jackson party formed in South Carolina and nominated Willie P. Mangum for president.

The Whigs viciously attacked Van Buren as an aristocratic dandy who had such a difficult time making up his mind that for a time the word *vanburenish* entered the language, meaning "evasive." One of the most scathing attacks on the Democratic nominee was a biography penned by the famous frontiersman Davy Crockett. Van Buren's supporters countered with the well-organized rallies and parades that had worked for Jackson.

To nobody's surprise, the election was close—Van Buren managed only 50.9 percent of the vote while garnering 46 more electoral votes than his opponents. What was shocking was that the strongest Whig candidate by far was the newcomer to politics, William Henry Harrison, who performed so well that within days after the election, he was deemed to be the Whig candidate for 1836.

| Electoral votes: | | Popular vote: | |
|---|---|---|---|
| VanBuren | 170 | Van Buren | 762,678 |
| Harrison | 73 | Whigs | 739,795 |
| White | 26 | Wirt | 91,602 |
| Webster | 14 | | |
| Mangum | 11 | | |

## THE PRIMARY FORMS OF LOCAL GOVERNMENT

The County, the Municipality, and the Town or Township are still the primary forms of local government in the United States today, although their structures and responsibilities have undergone a lot of growth and change. Some states have also created a fourth form of local government called a Special District, which is created to administer one particular service, such as education, sewage collection and processing, or health services.

Let's take a closer look at each form of government and see what the most common elected officials are.

---

## WHAT DOES IT MEAN?
### COUNTY

The word *county* comes from a French word that means "territory of a count." After the Normans invaded Britain in 1066, the word gradually replaced the Saxon term "shire" (as in "Hampshire"), which defined a large area controlled by a specific tribe.

Counties have been the largest administrative areas in Great Britain ever since, and settlers took the concept of a county with them to the new world.

---

## COUNTIES

Counties are the largest local governmental units in forty-eight of the fifty states, although these units are called parishes in Louisiana and boroughs in Alaska. Only Connecticut and Rhode Island have no county governments. Some cities in Virginia, Maryland, and Missouri are not part of any county. The number of counties has little relationship to a state's population. Iowa, with 2.8 million people, has ninety-nine counties; Arizona, with a population of four million, has just fourteen. The United States has 3,042 counties governed by about 61,000 elected officials.

County boundaries were created by the state and the responsibilities and limits of county government are determined by each state legislature. Over the last three decades, as people increasingly fled central cities for sprawling suburbs, county governments have been given more to do. An increasing number of city governments have been absorbed into county governments to reduce expenses and provide services more efficiently.

### What do counties do?

To me, the word *county* brings to mind two phrases "county highway" and "county jail." That's because almost all counties have long been responsible for building and maintaining a system of roads and protecting public safety with a sheriff's department, judicial system, and correctional facilities. The county courthouse is

also commonly home to probate administrators, a registrar of deeds, a county clerk, and an election commission.

Other responsibilities vary widely from state to state. Many counties are responsible for public welfare programs, health and hospital services, parks and recreational facilities, and water and air pollution control programs. Only in a handful of states are counties involved in education.

## Where do counties get their money?

Because counties were created primarily to carry out state programs, it's not surprising that two-thirds of the typical county budget comes from the state treasury. The other third is raised through local property taxes.

## What is a county board?

About four-fifths of all counties have an elected county board—for which there are at least thirty-four different titles across the United States. Although a handful of counties have boards of fifty members or more, the average size is three to five. In some counties, board members are each elected to represent a specific district within the county, while in other counties all board members are elected at large (that means every voter gets to select among all the candidates).

## What does a county board do?

Most county boards have both administrative and legislative duties. Those fancy words mean that the members act like managers. They supervise county programs and employees, and at the same time they introduce, debate, and vote on new laws and taxes.

## What is a county executive?

A county executive is an appointed or elected individual who serves as sort of mayor for a county. County executives run counties with no elected boards and they are becoming increasingly common in counties with boards.

---

### WHAT DOES IT MEAN?
### BOROUGH

Boroughs existed in England from the earliest times. Among the early Anglo-Saxons, the borough was a fort or fortified place. As law and order developed, it became a group of fortified houses and finally a town having special duties and privileges, including the right to send a representative to Parliament.

Today, there are two kinds of boroughs in Great Britain. A municipal borough is a city or part of a city (London has thirty-two boroughs, each with a major, alderman, and councilors). A parliamentary borough is a district that sends a member to Parliament, but has no governmental function.

The amount of power given to the executive by the county board varies widely. Some "strong" county executives make appointments and have veto power over board decisions; at the other end of the spectrum, some are merely managers with no independent decision-making authority.

## What other county officials are elected?

Most counties elect a number of administrators who are called "row officials." These include:
- County sheriff, who supervises the law enforcement and corrections departments
- Prosecutor or prosecuting attorney, who acts like a city district attorney
- A supervising judge or judges
- A county clerk, who records marriages, births, deaths, and other kinds of records
- A recorder of deeds, who deals with property rights and transfers.

How much control the county board or county executive has over the row officials varies from county to county.

## How can you find out about the structure of your county?

All counties have administrative offices located in a specific location, called the county seat. Call or visit the county seat to ask for information on who does what.

## MUNICIPALITIES

For most of us, our municipality is what we list before our state on our mailing address. A municipality can be a city (50,000 people or more), a town (less than 50,000), or a village (usually under 10,000 people). In the United States we have over 19,000 municipalities with more than 460,000 elected officials.

## What is a municipality?

A municipality is a kind of public corporation that is chartered by the state. This charter is like a contract that spells out in great detail what the municipality can and can't do. Although all state charters are different, almost all allow local governments to raise money through taxes and borrowing, spend money, buy and sell property, and provide a variety of public services.

## What do municipalities do?

Municipalities provide the local government services that counties don't provide. Although the list varies widely from state to state and from small hamlet to big city, those services may include:
- Education—operating local schools, building and maintaining school buildings, and operating libraries

---

## WHAT DOES IT MEAN?
## MUNICIPALITY

The word *municipality* comes from the Latin word *municipium*, which was used to identify towns or cities annexed by the Roman Empire that were granted certain rights of self-government. The term was later used in England to identify urban areas that were granted charters by the king. A charter is a kind of contract that spells out the duties and responsibilities of the local government. Most cities, towns, and villages in the United States are municipalities.

---

- Sewage treatment and refuse removal
- Fire fighting and protection
- Transportation—ranging from plowing local streets to operating a transit system
- City planning—issuing building permits, pursuing economic development, administering a zoning program, initiating urban renewal efforts
- Public safety—operating a police department and court system
- Health services—anything from inspecting restaurants to operating a hospital system
- Social services—administering welfare payments, child protection services, etc.
- Parks and recreation.

## What is the structure of municipal government?

Since Americans can seldom agree on anything, it's not surprising that there are four basic types of municipal government:
- The weak mayor-council plan
- The strong mayor-council plan
- The commission plan
- The council-manager plan.

## What is the weak mayor-council plan?

The weak mayor-council plan is the oldest form of local government in the United States, and it was the structure of nearly every municipality, small or large, until the latter part of the nineteenth century. Under this plan the mayor, elected by the voters at large, usually has limited appointive and veto powers and little control over the city administration. The council, elected either by districts or by the voters at large, has both legislative and executive powers, including the authority to appoint and supervise administrative department heads.

## What is the strong mayor-council plan?

As city government became more complex in the late nineteenth century, municipal governments became increasingly paralyzed by the difficulties involved in having

every administrative decision made jointly by all the council members. As part of a trend to that led to the strengthening of powers of chief executives at all levels of government, most large cities and towns adopted the strong mayor-council structure. Under this plan the mayor, elected by the voters at large, has considerable appointive and removal powers, a strong veto power, almost complete control of administrative department heads, and full responsibility for the city budget. The council, which is usually smaller under this system, is restricted mainly to lawmaking functions. Almost all large U.S. cities still have this form of government.

## What is the commission plan?

In 1900, the city of Galveston, Texas was completely destroyed by a powerful hurricane (I just love weather-related history!). There was so much work to be done rebuilding the city from scratch that the state legislature suspended Galveston's mayor-council government and replaced it with a commission composed of five members, each of which was responsible for administering a different part of the government. The commission was so effective that Galveston permanently adopted the system, with commissioners elected rather than appointed.

Galveston's positive experience led many other municipalities to adopt the commission plan. One positive effect of this structure was that it diminished the power of political parties. However, that was outweighed in many cases by the delays and confusion that sometimes resulted when there was a serious dispute among the members of the commission. Consequently, many cities that tried the commission plan have reverted to the mayor-council plan or adopted the newer council-manager plan—only about 125 U.S. cities still use it today, with Miami, Florida being the largest by far.

---

### WHAT DOES IT MEAN?

#### CITY

The word *city* is derived from the Latin word *civitas*, which means a community that administers its own affairs. In ancient Greece such an independent community was called a city-state; it consisted of a chief town and its immediate neighborhood. During the Middle Ages a city was usually identical with a cathedral town; accordingly, when King Henry VIII of England established new bishoprics in boroughs, he made these into cities. In modern Great Britain *city* is merely a complimentary title conferred by the monarch on important towns.

In the United States a city is a chartered municipal corporation. Charters are granted by state governments according to requirements prescribed by the legislature of that state; a city must usually attain a certain population, commonly 50,000, before it can be granted a charter.

# What is the council-manager plan?

Early in this century, an insurance company executive named Richard S. Childs began to explore ways to make city government more efficient. His solution was to copy private business by giving administrative control of a city not to a politician, but to a professional manager who would be hired for his or her qualifications, just as corporations hire chief executive officers. In 1912, Sumter, South Carolina became the first U.S. city to adopt the council-manager form of government, and Dayton, Ohio followed the next year.

Today, more than half of all municipalities with a population over 10,000 peo-

## WHO WAS...

Abraham Lincoln was born on February 12, 1809, near Hodgenville, Kentucky, the son of Nancy Hanks (1784?–1818) and Thomas Lincoln (1778–1851), pioneer farmers. His mother died in 1817, and in 1819 his father married Sarah Bush Johnston (1788–1869), a kindly widow, who soon gained the boy's affection.

Lincoln grew up a tall, gangling youth, who could hold his own in physical contests and also showed great intellectual promise, although he had little formal education. After moving with his family to Macon County, Illinois, in 1831, he struck out on his own, taking a cargo to New Orleans, Louisiana, on a flatboat. He then returned to Illinois and settled in New Salem, a short-lived community on the Sangamon River, where he split rails and clerked in a store. He gained the respect of his fellow townspeople and was elected captain of his company in the Black Hawk War (1832).

Defeated in 1832 in a race for the state legislature, Lincoln was elected on the Whig ticket two years later and served in the lower house from 1834 to 1841. He quickly emerged as one of the leaders of the party and was one of the authors of the removal of the capital to Springfield, where he settled in 1837. He was admitted to the bar in 1836 and began a successful law practice. In 1842 Lincoln married Mary Todd (1818–82), the daughter of a prominent Kentucky banker, and despite her somewhat difficult disposition, the marriage seems to have been reasonably successful. The Lincolns had four children, only one of whom reached adulthood.

His birth in a slave state notwithstanding, Lincoln had long opposed slavery. In the legislature he voted against resolutions favorable to the "peculiar" institution and in 1837 was one of two members who signed a protest against it. Elected to Congress in 1846, he attracted attention because of his outspoken criticism of the war with Mexico and formulated a plan for gradual emancipation in the District of Columbia. He was not an abolitionist, however. Conceding the right of the states to manage their own affairs, he merely sought to prevent the spread of human bondage.

In 1857, he joined the newly formed Republican party and in 1858 he became its senatorial candidate against Stephen Douglas. In a speech to the party's state convention that year he warned that "a house divided against itself cannot stand" and predicted the eventual triumph of freedom. Although Lincoln lost the election to Douglas, his eloquence in a series of campaign debates won him national recognition.

In 1860 the Republicans, anxious to attract as many different factions as possible, nominated Lincoln for the presidency on a platform of slavery restriction, internal improvements, homesteads, and tariff reform. In a campaign against Douglas and

ple have a popularly elected council (the largest city with a council-manager government is San Diego, California), which is responsible for making laws. The council, in turn, selects and employs an authority, usually called the city manager, a professional in the field of municipal administration, to manage the day-to-day affairs of the city, direct its administrative agencies, and hire administrators. In addition, a growing number of municipalities that still elect mayors also hire professional managers to handle part or most of the administrative work.

## ABRAHAM LINCOLN?

John C. Breckinridge, two rival Democrats, and John Bell, of the Constitutional Union party, Lincoln won a majority of the electoral votes and was elected President. Immediately after the election, South Carolina, followed by six other Southern states, took steps to secede from the Union.

When Lincoln took the oath of office on March 4, 1861, he was confronted with a hostile Confederacy determined to expand and threatening the remaining federal forts in the South, the most important of which was Fort Sumter in the harbor of Charleston, South Carolina. The Confederates, unwilling to permit continued federal occupation of their soil, opened fire on the fort, thus starting the Civil War. When Lincoln countered with a call for 75,000 volunteers, the North responded with enthusiasm, but the upper South seceded.

On July 22, 1862, Lincoln told his cabinet that he intended to issue an Emancipation Proclamation. Promulgated by the President in his capacity as commander-in-chief in times of actual armed rebellion, the proclamation freed slaves in regions held by the insurgents and authorized the creation of black military units. Lincoln was determined to place emancipation on a more permanent basis, however, and in 1864 he advocated the adoption of an antislavery amendment to the U.S. Constitution. The amendment was passed after Lincoln's reelection, when he made use of all the powers of his office to ensure its success in the House of Representatives (January 31, 1865).

A consummate politician, Lincoln sought to maintain harmony among the disparate elements of his party by giving them representation in his cabinet. Lincoln's political influence was enhanced by his great gifts as an orator. Able to stress essentials in simple terms, he effectively appealed to the nation in such classical short speeches as the Gettysburg Address and his second inaugural address. Moreover, he was a capable diplomat.

At his second inaugural, Lincoln, attributing the war to the evil consequences of slavery, summed up his attitude in the famous phrase "with malice toward none, with charity for all." A few weeks later, he publicly announced his support for limited black suffrage in Louisiana. This open defiance of conservative opinion could only have strengthened the resolve of one in his audience, John Wilkes Booth, a well-known actor of Confederate sympathies, who had long been plotting against the President. Aroused by the prospect of votes for blacks, he determined to carry out his assassination scheme and on April 14, 1865, shot Lincoln at Ford's Theater in Washington, D.C. President Lincoln died of his wounds the next day.

## Where do municipalities get their money?

Municipalities obtain most of their money through taxes—property taxes, income taxes, sales taxes, or use taxes. They also receive funds from state and federal governments, and they can raise money for capital projects by issuing bonds or incurring other forms of debt.

## What municipal officials are elected?

The strong mayor-council and council-manager plans both restrict the number of officials who are directly elected. Council members usually represent a specific district, which is often called a precinct or a ward. The mayor (sometimes a deputy mayor) is most commonly elected at large, although in some places the mayor is a member of the council who is elected by his or her peers. While county officials such as the sheriff and prosecuting attorney are elected, their equivalent positions in most municipal governments are filled by appointment.

The most prominent exception to this general rule involves members of the school board, who are generally elected by the people. Many municipalities also elect judges.

## How can you find out about the structure of your municipal government?

The office of your mayor or city manager can usually direct you to information about who does what in your locality.

## TOWNS AND TOWNSHIPS

Although many of you informally refer to your community as a town, the formal term applies to a form of government

### COUNTIES WITH 1990 POPULATION OVER ONE MILLION

| COUNTY NAME | APRIL 1, 1990 CENSUS |
|---|---|
| Los Angeles, CA | 8,863,164 |
| Cook, IL | 5,105,067 |
| Harris, TX | 2,818,199 |
| San Diego, CA | 2,498,016 |
| Orange, CA | 2,410,556 |
| Kings (Brooklyn), NY | 2,300,664 |
| Maricopa, AZ | 2,122,101 |
| Wayne, MI | 2,111,687 |
| Queens, NY | 1,951,598 |
| Dade, FL | 1,937,094 |
| Dallas, TX | 1,852,810 |
| Philadelphia, PA | 1,585,577 |
| King, WA | 1,507,319 |
| Santa Clara, CA | 1,497,577 |
| New York, NY | 1,487,536 |
| San Bernadino, CA | 1,418,380 |
| Cuyahoga, OH | 1,412,140 |
| Middlesex, MA | 1,398,468 |
| Allegheny, PA | 1,336,449 |
| Suffolk, NY | 1,321,864 |
| Nassau, NY | 1,287,348 |
| Alameda, CA | 1,279,182 |
| Broward, FL | 1,255,488 |
| Bronx, NY | 1,203,789 |
| Bexar, TX | 1,185,394 |
| Riverside, CA | 1,170,413 |
| Tarrant, TX | 1,170,103 |
| Oakland, MI | 1,083,592 |
| Sacramento, CA | 1,041,219 |
| Hennepin, MN | 1,032,431 |

# Population of U.S. Cities

Source: U.S. Bureau of the Census.

**(100 most populated cities ranked by April, 1990 census)**

| Rank | City | 1990 | Rank | City | 1990 |
|---|---|---|---|---|---|
| 1 | New York, NY | 7,322,564 | 51 | Wichita, KS | 304,011 |
| 2 | Los Angeles, CA | 3,485,398 | 52 | Santa Ana, CA | 293,742 |
| 3 | Chicago, IL | 2,783,726 | 53 | Mesa, AZ | 288,091 |
| 4 | Houston, TX | 1,630,553 | 54 | Colorado Springs, CO | 281,140 |
| 5 | Philadelphia, PA | 1,585,577 | 55 | Tampa, FL | 280,015 |
| 6 | San Diego, CA | 1,110,549 | 56 | Newark, NJ | 275,221 |
| 7 | Detroit, MI | 1,027,974 | 57 | St. Paul, MN | 272,235 |
| 8 | Dallas, TX | 1,006,877 | 58 | Louisville, KY | 269,063 |
| 9 | Phoenix, AZ | 983,403 | 59 | Anaheim, CA | 266,406 |
| 10 | San Antonio, TX | 935,933 | 60 | Birmingham, AL | 265,968 |
| 11 | San Jose, CA | 782,248 | 61 | Arlington, TX | 261,721 |
| 12 | Indianapolis, IN | 741,952 | 62 | Norfolk, VA | 261,229 |
| 13 | Baltimore, MD | 736,014 | 63 | Las Vegas, NV | 258,295 |
| 14 | San Francisco, CA | 723,959 | 64 | Corpus Christi, TX | 257,453 |
| 15 | Jacksonville, FL | 672,971 | 65 | St. Petersburg, FL | 238,629 |
| 16 | Columbus, OH | 632,910 | 66 | Rochester, NY | 231,636 |
| 17 | Milwaukee, WI | 628,088 | 67 | Jersey City, NJ | 228,537 |
| 18 | Memphis, TN | 610,337 | 68 | Riverside, CA | 226,505 |
| 19 | Washington, DC | 606,900 | 69 | Anchorage, AK | 226,338 |
| 20 | Boston, MA | 574,283 | 70 | Lexington-Fayette, KY | 225,366 |
| 21 | Seattle, WA | 516,259 | 71 | Akron, OH | 223,019 |
| 22 | El Paso, TX | 515,342 | 72 | Aurora, CO | 222,103 |
| 23 | Nashville-Davidson, TN | 510,784 | 73 | Baton Rouge, LA | 219,531 |
| 24 | Cleveland, OH | 505,616 | 74 | Stockton, CA | 210,943 |
| 25 | New Orleans, LA | 496,938 | 75 | Raleigh, NC | 207,951 |
| 26 | Denver, CO | 467,610 | 76 | Richmond, VA | 203,056 |
| 27 | Austin, TX | 465,622 | 77 | Shreveport, LA | 198,525 |
| 28 | Fort Worth, TX | 447,619 | 78 | Jackson, MS | 196,637 |
| 29 | Oklahoma City, OK | 444,719 | 79 | Mobile, AL | 196,278 |
| 30 | Portland, OR | 437,319 | 80 | Des Moines, IA | 193,187 |
| 31 | Kansas City, MO | 435,146 | 81 | Lincoln, NE | 191,972 |
| 32 | Long Beach, CA | 429,433 | 82 | Madison, WI | 191,262 |
| 33 | Tucson, AZ | 405,390 | 83 | Grand Rapids, MI | 189,126 |
| 34 | St. Louis, MO | 396,685 | 84 | Yonkers, NY | 188,082 |
| 35 | Charlotte, NC | 395,934 | 85 | Hialeah, FL | 188,004 |
| 36 | Atlanta, GA | 394,017 | 86 | Montgomery, AL | 187,106 |
| 37 | Virginia Beach, VA | 393,069 | 87 | Lubbock, TX | 186,206 |
| 38 | Albuquerque, NM | 384,736 | 88 | Greensboro, NC | 183,521 |
| 39 | Oakland, CA | 372,242 | 89 | Dayton, OH | 182,044 |
| 40 | Pittsburgh, PA | 369,879 | 90 | Huntington Beach, CA | 181,519 |
| 41 | Sacramento, CA | 369,365 | 91 | Garland, TX | 180,650 |
| 42 | Minneapolis, MN | 368,383 | 92 | Glendale, CA. | 180,038 |
| 43 | Tulsa, OK | 367,302 | 93 | Columbus, GA | 179,278 |
| 44 | Honolulu, CDP, HI | 365,272 | 94 | Spokane, WA | 177,196 |
| 45 | Cincinnati, OH | 364,040 | 95 | Tacoma, WA | 176,664 |
| 46 | Miami, FL | 358,548 | 96 | Little Rock, AR | 175,795 |
| 47 | Fresno, CA | 354,202 | 97 | Bakersfield, CA | 174,820 |
| 48 | Omaha, NE | 335,795 | 98 | Fremont, CA | 173,339 |
| 49 | Toledo, OH | 332,943 | 99 | Fort Wayne, IN | 173,072 |
| 50 | Buffalo, NY | 328,123 | 100 | Newport News, VA | 170,045 |

that's only found in some New England states. Towns are called plantations in Maine and locations in New Hampshire.

Township is a name for a local government unit that is used in twenty states, but most commonly in New Jersey, Pennsyl-vania, and Maryland. These townships are operated just like municipalities.

## What is a town?

Early New England settlers demonstrated their independence by refusing to ask for a Royal charter for their communities. And they put their democratic beliefs into practice by establishing a form of government in which all important decisions were made collectively by all the residents in a town meeting. At this meeting, residents enacted laws, appointed officials, levied taxes, and made administrative decisions.

The town meeting survives in many smaller New England communities, although the number of issues put to vote at such meetings has been reduced. Reflecting the rich tradition of citizen participation, towns tend to have a much larger number of elective offices than do municipalities. For example, voters in one small Connecticut town where a friend of mine lives choose between candidates for forty-seven positions—slates considerably larger than those placed in front of voters in New York, Chicago, Los Angeles, or almost any other big city!

## What are the other differences between a town and a municipality?

Except for the level of citizen participation, towns operate like municipalities, provide the same types of services, and raise money in the same ways. Most have a weak mayor-council structure. The mayor (sometimes called the first selectman) has administrative responsibilities, but doesn't have the power to veto legislation or hire other administrators.

### NUMBER OF COUNTIES IN EACH STATE

| | | | |
|---|---|---|---|
| Alabama ..........67 | Indiana.............92 | Nebraska .........93 | South Carolina .46 |
| Alaska.............25 | Iowa .................99 | Nevada ............16 | South Dakota ....67 |
| Arizona ............ 5 | Kansas............105 | New Hampshire 10 | Tennessee........95 |
| Arkansas..........75 | Kentucky ........120 | New Jersey .......21 | Texas .............254 |
| California........58 | Louisiana .........64 | New Mexico .....33 | Utah .................29 |
| Colorado..........63 | Maine...............16 | New York.........62 | Vermont...........14 |
| Connecticut .......8 | Maryland .........23 | North Carolina 100 | Virginia............95 |
| Delaware ..........3 | Massachusetts..14 | North Dakota ....53 | Washington......39 |
| Florida.............67 | Michigan..........83 | Ohio.................88 | West Virginia....55 |
| Georgia..........159 | Minnesota ........87 | Oklahoma ........77 | Wisconsin ........72 |
| Hawaii..............5 | Mississippi.......82 | Oregon ............36 | Wyoming .........23 |
| Idaho ..............44 | Missouri .........114 | Pennsylvania....67 | |
| Illinois ............102 | Montana...........56 | Rhode Island......5 | |

PRESIDENTIAL ELECTION 14

# 1840

## WILLIAM HENRY HARRISON

If Jackson's candidacy in 1832 opened the door to public participation in presidential politics, the election of 1840 saw the floodgates finally wide open. The Whigs had rallied behind William Henry Harrison shortly after the 1836 election, and by 1840, in the words of John Quincy Adams, "The whole country is in a state of agitation upon the approaching presidential election such as was never before witness." Borrowing a page from Andrew Jackson's book, the Whigs painted their candidate as a great war hero and a man of the people who lived in a simple log cabin—a vivid contrast to Van Buren, the incumbent, who the Whigs called an aristocratic, elitist snob.

In truth, Harrison had been born into one of the wealthiest and most prestigious families in Virginia. His father, Benjamin Harrison, several times elected the governor of Virginia, owned one of the greatest plantations in the South. William Henry Harrison obtained all of his military and civilian positions based on his father's influence rather than on his own abilities. He had been a barely adequate military commander and a mediocre territorial governor. His most recent political position before his nomination to run for the presidency had been as a county recorder in Ohio.

However, the Whig portrait held up brilliantly for one reason: Harrison, following the advice of his mentors, refused to utter a word about the issues during the entire campaign. His Democratic critics attacked him as "General Mum." But the Whig campaign slogan, "Tippicanoe and Tyler, too" (John Tyler of Virginia was his running mate) had a much more compelling ring. The Democratic ticket of Van Buren and Richard S. Johnson had suggested no alliterative phrase.

In the end, it probably wasn't campaign slogans or slanders that denied Van Buren a second term. Rather, severe economic hardships following the Panic of 1837 made many ordinary people desperate for a change. They flocked to the polls in records numbers (nearly 1 million more votes were cast in 1840 than in 1836), and although the popular vote was close, Harrison and Tyler smashed their opponents in the electoral college.

Ironically, the public never found out what kind of leader Harrison might have been. The President-elect caught a severe cold at his inauguration and died of pneumonia a month later. John Tyler became the first "accidental President" in American history and a man whose belief that the rights of the states superseded the power of the presidency horrified many of his fellow Whigs.

| Electoral votes: | | Popular vote: | |
|---|---|---|---|
| Harrison | 234 | Harrison | 1,274,624 |
| Van Buren | 60 | Van Buren | 1,127,781 |

## SPECIAL DISTRICTS

Special districts have been created to serve public needs by providing single services more efficiently than existing local governments. The best example of a special district is a rural school system that serves several small municipalities, each of which couldn't afford to operate a school system on its own. In addition to education, special districts are frequently established to provide sewerage, parks and recreation, fire protection, soil and water conservation, hospitals, or libraries.

Most districts are administered by a board with members called commissioners, trustees, or supervisors; board members may be either appointed or elected. With the establishment of new and more extensive suburban areas near large cities, the number of special districts continues to increase.

PRESIDENTIAL ELECTION 15

# 1844

## JAMES POLK

The campaign of 1840 had been waged largely on petty personal attacks; in stark contrast, the central issue of the 1844 race was one of the grand issues of the day: manifest destiny. This phrase (it probably rings a bell with most of you from those otherwise long forgotten history classes) represents a widely held belief held by many Americans that God had ordained that the United States should expand from coast to coast. Like most grand concepts, manifest destiny was based not just on a philosophical belief, but on hard political reality—areas like Texas and California had tremendous economic potential. Southerners, in particular, were salivating over the prospect of making Texas a slave state.

The annexation of Texas,and the war with Mexico that was likely to ensue if annexation was pursued, was the focus of the campaign. Martin Van Buren had been the odds-on favorite to win the Democratic nomination, but his opposition to annexation denied him a majority vote in the nominating convention. The deadlocked delegates took nine votes before settling on the first "dark horse" candidate in American presidential politics, James Polk of Tennessee. Polk wasn't a total unknown—he had been Speaker of the House of Representatives for four years during the Jackson administration and had gone on to a two- year term as governor of his home state. However, he had lost two subsequent gubernatorial elections and came to the convention seeking only the vice-presidential nomination. But his pro-annexation stance won him the unexpected honor, and George F. Dallas of Pennsylvania was named as his running mate.

The Whigs nominated Henry Clay, who was making his third run for the nation's highest office, and they were supremely confident that their nationally known candidate would easily triumph over a relative unknown. But Clay damaged his candidacy by waffling on the annexation issue. A strong opponent to acquiring Texas before his nomination, Clay began to soften his stance to win Southern votes. In the end, he lost the support of Southerners unsure of his position and Northern Whigs who were strongly antislavery. In an extremely close election, Polk gained a slim 31,000 popular vote plurality and victory in the electoral college. Some observers believe the difference was 62,000 votes garnered in the North by the antislavery Liberty Party.

Electoral votes:

Polk ..............................170
Clay............................ 105

Popular vote:

Polk ...............................1,338,464
Clay ..............................1,300,097
Birney ....................................62,300

PRESIDENTIAL ELECTION 16

# 1848
## ZACHARY TAYLOR

A sixty-four year old presidential candidate who had never voted? Sounds illogical, but that didn't stop the Whigs from attempting to regain the White House by nominating Mexican War hero General Zachary Taylor in 1848 (along with New York State comptroller Millard Fillmore for Vice-President). Taylor was a crusty career military man who hadn't expressed much interest in politics and didn't attend the Whig national convention. The party sent him a letter informing him that he'd been nominated for President, but failed to put sufficient postage on the envelope. The frugal Taylor refused to pay the postage due; when the Whigs didn't hear back from him in a few weeks, they eventually sent him another letter. Taylor's total inexperience upset many Whigs like Daniel Webster, but they finally stepped in line.

Part of the reason they stepped in line was factionalism among the Democrats. Slavery in the new states entering the Union had become a major issue in American political life. The Democratic party nominated Michigan Senator Lewis Cass (the first nominee from the former Northwest Territories) for President and War of 1812 General William O. Butler for Vice-President. Cass personally believed that the settlers of new territories should decide the question of slavery by popular vote, but the Democratic platform was silent on the issue. Antislavery Democrats reacted by forming the new Free Soil Party, which promised "Free Soil, Free Speech, Free Labor, and Free Men." The Free-Soilers nominated old warhorse Martin Van Buren for President and Charles Frances Adams (John Quincy's son) for Vice-President.

For the most part, Taylor followed the William Henry Harrison school of campaigning—say virtually nothing about the issues. He was the subject of a variety of vicious personal attacks, most of which centered around his rumored greed and lack of education. His supporters, in turn, went after Cass, dredging up some long-dismissed charges of graft and portraying him as a chronic liar. But neither candidate generated a great deal of enthusiasm.

In 1845, Congress had passed a law requiring that all presidential voting take place on the first Tuesday in November. And when the results were in, the 10 percent of the popular vote captured by Martin Van Buren and the Free Soil party made the difference in a very close election. Taylor bested Cass by just 36 electoral votes—the exact number of electoral votes for New York, Van Buren's home state.

Two years after taking office, Taylor succumbed to acute gastritis and Millard Fillmore assumed the presidency.

| Electoral votes: | | Popular vote: | |
|---|---|---|---|
| Taylor | 163 | Taylor | 1,360,967 |
| Cass | 127 | Cass | 1,222,342 |
| | | Van Buren | 291,263 |

# A Short History of Political Parties in America

5

"No free country has ever been without parties, which are a natural offspring of freedom."
—James Madison

If you've ever sat down to read the U.S. Constitution (if you have, you're a better citizen than I am), you'll notice that political parties are not mentioned at all. That's because the men who crafted that document believed that parties were dangerous and disruptive. However, the founders of our country had very little experience with either parties or the institutions of democracy. After all, during the centuries when laws were made by kings and their advisers, parties could not exist because there were no elected officials. The factions, or parties that did exist, were more like interest groups that tried to influence the decisions of the monarch rather than acting as parties who had the obligation of governing.

True political parties are the products of representative democracy. Parties began to emerge in Europe in the late-eighteenth and early-nineteenth centuries when elected legislatures became a dominant force in government. And it was inevitable that they would develop in the new United States, which was the world's most representative democracy.

## THE DEVELOPMENT OF POLITICAL PARTIES IN THE U.S.

"The two parties which divide the state, the party of conservatives and the party of innovators, are very old and have disputed the possession of the world ever since it was made."—Ralph Waldo Emerson

American political parties did spring up because of profoundly different opinions about the role of government that developed between two of the most powerful figures in American political life—Alexander Hamilton and Thomas Jefferson. Hamilton identified with the commercial and industrial interests that dominated

Northern states. He believed those interests were best served by a strong federal government dominated by a handful of wealthy aristocrats. In fact, he once referred to the American people as "the great Beast." In other words, he favored a government very much like that of Great Britain without the monarch. Jefferson, on the other hand, was a staunch believer in democracy. Perhaps because he had roots in the agricultural South, he believed in a limited government that reflected the will of the common man. To pursue their classic but fundamentally different objectives, Hamilton's supporters formed the Federalist party, while Jefferson's formed the Anti-Federalist party which was soon to be known as the Democratic-Republican party.

In the beginning, these parties were quite small, because most citizens were not allowed to vote. Party membership, therefore, consisted mainly of male business and property owners. By the third decade of the nineteenth century in the United States, the right to vote was extended to include most white males. When more people could vote, party memberships increased. By the middle of the twentieth century, after women had gained the right to vote in most nations, political parties became more dependent upon mass support.

Over the last two centuries, the names and roles of the two parties have changed. But the two-party system proved to be so functional and durable that it dominates government at all levels today. Let's take a look at the history of our two major political parties and explore why the two-party system has endured.

## A SHORT HISTORY OF THE DEMOCRATIC PARTY

A couple of interesting facts about the Democratic party:
- It was originally called the Republican party.
- Although the Republican party today is known as the "Grand Old Party," the Democratic party is a half century older.

The origins of the Democratic party, can be traced to the coalition formed supporting Thomas Jefferson in the 1790s, which sought to resist the policies of the Federalists who dominated George Washington's administration. This coalition was originally called the Anti-Federalist or Republican party, but soon became known as the Democratic-Republican party.

This party came into power when the House of Representatives broke an electoral vote tie and chose Jefferson over Aaron Burr as the President. Jefferson, James Madison and James Monroe easily defeated Federalist candidates until 1816, when the Federalist party disappeared.

Replacing the Federalists were a faction of the Democratic-Republican party who split off to become first the National Republican party, then soon after changed its name to the Whig party. In 1828, the Democratic-Republican party became just the Democratic party. Ironically, the philosophy of the party in the nineteenth century

was very conservative. It was willing to use national power in foreign affairs when American interests were threatened, but in economic and social policy it stressed the responsibility of government to act cautiously—if at all. Democrats argued that the national government should do nothing the states could do for themselves, and the states nothing that localities could do. The party's supporters in this period all had in common a dislike of government intervention in their lives. The Democrats' opponents, the Whigs, on the other hand, believed in using governmental power to promote, regulate, correct, and reform.

A major source of the party's cohesion was its strong organization, which enabled it to win the presidency six out of eight times through 1856. However, the party's fortunes changed in the mid-1850s over the issues of slavery and immigration. Many Northern voters, angry over the refusal of the Democrats to take a strong stand against slavery and to abandon their traditional relationship with immigrant workers who were flooding Northern cities, switched allegiance to the newly formed Republican party. The Democrats became a minority party with two strange areas of strength—Southerners and immigrants concentrated in Northern cities.

Democratic opposition to the Civil War allowed Republicans to charge them with disloyalty and made it an effective campaign slogan for the rest of the nineteenth century. This tactic, known as "waving the bloody shirt," always hurt the Democrats in close elections until powerful emotional memories faded. They did not regain control of either house of Congress until 1874 and did not win the presidency again until 1884. Until the Great Depression, the Democrats were the minority party in the nation, able to win only when the Republicans were badly split. For example, the Progressive split in Republican ranks in the early 1900s helped elect Woodrow Wilson twice. But they were unable to keep the presidency once World War I broke out.

In the mid-twentieth century the basic character of the Democratic appeal began to change, first slowly and then rapidly. In the 1930s and '40s the Democrats became a party of vigorous government intervention in the economy and in the social realm, willing to regulate and redistribute wealth and to protect those least able to help themselves in an increasingly complex society. The urban political machines had brought to the party a commitment to social welfare legislation in order to help their immigrant constituents. At first resisted by Southern Democrats and the other limited-government advocates of the party's traditional wing, the new look began to win out in the late 1920s. The Stock Market Crash of 1929, which lead to the Great Depression and the coming to power of Franklin D. Roosevelt with his New Deal, solidified and expanded this new commitment. Increasingly, under Democratic leadership, the government expanded its role in social welfare reform and economic regulation. Given the economic situation, this proved to be very attractive to the electorate. Traditional Democrats surged to the polls, new voters joined, and the party won over groups, such as the blacks,

## THE FOUNDERS
## OF OUR COUNTRY
## ON POLITICAL PARTIES

"The public good is disregarded in the conflicts of rival parties." —JAMES MADISON

"If I could not go to Heaven but with party I would not go there at all." —THOMAS JEFFERSON

" Ignorance leads Men into a party, and Shame keeps them getting back out again. " —BENJAMIN FRANKLIN

"Let me now warn you in the most solemn manner about the baneful effects of the spirit of party. " —GEORGE WASHINGTON

"There is nothing I dread so much as the division of the Republic into two great parties, each under its leader. This, in my humble opinion, is to be feared as the greatest political evil under our Constitution." —JOHN ADAMS

who had been Republicans for generations—at first haltingly, then enthusiastically and finally overwhelmingly. The result was the New Deal coalition that has dominated the country for more than thirty years.

The Democrats regained the White House with the election of John F. Kennedy in 1960 and passed much vigorous legislation, culminating in the Great Society policies of President Lyndon Johnson. These continued and expanded New Deal social commitments, this time to encompass civil rights and to aid minorities and the unorganized. As the party solidified its support among blacks, however, it lost Southern whites and Northern labor and ethnic voters. The country prospered, but conflicts over social, economic and military policy intensified.

Landslide victories by Republican presidential nominee Ronald Reagan over Jimmy Carter in 1980 and Walter Mondale in 1984 was heralded by many as a sign that Democrats were "out of the mainstream" on social, economic, and defense issues. In a complete turnaround from their positions a century before, Republicans, with their philosophy of limiting the role of government in people's lives and giving more power to the states, began to dominate a Democratic party who believed in a more activist governmental role.

## A SHORT HISTORY OF THE REPUBLICAN PARTY

The Republican party, a relative youngster compared to the Democratic party, was born in 1854. It was formed by founded by a coalition of people united on one issue—their opposition to the extension of slavery into the western territories. In

PRESIDENTIAL ELECTION 17

# 1852

## FRANKLIN PIERCE

The two major political parties had so much trouble selecting nominees that for a while it looked as if there might not be an election of 1852. Once again, the problem was slavery, which had become the dominant issue in American political life. After turmoil that threatened to tear the nation apart, Congress had adopted five bills collectively known as the Compromise of 1850. The South agreed that the slave trade would be abolished in the District of Columbia and that California would be admitted to the Union as a free state in return for three concessions: passage of the Fugitive Slave Law, which would provide that runaway slaves be returned to their masters; the New Mexico and Utah territories would be opened to slaveholders as well as non-slaveholders; and Texas, a slave state, would gain more territory.

Both parties wanted the Compromise to work and neither wanted to rock the boat by supporting a well-known candidate who may have alienated one side or the other in the past. So the Whigs went to the fifty-third ballot before naming Mexican War hero Gen. Winfield Scott for President and William A. Graham for Vice-President, on the forty-ninth ballot while the Democrats named virtually unknown Senator Franklin Pierce of New Hampshire. Senator William King of Alabama was chosen as the vice-presidential candidate. Both Scott and Pierce firmly supported the Compromise of 1850, and Scott in particular went out of his way not to utter a word that would offend the South.

Without a major issue, the campaign was waged on personality. Pierce had been a brigadier general who served under Scott in the Mexican War, but his opponents learned that he had twice fainted from the heat and fallen from his horse during battles. These embarrassing incidents, as well as the New Hampshire senator's fondness for the bottle, were the major focus of Whig jibes and jests. Scott's major personal flaw was that he was a prima donna who loved fancy uniforms and was extremely vain about his rank. The Democrats painted him as pompous, conceited, and politically ignorant.

As election day approached, however, Scott's Achilles heel was not his personality, but a fundamental weakening of the Whig party. Southern Whigs had deserted to the Democrats while Northern Whigs were lukewarm at best about their party's support of slavery. Pierce won 55 percent of the vote and captured all but four states in an election that proved to be the death knell for the Whigs.

| Electoral votes: | | Popular vote: | |
|---|---|---|---|
| Pierce | 254 | Pierce | 1,601,474 |
| Scott | 42 | Scott | 1,386,578 |

1856 they nominated John C. Fremont for the presidency, and he won about a third of the popular vote. But in 1860 their candidate, Abraham Lincoln, was elected to the presidency. However, an unfortunate consequence of their victory was that the South seceded from the Union, and the country was plunged into civil war.

The American Civil War and the Reconstruction period that followed gave the Republican party a solid core of strength and permanence. Republicans controlled most elective offices in the Northern states during the war, and for a generation afterward they were able to make full use of patriotic fervor to denounce the Democrats as traitors and friends of the South. This was an effective campaign tactic. "Waving the bloody shirt" against the South and the Democrats united all Republicans behind their memories of the great crusade to save the Union.

In the late-nineteenth century, the party's policy stances increasingly emphasized the promotion of industrial values, and Republican actions in office aided the emerging, highly centralized industrial economy. At the same time, Republicans were often openly hostile to the new waves of eastern European and Irish groups that were transforming the nation's cities. Republican state platforms frequently advocated government intervention to prohibit or limit liquor

# ELEPHANTS AND DONKEYS

Why is the elephant the symbol of the Republican party and the donkey the symbol of the Democratic party? The answer isn't flattering to either organization, because both stem from the stinging satirical cartoons drawn by Thomas Nast, the most famous political cartoonist in American history.

Nast was born in Germany in 1840, but moved to the United States as a boy and took classes at the National Academy of Design in New York City. He became a professional cartoonist at age fifteen and at eighteen became the staff cartoonist for *Harper's Weekly*. He became famous for his drawings during and after the Civil War, but he's best known today for his biting political cartoons that, among other things, helped end the power of a corrupt New York City political machine.

In 1837, another cartoonist had drawn a picture of President Andrew Jackson riding a donkey that represented the Democratic party. But Nast popularized the image beginning with an 1870 cartoon which mocked Democratic newspapers that sympathized with the South. The elephant symbol resulted from an erroneous news story in which a group of animals was reported to have escaped from the New York City Zoo and was roaming around Central Park. Just before the 1874 midyear elections, Nast drew a cartoon of a donkey (the Democratic party) disguised as a lion scaring a group of animals. The group included a huge elephant that was labeled "the Republican Party." Unflattering as they were, both images stuck.

By the way, Nast also drew the first picture of another symbol dear to our hearts—the jolly, fat, bearded Santa Claus.

consumption and to shape school curricula in order to promote certain Protestant and American values against the threats posed by the newcomers, who became closely allied with the Democratic party.

## PARTY STRENGTH IN THE U.S. CONGRESS IN THE LAST TWO DECADES

| Congress | Senate | | House | |
|---|---|---|---|---|
| | Dem. | Rep. | Dem. | Rep. |
| 94th—1975-76 | 61 | 38 | 291 | 144 |
| 95th—1977-78 | 61 | 38 | 291 | 143 |
| 96th—1979-80 | 58 | 41 | 276 | 159 |
| 97th—1981-82 | 46 | 53 | 243 | 192 |
| 98th—1983-84 | 46 | 54 | 269 | 165 |
| 99th—1985-86 | 47 | 53 | 253 | 182 |
| 100th—1987-88 | 55 | 45 | 258 | 177 |
| 101st—1989-90 | 55 | 45 | 256 | 176 |
| 102nd—1991-92 | 56 | 44 | 267 | 167 |
| 103rd—1993-94 | 56 | 44 | 258 | 176 |
| 104th—1994-95 | 47 | 53 | 204 | 230 |

The Republican party remained dominant throughout the 1920s. Despite opposition from agricultural and progressive Republicans, it continued to foster industrial economic values in a time of extraordinary prosperity. Herbert Hoover, first as Secretary of Commerce, then as President from 1929 to 1933, symbolized Republican commitment to unbounded national prosperity rooted in massive industrial expansion. The Great Depression, which began during Hoover's administration, destroyed America's belief in that dream of unlimited prosperity and its faith in the Republican party. The disastrous economic collapse and extraordinarily high unemployment that followed made a mockery of Republican claims.

In the 1950s and 1960s, the party represented itself as the movement of a better America—more homogeneous, simpler, happier, and unspoiled by the ruinous policies of the New Deal Democrats. The nomination of Sen. Barry M. Goldwater in 1964 brought conservative Republicanism to a dominant place in party councils for the first time since the 1930s. The conservatives thereafter controlled the party machinery and increasingly impressed their stamp on the party's principles and actions. They worked hard to win recruits in places where they had long been without influence, especially in the South and among urban, ethnic, working-class groups. The conservative tide paid dividends when the Republican candidate Ronald Reagan won an overwhelming victory over Jimmy Carter in 1980. Republican attacks on big government led to a landslide victory in the 1994 Congressional elections.

## WHY WE HAVE REMAINED A TWO-PARTY SYSTEM

The two-party system is a rarity in global politics—only five other countries (Australia, Austria, Great Britain, Canada, and New Zealand) also have two major political parties. But the two-party system is so much a part of American government that it almost seems as if someone deliberately designed it. However, as we've seen, the founders of our country didn't want political parties at all. Instead, the two-party system developed and flourished for a number of reasons.

### Voter beliefs

Perhaps the most extraordinary thing about the American people is that they overwhelmingly accept the basic tenets of our government, such as democracy, capitalism, freedom of religion, and freedom of speech. Over the course of two hundred years, parties that narrowly restrict their membership to a single religious point of view, ethnic group, economic class, or region of the country have failed to attract enough people to become viable political forces.

# WHY IS THE REPUBLICAN PARTY ALSO KNOWN AS THE GOP?

GOP stands for "Grand Old Party," and that nickname comes from an organization called the Grand Army of the Republic. Established by Union veterans of the U.S. Civil War, the Grand Army of the Republic worked to aid war veterans and their families, obtain pension increases, and preserve the memory of fallen comrades (they secured the adoption of *Memorial Day* in 1868). This organization was so closely allied with the Republicans that the party became known as the "Grand Old Party." The influence of the Grand Army of the Republic waned after 1900, and the last member died in 1956.

### Flexibility of the major parties

The two major political parties are called "umbrella parties," which means that they accept members with a wide range of viewpoints on almost every issue. Being inclusive rather than exclusive results in both parties adopting centrist or main-stream positions with which the majority of voters feel comfortable.

### The decentralization of the major parties

Both major parties have established organizations in almost all of the nation's 3,000 counties and 19,000 municipalities, and these local parties tend to be responsive to local interests and concerns. This diminishes the incentive for forming third parties. Also, a third party faces the awesome and expensive task of duplicating this huge party infrastructure.

## The structure of our electoral system

Almost all legislators at every level are elected by majority vote in a specific geographic district. Candidates from minor parties may get a portion of the vote, but seldom enough to get elected. In contrast, many European countries apportion representation according to the percentage of votes each party receives (that means a party that gets only 5 percent of the vote gets 5 percent of the seats in the legislative body).

# WHAT IS THE DIFFERENCE BETWEEN THE TWO-PARTY SYSTEMS IN THE U.S. AND IN GREAT BRITAIN?

Great Britain and the United States both have, in general, two-party systems of government. They do not operate in the same way, however. In Britain, elections are held for members of Parliament. After the election the leader of the winning party is named prime minister. This individual thus serves both in Parliament as a legislator and in the cabinet as an executive and policymaker.

This dual role cannot happen in the United States because of the constitutional separation of powers. The President cannot serve in Congress while in office. It is therefore possible for the presidency and the Congress to be controlled by different parties, a situation that cannot occur in Britain. This control of the Congress by one party and the presidency by another has generally been the rule instead of the exception since World War II. The disadvantage of the American system is the deadlock that can develop between the President and the Congress over policy when each is in the control of a different party.

## Election laws

Almost all of the nation's 7,500 state legislators belong to one of the two major parties, and they have shown little interest in passing legislation that makes it easier for minor party candidates to get on the ballot. This is particularly true for offices at the state and national level.

## Why do third parties form?

Third parties widely vary, but generally they fit into one of four types:

PRESIDENTIAL ELECTION 18

# 1856

## JAMES BUCHANAN

While the election of 1852 had been waged on petty personality, the election of 1856 was a referendum on the most important of all issues: would the U.S. remain one united nation? Long gone was the optimism generated by the Compromise of 1850; after the Kansas-Nebraska Act of 1854 negated the Missouri Compromise by opening these Northern territories to slave as well as non-slave holders, Kansas became the scene of a bloody civil war marked by brutal massacres. Thomas Hart Benton remarked, "We are treading upon a volcano that is liable at any time to burst forth and overwhelm the nation."

The controversy over the Kansas-Nebraska Act was so intense that it gave birth to a new political party—and the second of our two major parties today—the Republican party. The party was formed around its firm opposition to the expansion of slavery into the new territories, but the motives of its adherents were not all humanitarian—western farmers wanted to eliminate competition from slave holders and northern businessmen wanted to stall legislation favoring the economy of the South. The party was also conciliatory to a significant anti-immigrant movement that had coalesced into the Know-Nothings, a secret society and political party. In 1856, the fledgling Republicans nominated John C. Fremont, an army officer famous for his explorations of the Oregon Trail, the Great Basin, and California (Senator William Dayton of New Jersey was nominated for vice-president). The Know-Nothings and remnants of the old Whigs supported former president Millard Fillmore.

To retain the support of Northern party members, the Democrats nominated a conciliator, James Buchanan of Pennsylvania. Buchanan had been serving as ambassador to Great Britain since 1852 and thus had taken no part in the controversy over the Kansas-Nebraska Act.(John C. Breckinridge of Kentucky was tabbed as the vice-presidential candidate).

The Democratic campaign focused on one theme: a vote for Fremont was a vote to tear the country apart. The Republicans countered by emphasizing that they had were not opposed to the continuation of slavery in the Old South, but were insistent that expansion of slavery into new territories should end. Since the Republicans had no organization or support in the South, the campaign was waged entirely in the North and West, and it was the most vigorous since 1840. The results, a clear victory for Buchanan, showed that the majority of Americans favored national unity. But the surprisingly strength shown by the brand new Republican party deeply worried Southern leaders.

| Electoral votes: | | Popular vote: | |
|---|---|---|---|
| Buchanan | 174 | Buchanan | 1,832,955 |
| Fremont | 114 | Fremont | 1,339,932 |
| Fillmore | 8 | Fillmore | 871,731 |

- One-issue parties, which spring up when a specific controversy creates strong feelings among a portion of the population. Such parties have included the Free Soil party (opposed to slavery), the States'-Rights party (opposed to civil rights,) and the Prohibition party (opposed to alcohol.) However, Americans tend to be moderates and single-issue parties have never attracted significant long-term support.
- Economic protest parties often spring up in difficult times. Examples are the Greenback party of the late 1800s and Ross Perot's 1992 candidacy. The appeal of these parties fades when economic conditions improve.
- Splinter parties are formed by dissident members of a major party. Among these parties are Teddy Roosevelt's Bull Moose party of 1912 and Strom Thurmond's States'-Rights party in 1948. Because splinter movements almost always spell defeat for the mainstream party candidate and the splinter candidate, the dissidents either rejoin the party or, in the case of many Southern democrats in recent decades, move to the other party.
- Radical viewpoint parties are formed by people whose ideology makes it unlikely that the party will ever win mainstream support. Examples include the Socialist party, the American Communist party and the Libertarians. The overwhelming tendency toward centrist positions of American voters makes it very unlikely a radical party will ever win major support.

## A GUIDE TO MAJOR AMERICAN THIRD PARTIES

Ready for a history quiz? First question: Who were the Know-Nothings? A term that refers to all politicians—from a practical standpoint, you're probably right. But from a historical standpoint, you're wrong. Let's learn about this and some other notable political parties.

### The Federalist Party
It developed from the Constitutional Convention of 1787, at which the advocates of a strong national government came to be known as Federalists, and their leaders included Alexander Hamilton and John Adams. The Federalists were largely aristocratic and pro-British, representing chiefly the commercial interests of the Northeast. However, an increasing number of hostile acts by the British (which eventually led to the War of 1812) led to a growing resentment of the Federalists, and the party disappeared completely by 1816.

### The Whig Party
The Whigs (the name comes from a British opposition party) were the major opposition to the Democrats from the mid-1830s to the mid-1850s. The party was formed about 1834 by a variety of people united only in their opposition to the

Democratic party. In 1840 the Whig ticket consisted of William H. Harrison for President and John Tyler for Vice-President. The Whigs triumphed, but Harrison died after one month in office, and Vice-President Tyler, who had been a Jacksonian Democrat, acceded to the presidency. Tyler feuded with the Whigs and his membership in the party was withdrawn. Conflicts over slavery and territorial expansion splintered the party until it disappeared in the 1850s.

## The Free-Soil Party

This party was organized in 1848 specifically to oppose the extension of slavery. The Free-Soil convention nominated Martin Van Buren and Charles Francis Adams as candidates for President and Vice-President, respectively, and adopted a platform opposed to the extension of slavery and called also for a homestead law and a tariff for revenue only. The slogan of the party was "Free Soil, Free Speech, Free Labor, and Free Men." The party polled 291,263 votes in the election of 1848; it carried no states, but played a decisive role in the election of President Zachary Taylor. The party also elected two U.S. senators and fourteen representatives. The influence of the party declined until it was absorbed into the new Republican party in 1854.

## The Know-Nothings

This party was organized in 1849 by clandestine societies that discriminated against immigrants and members of the Roman Catholic church. Such societies included the Order of the Sons of America in Pennsylvania and the Order of the Star-Spangled Banner in New York. Between 1825 and 1855 more than 5 million foreigners, mostly Roman Catholics, entered the United States. The Know-Nothings became powerful because of popular fear that these immigrants were growing in strength. The Know-Nothing party's name was derived from its practice of secrecy; a member questioned about the party always answered "I don't know." In 1854, its candidates won the governorships in Massachusetts and Delaware. The party was also successful in several state gubernatorial elections the following year. In the presidential election of 1856, however, the party attempted to straddle the slavery issue and in so doing lost a great majority of its partisans in the North and West to the aggressive Republican party.

## The Greenback-Labor Party

This was a popular name for the National party, organized in 1878 by workers and farmers as a means of relieving their economic difficulties resulting from the depression of the 1870s. Their program called for the issuance of the greenback, or paper currency not backed by gold, for a monetary policy based on bimetallism, a reduction in working hours, the establishment of a labor bureau in the federal government, and the curtailment of Chinese immigration, which was viewed as a cause of lowered wages. The congressional elections of 1878 marked the height of power of the Greenback-

# 1860

# ABRAHAM LINCOLN

The optimism about the continued unity of the United States that accompanied the inauguration of James Buchanan was shattered just two days later in a controversial decision by the Supreme Court in a case involving a 62-year-old slave named Dred Scott. When his master moved him from Missouri, a slave state, to Minnesota, a free state, Scott filed suit in federal court arguing that he should be freed. The Court dashed his hopes by ruling that blacks, slave or free, were not citizens of the United States and thus had no legal standing to file suit. In his majority opinion, Chief Justice Roger Brooke Taney went beyond the narrow issue to declare that slavery was protected by the Constitution and that neither the federal government nor territorial governments had any legal authority to ban slavery.

This decision not only outraged Republicans, but also northern Democrats who believed that the citizens of each territory had the right to decide the issue of slavery. When the Democrats convened their 1860 national convention in Charleston, South Carolina, they split along Northern-Southern lines almost immediately. The Southerners nominated Vice President John C Breckinridge (Joseph Lane of Oregon for vice-president), while the Northerners named Stephen Douglas of Illinois (Hershel V. Johnson for vice-president).

Sensing a great opportunity, the Republican convention chose a lesser-known candidate who had made few political enemies—Abraham Lincoln of Illinois (Hannibal Hamlin of Maine for vice-president). Lincoln was a self-made man of moderate political views who had developed a reputation as a folksy orator in a previous series of campaign debates with no other than Stephen Douglas. A splinter group consisting primarily of former Whigs who believed in saving the Union at any cost formed the Constitution party and nominated former Speaker of the House John Bell of Tennessee to run for president.

The election that has been called the most momentous in U.S. history became two separate campaigns: Breckinridge vs. Bell in the South and border states, and Lincoln vs. Douglas in the North and West. It soon became apparent that the South would not tolerate a Lincoln victory. With such enormous stakes, Stephen Douglas embarked on the very first national presidential campaign tour.

But his efforts were in vain. Although Lincoln captured only 40 percent of the popular vote, his strength in the large Northern states gave him 180 electoral votes, a clear majority. A little more than a month after the election, on December 20, 1860, South Carolina voted to secede from the Union, and the other Southern states soon followed. Lincoln was inaugurated president of a nation divided.

| Electoral votes: | | Popular vote: | |
|---|---|---|---|
| Lincoln | 180 | Lincoln | 1,865,593 |
| Breckinridge | 72 | Douglas | 1,382,713 |
| Bell | 39 | Breckinridge | 848,356 |
| Douglas | 12 | Bell | 592,906 |

Labor party, which polled about one million votes and elected fourteen representatives to Congress. Improving economic conditions killed the party in the mid-1880s.

## The People's Party or Populist Party

This party was the successor of the Greenback-Labor party of the 1880s. Founded in 1891 at a convention in Cincinnati, Ohio, the party adopted a platform calling for free coinage of silver and the issuance of large amounts of paper currency, inflationary measures that it hoped would ease the financial burdens of the nation's debt-ridden farmers. Its other demands included abolishing the national banking system, nationalizing the railroads, instituting a graduated income tax, electing U.S. senators by direct popular vote, and allowing people to participate directly in government by means of referendum. In 1892 the party nominated James Baird Weaver (1833-1912) for the presidency. Weaver lost, but he received more than a million popular votes and 22 electoral ones, and several Populist candidates were elected to Congress. In 1896 the Populists won control of the Democratic convention in St. Louis and secured the nomination of William Jennings Bryan, who favored the Populist program, as candidate for the presidency. The party ceased to exist after the 1908 election, but some of its ideas, such as direct election of senators, were later incorporated into our system of government.

## The Progressive Party

This name was taken by no less than three political parties in United States history. The first, known colloquially as the Bull Moose party, was founded by former president Theodore Roosevelt after he lost the 1912 Republican nomination to William Taft. Roosevelt got 27 percent of the vote, more than Taft, but all this accomplished was to allow Democrat Woodrow Wilson to win the election. Most Progressives soon rejoined the Republican party, and the Progressive party died out in 1917.

The second was the League for Progressive Political Action, popularly called the Progressive party which was founded in 1924 to pursue its goals of government ownership of public utilities and labor reforms such as the right to collective bargaining. The party nominated Senator Robert La Follette for President and Montana Democratic Senator Burton K. Wheeler for Vice-President. Although he was overwhelmingly defeated by the Republican candidate, the incumbent President Calvin Coolidge, La Follette polled more than 4.8 million votes, about 16.5 percent of the total ballots cast, and 13 electoral votes.

The third Progressive Party was formed in 1948 by dissident Democrats (for a change), who favored high-level international conferences to lessen tension with the USSR, full constitutional rights for all minority and political groups, federal curbs on monopolies, and anti-inflation measures such as price and rent controls. Defeated by the Democrats under the incumbent president Harry S. Truman, the Progressives

received more than 1 million popular votes, but after 1948 they no longer played a role in national politics.

## The Socialist Party

The first political party in the United States dedicated to the promotion of socialism was founded in 1901. By 1912 party membership had increased to approximately 118,000. Eugene V. Debs, presidential candidate of the party in 1904 and 1908, received 900,672 votes (6 percent of the popular vote), in the 1912 presidential election. In that year the party had more than 1,000 members in public office. The party played an important role in the growth of trade unions in the United States. The antiwar stance taken by many party members during World War I seriously weakened the party. However, the party continued to nominate presidential candidates until 1972, and it still survives today.

## The States'-Rights Party

This party was born at the Democratic party convention of 1948, when the Northern majority got an extensive program of civil rights incorporated into the election platform. Opponents of these measures, chiefly political leaders of the Southern states, declared the program an outright abrogation of states' rights and withdrew from the Democratic party to form a new political party known as the States'-Rights Democrats, often referred to as the Dixiecrats. The new party nominated the governor of South Carolina, Strom Thurmond (1902- ) for the presidency; in the 1948 election he received slightly more than 1 million popular and 38 electoral votes. Afterwards, however, most states'-rights leaders returned to the Democratic party.

## The American Independent Party

In 1968, dissatisfied with the civil rights platform of the Republican party, the former governor of Alabama, George Wallace formed the American Independent party and won the electoral votes of five states (Alabama, Arkansas, Georgia, Louisiana, and Mississippi), as the candidate of the American Independent party. The party folded after the election.

## The Perot Movement

Billionaire H. Ross Perot captured an impressive 19 percent of the popular vote as an independent candidate for president in 1992. Perot's success resulted from a number of factors, including economic uncertainty, lukewarm appeal of both major party candidates, and a growing voter distrust of both major political parties.

PRESIDENTIAL ELECTION 20

# 1864

## ABRAHAM LINCOLN

Although conventional political wisdom deems a wartime president undefeatable, in early 1864 even Abraham Lincoln's closest advisors doubted that he would win another term. The Civil War was the bloodiest in U.S. history, with 620,000 men killed (out of a population of 35 million) and perhaps twice as many wounded. Throughout the course of this horrific conflict, Lincoln was blamed for every Union defeat and every war-related shortage. Although Republicans and some Democrats held a National Union convention to renominate the president, Radical Republicans who urged harsh retribution against the South and full black suffrage held their own convention to nominate John Fremont, the 1856 Republican candidate, to run for president. Lincoln's prospects looked ever more bleak.

Then a series of events combined to turn the tide. Lincoln had initiated the first by naming Ulysses S. Grant as Commander in Chief of the Union forces. Grant quickly separated himself from the indecisive and ineffective previous commanders and he became so popular that Republicans approached him about replacing Lincoln on their ticket. Grant warmed the president's heart by flatly refusing.

Next, the Democrats cooperated by nominating Gen. George B. McClellan, who Lincoln had dismissed as Commander-in-Chief for his timidity in 1862. Although Democrats employed vicious campaign tactics that accused Lincoln of every sin from adultery to drunkenness, their candidate lacked the charisma or the strong record of leadership that would win the affections of the voters.

Finally, and most importantly, Grant's leadership and the massive Northern superiority in men and materials dramatically turned the tide of the war. In particular, the public's imagination was captured by General William Sherman's capture of Atlanta and his subsequent march though the South. It became clear that a victory by Union forces was inevitable.

But even though the war news began to swing public opinion to his side, the astute Lincoln took the time to shore up his political support. Although he favored accomplishing the restoration of the Union through quickly readmitting the Southern states, he made enough concessions to the less charitably minded Radical Republicans. As a result, John Fremont dropped out of the presidential race.

By election day, the results were a forgone conclusion. Lincoln captured 55 percent of the popular vote and won a smashing victory in the electoral college. Characteristically, the president downplayed the meaning of his landslide, remarking that the voters didn't conclude "that I am either the greatest or best man in America; but rather they have concluded that it is not best to swap horses while crossing the river."

| Electoral votes: | Popular vote: |
|---|---|
| Lincoln ........................................ 212 | Lincoln ............................. 2,206,938 |
| McClellan ..................................... 21 | McClellan ........................ 1,803,787 |

# What Is the Structure of Political Parties and What Do They Do?

## 6

When I was growing up in a small Southern town, many adults strongly identified with a political party—they were Democrats in the same way that they were Baptists or Virginians. Although two-thirds of American voters have registered as Democrats or Republicans, this kind of strong identification is increasingly rare today. Numerous studies have shown that as voters we've become much more issue-oriented and candidate-oriented than party-oriented. But even though the days when powerful political machines could automatically deliver huge blocs of votes are gone, parties continue to play an important role in the effective functioning of the election system at all levels. In this chapter, we'll take a look at how the relationship between voters and political parties has evolved over the years, then explain how parties are structured today and what services they provide.

## PARTIES AND THE PEOPLE

Early in our history, political decisions were made by a handful of top party leaders—the first major national convention wasn't held until the Democrats organized one in 1832. The reasons for this were, to a great extent, logistical; travel was expensive and time-consuming, and relatively few Americans had the luxury of leaving their farms or businesses to attend a political meeting. At the same time, only a small portion of the population was eligible to vote. In 1824, the first election for which popular vote totals are available, only 4 percent of the U.S. population cast a vote for president, compared with 42 percent of the total population in 1992.

The number of people eligible to vote gradually expanded, but two factors contributed to the great power wielded by party organizations. The first, and most important, was the spoils system, which received its name from William L. Marcy,

who declared in 1832 that he perceived "nothing wrong in the maxim that to the victors belong the spoils of the enemy." Starting from the election of Andrew Jackson in 1828 and throughout most of the nineteenth century, political bosses from President to precinct captain dolled out government jobs and government contracts to their supporters. In return, they demanded, and got votes, campaign services, and campaign contributions. Prospective candidates who didn't have the support of party leaders had little chance of being nominated.

---

## WHAT DOES IT MEAN?
### BOSS

*Boss*, used as a designation for the person who gives the orders, came into English from the Dutch *baas* meaning "master" probably around the middle of the seventeenth century. It came in by way of New Amsterdam, or New York, as it was renamed when English colonists took it over.

It seems to have enjoyed considerable popularity that resulted from an American aversion to *master*, which was common in British use. Boss became a verb in the 1850s, and the noun was applied to the political boss in the 1860s. The political use got a big boost from the notoriety of Boss Tweed of New York in the 1870s, and it was probably also helped by its frequent appearance in *Time* magazine in the years following World War II. It may have been *Time*'s use that led Harry Truman to remark, "When a leader is in the Democratic Party, he's a boss; when he's in the Republican Party, he's a leader."

---

A second factor that contributed to the power of parties was that most Americans had little or no access to information about the issues facing their government. Today, we're inundated with information about issues, and we see the candidates on the news every night; in the 1800s, many people didn't even know who the candidates for national and state office were, much less ever see them in person. In the absence of information, many voters relied on the judgment of their political party and routinely cast votes for party nominees.

The winds of reform began to blow in the late 1800s when the public became outraged at the massive corruption perpetrated by political machines such as New York City's Tammany Society and its head, Boss Tweed. Reformers called for legislation to fill government jobs by competitive examinations rather than through patronage. Finally, in 1883, Congress established a civil service system by passing the Pendleton Act. As more state and local governments adopted the merit system in hiring, the power of the political machines was greatly diminished. With every technological advance—first the telegraph, then the motor vehicle, then radio—people had more and more access to information, and with that access they began to make up their own minds more often than they had in the past.

Although the day of the powerful political bosses is long gone, party organizations have survived, not only at the national and state level, but in a great majority of the 100,000 voting districts in the United States. Any citizen who wants to become more involved in the political process has to learn how they work.

## WHO ARE MEMBERS OF POLITICAL PARTIES?

Political parties today are made up of three different groups, or constituencies:

### Voters who identify with a party

Anyone who registers to vote as a Democrat or Republican is officially a member of the party. Studies have also shown that about two-thirds of the voters who register as independents are "leaners," a political term for a voter who usually supports the candidates of one party or another.

The ultimate power of a political party at any level has always been directly dependent on how much of the electorate they can sway to their candidates. Today, however, the image of the candidates and their stands on specific issues play as much or more of a part in voting decisions as does party affiliation.

### Elected officials

The Congress, state legislatures, and many local government bodies are structured around party affiliations. In Congress, for example, the Democratic and Republican caucuses select the majority and minority leaders, assign members to committees, chose committee chairmen, and formulate positions on issues and legislation. The positions by which parties are identified today are largely those adopted by legislative members of a party, rather than by the separate party organization—in other words, we tend to identify the Republican position by the stance taken by Republicans in Congress, not by the Republican National Committee. The same is true on state and local issues.

### Party officers and officials

As we've seen, the party leaders used patronage to control political power. Today, these leaders, the vast majority of whom are volunteers, operate more like support staff to candidates.

## WHAT ARE THE FUNCTIONS OF POLITICAL PARTIES?

### They serve as personnel agencies

Parties actively recruit and screen attractive candidates for elected offices from town council to the presidency of the United States. While there is no shortage of people who want to run for the more glamorous national and state offices, voters would def-

# WHAT IS CIVIL SERVICE?

Until the second half of the nineteenth century, elected government officials in the United States regarded appointive posts under their jurisdiction as political prizes to be distributed among influential or faithful supporters. The abuses inherent in this system, which became known as the spoils system, were especially pronounced during the three decades following 1845. Washington, D.C. became the Mecca of a multitude of federal office seekers.

Public indignation over the spoils system began to grow throughout the country, leading to the establishment in 1877 of the New York Civil Service Reform Association and to the founding of similar organizations in other cities. But the issue came to a head in 1881, when President James Garfield was assassinated by a man who was angry that he had not been appointed to a federal job. The National Civil Service Reform League, established in 1881, shortly before Garfield's death, led the subsequent fight for congressional action. In 1883 Congress passed the Civil Service Act, sometimes referred to as the Pendleton Act, legislation that created the foundations of the American civil service system. Among the major features of the act are provisions for the selection of civil service personnel by open competitive examinations; guarantees to civil service employees against coercion in any form for political reasons, or solicitation in government buildings or by other federal employees for political purposes; and allocation to the states and territories, in proportion to population, of appointments from lists of eligible applicants to fill positions in the departmental service in Washington, D.C. Administration of the act was assigned to an appointive board called the Civil Service Commission, which was empowered to frame the necessary rules and regulations. In addition, the President of the United States was authorized to determine, by executive order, the classes of positions subject to the jurisdiction of the commission. In 1883 the total number of positions was 13,900, slightly more than 10 percent of all positions; a century later, the civil service encompassed more than 85 percent of all federal civilian jobs in the United States.

Civil service reforms in the United States were not confined to the federal government. In 1883, the year Congress passed the Civil Service Act, the New York State legislature adopted a similar bill, placing administrative employees of the state under the merit system. Other states followed suit. Beginning in 1940 the U.S. government required the establishment of state merit systems for employees in state departments receiving federal grants for salaries. Consequently, all fifty states have merit systems in such programs as employment services, unemployment insurance, public welfare assistance, and public health.

initely have far fewer choices in selecting qualified people for seats on local councils, commissions, and boards without the efforts of local parties to fill a ticket. This is even true in local areas where elections to local offices are officially non-partisan.

### They educate voters
Parties conduct a wide range of voter information programs, ranging from public forums, to debates, to publication of reports and position papers.

### They facilitate compromise
Our umbrella parties attract people with diverse opinions and they often serve to establish a more moderate approach to issues by selecting compromise candidates who are supported by a majority of their members.

### They provide campaign funds
Parties conduct fund-raising activities and advise candidates in their own search for monetary support.

### They provide campaign services
Parties help provide office staff, support services, advice on campaign strategy, and assistance in developing campaign materials and advertising.

### They get out the vote
Parties urge voters to get to the polls through telephone calls and home visits, and they often provide transportation to and from polling places.

### They serve as a government watchdog
A party that is not in power criticizes decisions and policies of the ruling party, publicity that often discourages the ruling party from holding to an extreme course and exposes corruption or abuses of authority.

## THE STRUCTURE OF PARTIES TODAY

Unlike parties elsewhere in the world, the Democratic and Republican parties in the United States don't have rigid discipline and hierarchy—the national organization doesn't dictate procedures or policies, and doesn't even collect money or dues. The strength of the party organization and the type of functions it undertakes varies widely among the three levels of party organizations and between organizations at each level. The only common goal that every organization shares is the desire to place its candidates in elective office.

Let's take a look at the three levels of party organization.

# HOW DID WOMEN WIN THE RIGHT TO VOTE?

The battle for the right of women to share on equal terms with men the political privileges afforded by representative government and, more particularly, to vote in elections and referendums and to hold public office, was waged in this country even before the American Revolution. In 1647 a wealthy Maryland landholder named Margaret Brent (1600-1671) attempted, boldly but unsuccessfully, to secure "place and voice" in the legislature of the colony. In Massachusetts women property holders voted from 1691 to 1780. The Continental Congress debated the woman-suffrage question at length, deciding finally that the individual states should formulate voting rules.

Nonetheless, in colonial and early-nineteenth century America, as elsewhere in the world, women commonly were regarded as inferior beings. Their children, property, and earnings belonged by law solely to their husbands, and various legal and social barriers made divorce almost unthinkable. In most respects American women were legally on a par with criminals, the insane, and slaves.

The beginning of the successful campaign for women's suffrage officially began in July 1848, when the first women's rights convention met at a Wesleyan church chapel in Seneca Falls, New York. More than one hundred persons attended the convention, among them many male sympathizers. After serious discussion of proposed means to achieve their ends, the delegates finally agreed that the primary goal should be attainment of the franchise. The convention then adopted a Declaration of Sentiments patterned after the American Declaration of Independence.

Although many prominent Americans, including the famed editor Horace Greeley and the abolitionist William Lloyd Garrison, warmly supported it, many citizens and the majority of newspapers responded with ridicule, fury, and vilification. Suffragists were called the "shrieking sisterhood," branded as unfeminine, and accused of immorality and drunkenness. Later, when suffragist leaders undertook speaking tours in support of women's rights, temperance, and abolition, they were often subjected to physical violence.

It wasn't until 1890, with the formation of the National American Woman Suffrage Association, that real progress was made. Largely as a result of agitation by the association, suffrage was granted in the states of Colorado (1893), Utah and Idaho (1896), and Washington (1910). In addition, the association in 1910 secured 500,000 signatures for a petition urging federal woman-suffrage legislation. California granted women the vote in 1911; Kansas, Oregon, and Arizona followed in 1912; Nevada and Montana in 1914; and New York in 1917.

The American suffragist movement scored its climactic victory shortly after World War I. In 1919 Congress approved the Nineteenth Amendment to the U.S. Constitution, which provided that "The right of citizens of the United States to vote shall not be denied or abridged by the United States or by any State on account of sex." Later ratified by thirty-six state legislatures, the Nineteenth Amendment became the law of the land on August 26, 1920.

## The national committee

Until recently, the primary job of the national committee of the Democratic or Republican party was to win the presidency. The national organizations virtually disappear between presidential elections. Today, however, the national committees put as much effort into winning congressional seats as they do into the presidential election. They have evolved into effective fundraising organizations, so much so that they can disperse some funds to state and local party organizations.

---

### WHAT DOES IT MEAN?
### SUFFRAGE

The word *suffrage* comes from the Latin *suffragium*, which means "vote" or "political decision." In English, it means the right to vote, for which we also use the term "franchise." Even though it means anyone's right to vote, the term has come to be used primarily for a woman's right to vote, or woman's suffrage. Suffragettes were women who fought to pass laws giving them the same right to cast ballots as men.

---

## State organizations

With the disappearance of patronage, state party organizations have lost much of their power to select candidates for statewide offices. An increasing number of gubernatorial candidates establish their own organizations to run in statewide primaries. As a result, state parties have evolved into organizations that provide campaign services. As Colorado Democratic state chairman Buie Seawell put it, "I see the state party organization as a sort of quartermaster corps, delivering services that achieve economies of scale. Many of the services the state party performs would cost ten times as much if the individual candidates went out and bought them on the open market." These services include maintaining computerized voter lists, preparing direct mail campaigns, operating phone banks, conducting polls, and serving as a data bank for demographics and issue-related facts.

The state organization is headed by a state chairperson. In one-third of the states the position is paid for; in the other two-thirds, it is filled by volunteers). In most states, day-to-day operations are under the direction of a paid professional manager. State committees elect delegates to the national party committee.

## Local party organization

In our democracy, all government policy is ultimately determined by the choices made by individual voters in local polling places. Because local party organizations are closest to these voters, they still play an important role in the political process. Although some political analysts discount the influence of local organizations in an age in which television brings candidates into our living rooms, the consensus is that, in the words

of one national consultant, "We still need local parties to handle the ground war."

The ground war includes carrying on registration drives, arranging rallies, setting up phone banks, facilitating the use of absentee ballots, assisting the candidates in fundraising, and even picking up voters and driving them to the polls. It is this assistance and encouragement provided by local parties that persuades many people to make the decision to run for office.

The base unit of the local organization is the precinct, or election district. The chief official is the committeeman, or precinct captain. The next higher level of

# WHAT WAS THE TAMMANY SOCIETY?

Tammany Society, often referred to as Tammany Hall, after the name of its headquarters, was founded in New York City in 1789 by William Mooney (1756–1831), a former soldier and a prominent anti-Federalist. It was named for a seventeenth century Delaware Indian chief known for his wisdom. Tammany was originally organized into thirteen tribes, one in each of the thirteen states; its officers were accorded Indian titles, such as "sachem" and "sagamore;" and its meeting places were referred to as wigwams. The national character of Tammany was relatively short-lived. In New York City, Aaron Burr gained control of the society in 1798, organizing it as a political machine that helped elect Thomas Jefferson to the presidency and Burr to the vice-presidency in 1800. In 1836, the grand sachem of Tammany, Martin Van Buren, was elected President.

The society first attained a dominant political influence in New York City in 1855, when one of its leaders, Fernando Wood, was elected mayor. About thirteen years later the notorious William Marcy Tweed was elected grand sachem or head of Tammany; his regime, which lasted until 1871, was marked by a notable rise in corruption in the municipal administration. Tammany Hall exercised a profound influence over city and state politics. It continued to have a reputation for corrupt practices and was regularly opposed by reform groups. In 1926 the Tammany candidate Jimmy Walker was elected mayor of New York. Charges of corruption were leveled at his administration, and the findings of an investigation conducted at the insistence of the state legislature caused Walker to resign in 1932. Excluded from power during the administration (1933–45) of reform mayor Fiorello H. La Guardia, the Tammany Democrats returned to office in the late 1940s, but were weakened in subsequent years by a growing Democratic reform movement. After the defeat of Democratic leader Carmine De Sapio (1908– ) in 1961, the name Tammany Hall gradually passed out of use.

# WHO WAS ANDREW JACKSON?

Born March 15, 1767, of a Scottish-Irish immigrant family in the Waxhaw settlement on the western frontier of South Carolina, Andrew Jackson was orphaned at the age of fourteen and was brought up by an uncle who was a well-to-do slave owner. He became a lawyer at the age of twenty and, blessed with great courage and an iron-willed determination that inspired fear and respect among those who crossed his path, Jackson quickly became one of the leaders in the new state of Tennessee. After helping to draft the Tennessee constitution in 1796, Jackson was elected the state's first congressman, serving one year in the U.S. House of Representatives and then for a year in the U.S. Senate. In 1798 he was appointed judge of the superior court in Tennessee.

In 1802, Jackson was appointed major general of the Tennessee militia, and his successes as a military leader in the War of 1812 made him a national hero. His crowning achievement was accomplished on January 8, 1815, when his motley army won an amazingly one-sided victory at New Orleans over a British army composed largely of veterans.

After serving as governor of Florida, Jackson accepted a seat in the Senate in 1823, and the following year he became one of five presidential candidates. Jackson received a plurality of electoral votes, but in the absence of a majority, the names of the three leading vote-getters were placed before the House in accordance with the provisions of the U.S. Constitution. When the House chose John Quincy Adams president, Jackson fared far better in winning a smashing victory in 1828.

Brilliant propagandists, the Democrats had depicted Old Hickory (Jackson's nickname) as a man devoted to the common people. However, he had a dramatic influence on the federal government and the institution of the presidency, in addition to being a vastly popular President. First of all, Jackson helped revolutionize and strengthen the presidency. He vetoed more bills, for example, than had all his predecessors combined. Furthermore, in vetoing bills merely because he disliked them, he repudiated the tradition originated by George Washington that the veto was a hangover from monarchy, rarely to be exercised by presidents in a republic. Since Jackson's time it has been commonplace for presidents to repeat the Jacksonian assertion that the President represents the will of the people better than does Congress. Jackson's chief political legacy to the nation was what political scientists call the strong presidency and a tradition whereby leaders and parties constantly proclaim their love of the people.

On a more negative note, Jackson was the first President to practice wholesale patronage. George Washington and John Adams had set a precedent for their successors by appointing only the most qualified men to positions of authority in the government. Although subsequent presidents did allow politics to intrude into their appointments, Jackson was the first to replace nearly all longtime federal officeholders with appointees of his own party. Jackson claimed that he was substituting commoners for aristocrats and preventing the build-up of an entrenched democracy, but the result was a significant strengthening in the powers of the President and the power of the Democratic party.

Many of Jackson's other actions, especially his management of the nation's finances and his aggressiveness in foreign affairs, were extremely controversial. Nevertheless, when Jackson retired from the White House in 1837, he was beloved by the people. After leaving office he withdrew to the Hermitage, his magnificent residence outside Nashville, where he died on June 8, 1845.

leadership in cities is the ward committeeman and, in rural areas, the county chairman. Above these are organizations for the city and congressional district. Each local organization elects representatives to serve on the state party committee.

PRESIDENTIAL ELECTION 21

# 1868
## ULYSSES S. GRANT

Gen. Robert E. Lee's surrender at Appomattox marked the end of the shooting war but also the beginning of one of the most bitter political wars ever waged between the President and Congress. The issue was Reconstruction, the terms on which the Southern states would be readmitted to the Union. Andrew Johnson, who took over as chief executive when Lincoln was assassinated, believed in relatively lenient terms for readmission and that Reconstruction should be directed by his office. Congress, however, was controlled by the self-proclaimed Radical Republicans, who believed in harsh treatment (including military occupation) of the Southern states and full civil rights for former slaves. Radical Republicans were so infuriated by Johnson's repeated vetoes that they succeeded in trying him on charges of "high crimes and misdemeanors" in the Senate. Johnson came within one vote of being the only president ever impeached.

Obviously, there was no way the Republicans would nominate Johnson to run for reelection. Instead, they turned to Gen. U.S. Grant, the "man who saved the Union," as their presidential candidate and completed the ticket by naming Schuyler Colfax of Indiana for vice-president. The Democrats took many votes before handing the nomination to former New York governor Horatio Seymour, who was so reluctant to run that he was nicknamed "the Great Decliner." Gen. Francis Blair was the vice-presidential nominee.

Reconstruction in general, and the issue of suffrage for blacks in particular, were the major issues in the race. The Democrats believed in reuniting the Union as quickly as possible and they urged that the Southern states be allowed to control the right to vote in their own states. They blasted Grant as an inexperienced and ignorant drunkard who wanted to "Africanize" the South. The Republicans responded by charging that Democrats were traitors who secretly supported the Rebels during the War. An incident that took place in Mississippi symbolized their campaign strategy. An Ohio man sent as a Reconstruction official was beaten by the Ku Klux Klan. He sent his blood-stained nightshirt to a Republican congressman, who brandished it during a fiery attack on the Democrats. For nearly four decades, "waving the bloody shirt," or attacking the South, was a major Republican tactic.

The sentiment in the country about Reconstruction was equally divided, and the difference in the results was probably the votes of approximately 500,000 freed slaves. Grant won a 310,000 plurality in the popular vote, which translated into a comfortable margin in the electoral college.

| Electoral votes: | | Popular vote: | |
|---|---|---|---|
| Grant | 214 | Grant | 3,015,071 |
| Seymour | 80 | Seymour | 2,709,615 |

# WHAT DOES A NATIONAL COMMITTEE DO?

Want more information on what the national committee of a political party does and how it is organized? Here's how the Democratic National Committee describes itself:

The Democratic National Committee (DNC) plans the party's quadrennial presidential nominating convention; promotes the election of party candidates with both technical and financial support; and works with national, state, and local party organizations, elected officials, candidates, and constituencies to respond to the needs and views of the Democratic electorate and the nation.

The committee meets twice a year, while the Executive Committee, a smaller, governing body made up of members of the full committee, meets four times a year. All DNC meetings are open to the public.

The committee's staff encompasses over ten departments: Press and Research, Direct Mail, MIS, Chairman's Office, Constituent Services, Vice Chairs' Staff, Political, Finance, Legal, Accounting, and the Secretary's Office. Associated organizations include the Democratic Governors Association, the Association of State Democratic Chairs, and the College Democrats.

Anyone who is registered to vote as a Democrat is a member of the party, but there are only approximately four hundred members of the Democratic National Committee. There are nine elected officers of the National Committee: the Chairman, five Vice Chairs, Treasurer, Secretary and National Finance Chair. Membership on the National Committee is composed of individuals selected by the Democratic party organizations in each state (including the District of Columbia and Puerto Rico), the U.S. territories (American Samoa, Guam and the Virgin Islands), and Democrats living outside of the United States and those territories indicated above ("Democrats Abroad").

Each jurisdiction is represented by its chair and the next highest ranking officer of the opposite sex. An additional 200 votes are distributed to the states and territories based on population, with each receiving a minimum of two. These delegations must be equally divided between men and women. Also seated on the DNC are two U.S. senators and U.S. representatives, two members of the College Democrats, and three representatives each from: Democratic governors, mayors, state legislators, county officials, municipal officials, Young Democrats, and members of the National Federation of Democratic Women. Fifty members are appointed by the DNC Chairman and are considered "members-at-large."

PRESIDENTIAL ELECTION 22

# 1872
## ULYSSES S. GRANT

Ulysses S. Grant may have been a master of military strategy, but he was possibly the worst personnel manager ever to serve in the Oval Office. His appointees, who included huge numbers of friends and relatives, ranged from incredibly incompetent to astonishingly corrupt. The situation was so bad that a significant number of people from Grant's own party, called Liberal Republicans, split off and held their own convention to nominate a presidential candidate who would institute civil service reform and end Radical Reconstruction. When the Democrats indicated they would also nominate the Liberal Republican candidate, it appeared that Grant was in serious trouble.

Then the Liberal Republicans, for reasons that remain unfathomable to this day, gave the advantage back to Grant by nominating one of the least likely of all presidential candidates—the journalist Horace Greeley. Greeley, who had been the founder and editor of the *New York Tribune* for thirty-one years, had the advantage of being nationally known. However, his eccentricity and unpredictability was part of his public image. He had temporarily embraced a wide variety of philosophies from vegetarianism to socialism—in fact, he employed Karl Marx as his European corespondent for many years. He struck many people as a crotchety old professor, not a proper presidential candidate.

Reluctantly, the Democrats went along with the Liberal Republicans and nominated the same ticket of Greeley for President and Governor Benjamin Gartz-Brown of Missouri for Vice-President. But many Democrats were appalled; one remarked that the choice between Grant and Greeley was like choosing between "hemlock and strychnine." The regular Republicans unanimously renominated President Grant and named Massachusetts Senator Henry Wilson for Vice-President.

The campaign was best summed up by the *New York Sun*, which used the phrase "a shower of mud." Greeley was so mercilessly attacked that he complained that "I hardly know if I am a candidate for the presidency or the penitentiary." However, he responded by embarking on a long campaign tour in which he blasted Grant for the corruption in his administration and the Republicans in general for "waving the bloody shirt." His attacks won him some intellectual points, but he never convinced voters he was a legitimate candidate. Grant won a landslide victory in the popular vote and in the Electoral College.

The campaign took a terrible toll on Greeley. And just before Election Day, his wife died. Emotionally and physically devastated, he entered a mental sanitarium a few days after the election and died three weeks later, on November 28, 1872. His 63 electoral votes went primarily to his vice-presidential candidate, Gartz-Brown.

| Electoral votes: | Popular vote: |
|---|---|
| Grant .....................................286 | Grant.............................3,597,070 |
| Gartz-Brown and others ...........63 | Greeley .........................2,834,079 |

# How to Get Involved in Party Politics

## 7

"A POLITICAL PARTY IS NOT MADE TO ORDER. IT IS THE SLOW DEVELOPMENT OF POWERFUL FORCES WORKING IN OUR SOCIAL LIFE. SOUND IDEAS SEIZE UPON THE HUMAN MIND. OPINIONS RIPEN INTO FIXED CONVICTIONS. MASSES OF MEN ARE DRAWN TOGETHER BY COMMON BELIEFS AND ORGANIZED AROUND CLEARLY DEFINED PRINCIPLES."
—ROBERT LA FOLLETTE

If you're unhappy or cynical about government and the political process, imagine the following situation. You're sitting in a meeting with the top executives of your company. The subject is your job and your future with the company. Proposals are being bandied about that could give you more responsibility, more money, and job security, while others would leave you unemployed and stripped of your pension and benefits. Unfortunately, for some inexplicable reason, you find yourself paralyzed—unable to speak, write, or participate in any way while these important issues are being debated.

This situation sounds bizarre, until you realize that it accurately portrays the situation of most of us who have absolutely no input into decisions that profoundly affect our lives that are made by local, state, and the federal government. In this book, we'll explain lots of ways all of us can have an impact on government. The first is getting involved with a political party.

## POLITICAL PARTIES 'R' US

As we discussed in the previous chapters, the core strength of both major political parties are the voters who cast their ballots for each party's candidates. Long gone are the days of the political bosses who controlled parties with an iron fist. If we don't like the positions a party is taking or the candidates they nominate, we have two choices:
- Vote for the candidates of the other party
- Get more involved to influence our party's positions and candidates selection.

I have yet to encounter any party organization on any level that didn't enthusiastically welcome newcomers who want to participate. Here are some ways you can have a voice.

## Register to vote

It is absolutely shocking to me that in 1992, a presidential election year, 59,106,000 Americans age eighteen and over—32 percent of our population—were not even registered to vote. I'm an amiable sort of person, but one thing that gets my dander up is hearing someone complain about politicians or the government, then discover that they're not even registered to vote! We should participate not only for the health of our democracy, but as an example for our children.

## Register a party affiliation

When we register to vote, we can, in most states, register a party affiliation or register as independents. About 68 percent of Americans currently register as Democrats or Republicans, while 32 percent register as independents. However, studies have shown that only 10 percent to 12 percent of all voters are truly independent—that is, they are equally likely to vote for candidates from either party. The other 20 percent of registered independents informally identify with one party.

What are the disadvantages of affiliating with a party? There are no financial obligations to registering as a Democrat or Republican, but those registered with a party do receive additional campaign mailings, fundraising solicitations, and "get out the vote" telephone calls that some people find annoying.

On the other side, there are some real advantages in affiliating with a party. First of all, in many states, only registered Democrats or Republicans can vote in primary elections. Unaffiliated voters in these states don't have a voice in selecting candidates for the presidency, Congress, the governorship, state legislature, and local offices.

Second, registered Democrats and Republicans can participate and vote in party caucuses that choose many candidates, establish party positions on important issues, determine how party funds are going to be spent, and elect delegates to state party committees. In many voting districts across the country, only a few dozen people participate in such caucuses, which means that individuals can have a significant impact.

Finally, you normally have to be a registered member of a party to win that party's nomination for elective office. As we've discussed, it is much more difficult to win any election without the backing of one of the major parties.

## Educate yourself about the candidates

Anyone who reads the front page of the newspaper and watches local newscasts can't help but absorb a significant amount of information about the people running for major offices such as President, senator, congressman, or governor. But the average ballot lists many more candidates competing for other state and local positions. Why should you take the time to learn about them? My answer is another question: If you were hiring someone to manage your personal finances and investments, would you be content to pick a name from a hat? Of course not. You'd want to thoroughly review a person's

resume, check references, and ask questions about their goals and philosophy.

Now, doesn't it stand to reason that all of us should be equally careful before we choose a candidate to manage our tax dollars, supervise the education of our children, plan the growth of our community, and make decisions about health and welfare issues? Of course we should. The first and most fundamental way we can have an impact on our political party is to make informed decision when we step into the voting booth for primary elections or cast a vote at a party meeting.

As a television journalist, I find it a little painful to admit that watching local newscasts isn't a very good way to become an informed voter—thirty-second sound bites can provide very misleading impressions.

There are a lot better ways to get information.

• Attend party meetings or caucuses in which candidates make speeches or answer questions. Candidates are most accessible when they are seeking a party's nom-

# WHAT DOES IT MEAN?
## REGISTRATION

Registration is a method usually used to identify voters who are qualified to participate in an election. That's used in every U.S. state except North Dakota. Voters must commonly register before an election (only Maine and Wisconsin allow registration on election day) by submitting to the appropriate city, municipal, or country official proof that they meet the qualifications for voting—for example, that they are residents of that election district, that they are old enough to vote, that they are not registered anywhere else, that they are citizens of the United States, and that they have no criminal convictions that bar them from voting. The Fifteenth Amendment of the U.S. Constitution provides that "the right to vote shall not be denied or abridged by the United States or by any state on account of race, color, or previous condition of servitude."

In the United States, voters were first required to register in Massachusetts in 1800. Not until after the American Civil War, however, were registration procedures adopted by most states as a method for preventing such fraudulent voting techniques as "repeating," or the casting of more than one ballot, which was once notoriously prevalent throughout many urban areas.

Most states have found that the permanent registration of voters is an adequate safeguard against repeating. Some jurisdictions, however, notably larger cities, have adopted a system of periodic registration that requires the voter to reregister at specific intervals so that voting lists may be kept current and accurate.

If you aren't registered, call your city or county registrar of voters and find out how to sign up. More than half of all states allow mail-in registration, and a recent federal law requires states to allow residents to register to vote when renewing their drivers' licenses.

PRESIDENTIAL ELECTION 23

# 1876

# RUTHERFORD B. HAYES

It was ironic that the national celebration of the U.S. centennial should be marred by the stench of scandal that made the Grant administration perhaps the most corrupt in U.S. history. Lack of confidence in the government contributed to the economic hard times produced by the Panic of 1873. Although Grant wanted to seek a third term, his party was in no mood to give him the nomination.

In fact, the public was so fed up with scandal that both major parties went out of their way to nominate reformers with sparkling reputations. The Republicans turned to Ohio Governor Rutherford B. Hayes, a strong proponent of civil service reform, and they also named New York Congressman William A. Wheeler as Vice-President. The Democrats made the obvious choice of former New York City District Attorney and New York Governor Samuel Tilden, who had made headlines by throwing Boss Tweed in jail and smashing the corrupt Canal Ring. The Democrats chose Thomas A. Hendricks of Indiana as their vice-presidential candidate.

Surprisingly, the platforms of the two parties were very similar. Both called for civil service reform, a return to honesty in government, and the end of military occupation in the South. With no issues to contest, the parties resorted to slander—the Democrats attacked the Republicans for the scandals of the Grant administration while the Republicans "waved the bloody shirt" and once again blasted the Democrats for starting the Civil War.

On election night, it looked as if Tilden had won, besting Hayes by 250,000 popular votes, and coming one vote short of winning a majority in the Electoral College with four states in dispute. However, the picture changed when the Republican machine took over. While it soon became clear that Oregon's votes belonged to Hayes, both parties charged gross election fraud in South Carolina, Florida, and Louisiana. As a result, two separate election results were submitted to the Congress by each state.

Because the Democrats controlled the House and the Republicans controlled the Senate, Congress was unable to resolve the dispute. Finally, Congress appointed an Election Commission consisting of seven Democrats, seven Republicans, and one independent as chairman. Just before the Commission met, the chairman had to step down because he was appointed to the Senate from Illinois, and a Republican took his place. By an 8-7 vote, the Commission gave all states to Hayes—despite overwhelming evidence the Tilden had won Florida and Louisiana. Although both parties were tainted by fraud, for the first time in American history a presidential election had been stolen.

| Electoral votes: | | Popular vote: | |
|---|---|---|---|
| Hayes | 185 | Hayes | 4,033,950 |
| Tilden | 184 | Tilden | 4,284,757 |

ination, and this is a time when your opinion and your vote count the most.

- Read campaign literature and position papers.
- Follow the campaigns in the newspaper. You may have to delve into the back pages, but you will become better informed.
- Call or write candidates to ask questions or express concerns. All kinds of charges, countercharges, and rumors circulate during a campaign that may cast a candidate in an unfavorable light or cause confusion about his or her position on a specific issue. As a journalist, I can tell you that the fairest way to get to the truth of the matter is to talk directly to the candidate. The vast majority of candidates welcome the opportunity to communicate directly with a voter. Those that don't welcome direct questions may not be the type of people you want to vote for, regardless of their state positions on the issues.

---

## WHAT DOES IT MEAN?
### CAUCUS

The derivation of the word is not clear (it may come from an Algonquian Indian word), but *caucus* has come to mean a meeting of members of a political party or faction for the purpose of making such decisions as what candidates to support, what positions will be taken on certain issues, etc. The first significant American use of the word was as the title of an eighteenth-century political organization in Boston, the Caucus Club, which was influential in local elections. Between 1800 and 1824 candidates for the presidency of the United States were regularly chosen by caucuses of the members of Congress belonging to the respective political parties. Subsequently these candidates were selected by conventions, but congressional caucuses have continue to decide the official party position on legislation.

Similar political caucuses exist in many state and local legislative bodies. Some state and local party organizations still choose their candidates in caucuses, although direct primaries are becoming more and more popular. About 25 percent of the delegates to the presidential nominating conventions are selected by caucuses.

---

## Put your money where your mouth is

I'm sure you've heard the saying, "Money is the mother's milk of politics," and because that statement is true, campaign financing is at the root of many people's suspicions about the integrity of politicians. I don't know a single person who believes that candidates relying on contributions from political action groups and large contributors is a good thing.

The problem, however, is that I also don't know many people who contribute anything to their political party or the party's candidates. If we don't want candidates to be obligated to large contributors, those funds are going to have to be provided by lots of small contributions from ordinary citizens like you and me. Another saying is also true: "Nothing worthwhile in life is free." If we want good,

# POLITICAL PARTIES

Our two-century-old two-party system is far from typical. Here's a brief look at the party system in some other major countries.

## GREAT BRITAIN

Although minor parties typically capture 40 to 50 of the 651 seats in Parliament in an election, Great Britain has functioned basically as a two-party system for more than a century. The majority party forms His or Her Majesty's Government, and the second party is officially recognized as His or Her Majesty's Own Loyal Opposition. The Opposition leader is paid a salary from public funds for that role. Since the end of World War I, the Conservative party and the Labour party have been dominant. The Labour party is generally socialist while the Conservative party leans toward the right end of the political spectrum..

## FRANCE

France has often had numerous political groups, but the rules of French legislature encourage mergers or coalitions of parties. Over the last two decades, four major parties—two centrist and two leftist groups—have dominated French politics.

## ITALY

Italy has ten major political parties and dozens of minor ones. Among them are the Partito Democrazia Cristiana (Christian Democratic party), which has been part of all postwar governments—it represents a wide range of views, which sometimes results in internal dissension. The Democratic Party of the Left (formerly the Communist Party of Italy) is one of the largest Communist parties in Western Europe.

## GERMANY

The German Bundestag has six major parties ranging from the conservative Christian Democratic Union and Christian Social Union to the Party of Democratic Socialism, the remnant of the East German Communist Party.

## SPAIN

Spain has many political parties that cover the entire range of the political spectrum from far right to communist, as well as Catalan and Basque nationalist parties. The two major groups have been the Socialist Workers party and the conservative Popular party.

## RUSSIA

Since the late 1980s, Russia has undergone a dramatic change from a single-party, totalitarian state to a chaotic, fractious, emerging multiparty democracy. The Communist party of the Soviet Union (CPSU) has been replaced by

# IN OTHER COUNTRIES

hundreds of political groupings, factions, movements, and parties that can be divided into three general categories: democratic, Communist-nationalist, and centrist. The parties range in size from a few members to more than half a million members.

## CHINA

According to the constitution of 1982, China is a socialist dictatorship of the proletariat led by the Communist party and based on a united front that includes other democratic parties. In practice, the Chinese Communist party has all the power and fills the vast majority of significant government positions. The Chinese Communist party has more than 48 million members (although this represents only about 4 percent of the total population) and is the world's largest Communist party.

## INDIA

In a century, India has gone from a one-party to a multiparty nation. The Indian National Congress, founded in 1885, led India in the struggle for independence and provided the country's prime ministers until 1977. In 1969 a group of Congress members left the party to form the small Indian National Congress-Organization (or O), the nation's first officially recognized opposition party. Today, India has more than three dozen political parties.

## MEXICO

The Partido Revolucionario Institucional (PRI) is the largest and most important political party in Mexico. It was formed in 1928 as the Partido Nacional Revolucionario (National Revolutionary party) and has been continuously in power since that time, although under several different names. Opposition parties began to seriously challenge the PRI in the 1980s.

## JAPAN

The Liberal-Democratic party and the Japan Socialist party were the two largest groups in parliament until 1993, when three newly formed conservative parties attracted many voters and gained control.

## AUSTRALIA

There are three major political parties in Australia: the Australian Labor party, the National Country Party of Australia (NCP), and the Liberal Party of Australia. The aims of the Liberal party and the NCP ordinarily have much in common, and the two parties usually work in coalition. For practical purposes, Australian politics operates on a two-party system, which results in relative stability of government.

# NATIONAL AND STATE PARTY ORGANIZATIONS

**Democratic
National Committee**
430 S. Capitol St. SE
Washington, DC 20003
202-863-8000
202-863-8081 (Fax)
**Republican
National Committee**
310 1st St. SE
Washington, DC 20003
202-863-8500
202-863-8820 (Fax)
**Democratic
State Committees**
**Alabama** Democratic Party
290 21st St. N, Suite 300
Birmingham, AL 35203
205-326-3366
**Alaska** Democratic Party
1443 W. Northern
   Lights Blvd.
Anchorage, AK 99503
907-258-3050
**Arizona** Democratic Party
1509 North Central Ave.
Phoenix, AZ 85004
602-257-9136
**Arkansas** Democratic Party
1300 W. Capitol Ave.
Little Rock, AR 72201
501-374-2361
**California** Democratic Party
8440 Santa Monica
Los Angeles, CA 90069
213-848-3700
**Colorado** Democratic Party
770 Grant
Denver, CO 80203
303-830-8989
**Connecticut**
Democratic Party
380 Franklin Ave.
Hartford, CT 06114
203-296-1775
**Delaware** Democratic Party
609 W. Newport Pike
Wilmington, DE 19804
302-996-9458
**DC** Democratic Party
1101 F St. NW
Washington, DC 20004
202-682-1253

**Florida** Democratic Party
P.O. Box 1758
Tallahassee, FL 32302
904-222-3411
**Georgia** Democratic Party
1100 Spring St.
Atlanta, GA 30309
404-872-1992
**Hawaii** Democratic Party
50 S. Beretania St.
Honolulu, HI 96813
808-536-2258
**Idaho** Democratic Party
P.O. Box 445
Boise, ID 83701
208-336-1815
**Illinois** Democratic Party
13126 Merchandise Mart
Chicago, IL 60654
312-464-1900
**Indiana** Democratic Party
1 N. Capitol Ave.
Indianapolis, IN 46204
317-231-7100
**Iowa** Democratic Party
2116 Grand Ave.
Des Moines, IA 50312
515-244-7292
**Kansas** Democratic Party
P.O. Box 1914
Topeka, KS 66601
913-234-0425
**Kentucky** Democratic Party
P.O. Box 694
Frankfort, KY 40602
502-695-4828
**Louisiana** Democratic Party
263 Riverside Mall
Baton Rouge, LA 70801
504-336-4155
**Maine** Democratic Party
51 Sewall St.
Augusta, ME 04330
207-622-6233
**Maryland** Democratic Party
224 Main St.
Annapolis, MD 21401
410-280-2300

**Massachusetts**
Democratic Party
45 Bromfield St.
Boston, MA 02108
617-426-4750
**Michigan** Democratic Party
506 Townsend St.
Lansing, MI 48933
517-371-5410
**Minnesota** Democratic Party
352 Wacouta St.
St. Paul, MN 55101
612-293-1200
**Mississippi**
Democratic Party
832 N. Congress St.
Jackson, MS 39202
601-969-2913
**Missouri** Democratic Party
P.O. Box 719
Jefferson City, MO 65102
314-636-5241
**Montana** Democratic Party
616 Helena Ave.
Helena, MT 59601
406-442-9520
**Nebraska** Democratic Party
715 S. 14th St.
Lincoln, NE 68508
402-475-4584
**Nevada** Democratic Party
706 Braken Ave.
Las Vegas, NV 89104
702-388-9600
**New Hampshire**
Democratic Party
148 N. Main St.
Concord, NH 03302
603-225-6899
**New Jersey**
Democratic Party
150 W. State St.
Trenton, NJ 08608
609-392-3367
**New Mexico**
Democratic Party
315 8th St. SW
Albuquerque, NM 87102
505-842-8208

**New York**
Democratic Party
307 Hamilton St.
Albany, NY 12210
518-462-7407
**North Carolina**
Democratic Party
220 Hillsborough St.
Raleigh, NC 27603
919-821-2777
**North Dakota**
Democratic Party
1902 E. Divide Ave.
Bismarck, ND 58501
701-255-0460
**Ohio** Democratic Party
37 W. Broad St.
Columbus, OH 43215
614-221-6563
**Oklahoma**
Democratic Party
116 E. Sheridan Ave.
Oklahoma City, OK73104
405-239-2700
Democratic
Party of **Oregon**
711 SW Alder
Portland, OR 97205
503-224-8200
**Pennsylvania**
Democratic Party
510 N. 3rd St.
Harrisburg, PA 17101
717-238-9381
**Rhode Island**
Democratic Party
1991 Smith St.
North Providence, RI 02911
401-421-1994
**South Carolina**
Democratic Party
P.O. Box 5965
Columbia, SC 29250
803-799-7796
**South Dakota**
Democratic Party
P.O. Box 737
Sioux Falls, SD 57101
605-335-7337

**Tennessee**
Democratic Party
1808 West End Ave.
Nashville, TN 37203
615-327-9779
**Texas** Democratic Party
815 Brazos St.
Austin, TX 78701
512-478-8746
**Utah** Democratic Party
453 Bearcat Dr.
Salt Lake City, UT 84115
801-484-1200
**Vermont** Democratic Party
P.O. Box 336
Montpelier, VT 05601
802-229-5986
**Virginia** Democratic Party
1108 E. Main St.
Richmond, VA 23219
804-664-1966
**Washington**
Democratic Party
P.O Box 4027
Seattle, WA 98104
206-583-0664
**West Virginia**
Democratic Party
405 Capitol St.
Charleston, WV 25301
304-342-8121
**Wisconsin** Democratic Party
222 State St.
Madison, WI 53703
608-255-5172
**Wyoming** Democratic Party
P.O. Box 2036
Cheyenne, WY 82003
307-637-8940

**Republican**
**State Committees**
**Alabama** Republican Party
2904 Claremont Ave.
Birmingham, AL 35205
205-324-1990
Republican Party of **Alaska**
1001 W. Firewood Lane
Anchorage, AK 99503
907-276-4467

**Arizona** Republican Party
3501 N. 24th St.
Phoenix, AZ 85016
602-957-7770
Republican
Party of **Arkansas**
1 Riverfront Plaza
North Little Rock, AR 72114
501-372-7301
**California** Republican Party
1903 W. Magnolia Blvd.
Burbank, CA 91506
818-841-5210
**Colorado** Republican Party
1275 Tremont Place
Denver, CO 80204
303-893-1776
**Connecticut**
Republican Party
78 Oak St.
Hartford, CT 06106
203-547-0589
**Delaware** Republican Party
2 Mill Rd.
Wilmington, DE 19806
302-651-0260
**District of Columbia**
Republican State
Committee
440 1st St. NW
Washington, DC 20001
202-662-1382
Republican Party of **Florida**
719 N. Calhoun St.
Tallahassee, FL 32303
904-222-7920
**Georgia** Republican Party
3091 Maple Dr. NE
Atlanta, GA 30305
404-365-7700
Republican
Party Of **Hawaii**
100 N. Beretania St.
Honolulu, HI 96817
808-526-1755
**Idaho** Republican Party
612 W. Hayes St.
Boise, ID 83702
208-343-6405

**Illinois** Republican Party
320 S. 4th St.
Springfield, IL 62701
217-525-0011
**Indiana** Republican Party
200 S. Meridian St.
Indianapolis, IN 46225
317-635-7561
Republican Party of **Iowa**
521 E. Locust St.
Des Moines, IA 50309
515-282-8105
**Kansas** Republican Party
214 SW 6th Ave.
Topeka, KS 66603
913-234-3416
Republican
Party of **Kentucky**
P.O. Box 1068
Frankfort, KY 40602
502-875-5130
**Louisiana** Republican Party
650 N. 6th St.
Baton Rouge, LA 70802
504-383-7234
**Maine** Republican Party
3 Wade St.
Augusta, ME 04332
207-622-6247
**Maryland** Republican Party
1623 Forest Dr.
Annapolis, MD 21403
410-269-0113
**Massachusetts**
Republican State Committee
114 State St.
Boston, MA 02109
617-367-1992
**Michigan**
Republican State Committee
2121 E. Grand River Ave.
Lansing, MI 48912
517-487-5413
Independent Republicans of
**Minnesota**
8030 Cedar Ave.
Minneapolis, MN 55425
612-854-1446
**Mississippi**
Republican Party
555 Tombigbee St.
Jackson, MS 39201
601-948-5191

**Missouri** Republican Party
204 E. Dunkin St.
Jefferson City, MO 65101
314-636-3146
**Montana** Republican Party
1419 B Helena Ave.
Helena, MT 59601
406-442-6469
**Nebraska** Republican Party
421 S. 9th St.
Lincoln, NE 68508
402-475-2122
**Nevada** Republican Party
595 Humboldt St.
Las Vegas, NV 89109
702-786-6245
**New Hampshire**
Republican Party
134 N. Main St.
Concord, NH 03301
603-225-9341
**New Jersey**
Republican Party
312 W. State St.
Trenton, NJ 08618
609-989-7300
**New Mexico**
Republican Party
2901 Juan Tabo NE
Albuquerque, NM 87112
505-298-3662
**New York** Republican Party
315 State St.
Albany, NY 12210
518-462-2601
**North Carolina**
Republican State Committee
P.O. Box 12905
Raleigh, NC 27605
919-828-6423
**North Dakota**
Republican Party
P.O. Box 1917
Bismarck, ND 58502
701-255-0030
**Ohio** Republican
State Committee
172 E. State St.
Columbus, OH 43215
614-228-2481

**Oklahoma**
Republican Party
4031 N. Lincoln Blvd.
Oklahoma City, OK 73105
405-528-3501
**Oregon** Republican Party
9900 SW Greenburg Rd.
Portland, OR 97223
503-620-4330
**Pennsylvania**
Republican Party
112 State St.
Harrisburg, PA 17101
717-234-4901
**Rhode Island**
Republican Party
18 Bridge St.
Providence, RI 02903
401-453-4100
**South Carolina**
Republican Party
720 Gracern Rd.
Columbia, SC 29221
803-798-8999
**South Dakota**
Republican Party
P.O. Box 1099
Sioux Falls, SD 57101
605-224-7347
**Tennessee**
Republican Party
P.O. Box 1150368
Nashville, TN 37215
615-292-9497
Republican Party of **Texas**
211 E. 7th St.
Austin, TX 78701
512-477-9821
**Utah** Republican Party
637 E. 400 South
Salt Lake City, UT 84102
801-533-9777
**Vermont** Republican
State Committee
43 Court St.
Montpelier, VT 05602
802-223-3411
**Virginia** Republican Party
115 E. Grace St.
Richmond, VA 23219
804-780-0111

| Washington State | Republican |
| Republican Party | Party of **Wisconsin** |
| 16400 S. Center Pkwy. | 121 S. Pinckney St. |
| Seattle, WA 98186 | Madison, WI 53703 |
| 206-451-1984 | 608-257-4765 |
| **West Virginia** | **Wyoming** |
| Republican State Committee | Republican State Committee |
| P.O. Box 20019 | 212 N. Wolcott St. |
| Charleston, WV 25362 | Casper, WY 82601 |
| 304-344-3446 | 307-234-9166 |

honest government, we should expect to bear part of the cost.

Of course, not all contributions have to be in cash, especially in local campaigns. The loan of an empty office or storefront, use of a photocopying or fax machine, computer time and software, use of a telephone, etc. can make all the difference in the world. Contact your party or your candidate's headquarters to see what they need that you can provide.

## Volunteer your time

No political party and no candidate has ever had enough volunteers. Regardless of your personality or situation, there's always a way you can help. Among the many types of jobs volunteers do are:

- Raising money
- Calling voters
- Passing out campaign literature
- Putting up signs and posters
- Driving people to the polls on election day
- Stuffing envelopes
- Typing mailing lists
- Hosting candidate coffees or teas
- Serving as poll watchers on election day

## How to find your local party organization

Political parties are usually listed in the white pages of the telephone directory. You can also write or call the national party committee or the state party committee listed in this chapter.

# WHO WAS MARTIN VAN BUREN?

Martin Van Buren, the eighth President of the United States and a shrewd political leader who was responsible for forming the coalition that became the modern Democratic party, was born on December 5, 1782, in Kinderhook, New York. He was well educated by private tutors, and he became both an unusually successful lawyer and a master politician. He served in the New York State Senate from 1812 to 1820 and was the state attorney general from 1816 to 1819. In 1821 the state legislature that he had come to dominate elected him to the U.S. Senate.

In New York, Van Buren was the leader of the Regency, an upper-class clique that ran the state's Democratic-Republican party with an iron hand. The principle they admired most was unquestioning party loyalty to the policies they had hammered out. After the election of 1824, Van Buren, who knew little about Andrew Jackson's beliefs, nevertheless became the guiding spirit in organizing a national Democratic party that in 1828 succeeded in electing Jackson to the presidency. He had perceived Jackson as a winner.

As a reward for Van Buren's loyalty and in recognition of his ability, Jackson named him secretary of state. In 1832, when Jackson ran for reelection to a second term, Van Buren was nominated as Vice President. With Jackson's enthusiastic support the Democrats nominated Van Buren for President in 1836, and he won easily, becoming the first New Yorker in the White House.

Unfortunately, in the president's office, Van Buren's political magic wasn't able to overcome the severe economic depression that followed the financial panic of 1837, for he failed to command the support of many within his own party. Even his foreign policy successes weren't enough to prevent him from being defeated by William Henry Harrison in 1840.

In later years, Van Buren left the Democratic party he loved so much because he was morally opposed to the proslavery stance the party had adopted. In 1848, he accepted the presidential nomination of the new antislavery Free-Soil party but was soundly beaten in the election. In his later years Van Buren wrote an autobiography designed to vindicate his administration. He did not succeed. He died in Kinderhook on July 24, 1862.

# 1880

## JAMES A. GARFIELD

After more than two decades of tumultuous elections that dealt with the explosive issues related to the Civil War, the 1880 election was relatively tranquil. Unfortunately, the greater sense of national unity came at the expense of African-Americans. The brief period of nearly equal rights they had enjoyed during Reconstruction quickly ended when the white aristocracy regained control of the Southern states. Although the Fifteenth Amendment had given blacks the right to vote, poll taxes, literacy tests, and physical intimidation made exercising that right difficult or impossible to achieve. Civil rights would not be a major issue for another three-quarters of a century.

The major issue facing Congress was civil service reform, and both major parties nominated candidates who supported change. Because so many leading Republicans had been touched by scandal, it took the party convention 36 ballots to nominate a dark horse, Ohio Congressman James Garfield. New York party boss Chester A. Arthur won the vice-presidential nod. The Democrats went for a Civil War hero, Gen. Winfield Scott Hancock, and named William H. English of Indiana for Vice-President.

Garfield's assets were his humble origins (he was born in a log cabin to a very poor family), a talent for speaking in folksy homilies ("A pound of pluck is worth a ton of luck"), and a substantial record of achievement as leader of the House Republicans. Hancock had a distinguished military career highlighted by his major contribution to the critical Union victory at Gettysburg, and he had been an effective military governor of Texas and Louisiana during Reconstruction. Neither candidate advocated a position strongly opposed by the other.

With no fire coming from the candidates, Republican and Democratic partisans turned to personal attacks. Hancock was portrayed as an overrated military man with no understanding of major political issues. The Republicans issued a pamphlet purporting to summarize his statesmanship and political achievements; all of the pages were blank. The Democrats had a bit more substantial ammunition, because Garfield had received $329 from the infamous Credit Mobilier. Garfield insisted the money was a loan that had been repaid.

Considering the lack of passion in the campaign, a remarkable 78.4 percent of registered voters made it to the polls, and they split their vote very evenly. Garfield won a slim 7,000 vote margin. But Republican strength in the large Northern industrial states gave him a convincing electoral college win.

Ironically, Garfield's support of civil service reform may have cost him his life. Charles J. Guiteau, a disappointed office seeker, shot the President on July 2, 1881, and Garfield died from his wounds a little more than two months later. Chester A. Arthur assumed the presidency.

| Electoral votes: | | Popular vote: | |
|---|---|---|---|
| Garfield | 214 | Garfield | 4,449,053 |
| Hancock | 155 | Hancock | 4,442,030 |

# Who Runs for Office and Why You Should Run

8

"WE'D ALL LIKE T' VOTE FOR TH' BEST MAN, BUT HE'S NEVER A CANDIDATE."
—FRANK MCKINNEY HUBBARD

If you ask anyone what's the main qualification for running for political office these days, you'll probably get the answer, "Lots of money." That's primarily because of a well-publicized trend in congressional and gubernatorial elections that reached an extreme in the 1994 California senatorial election. The Republican candidate, oil tycoon Michael Huffington, spent somewhere between $10 and $15 million of his own money in an effort that fell just short of defeating incumbent Democrat Diane Feinstein. What was Huffington's main qualifications to run for the Senate? He was a first-term congressman who had spent an astonishing $5.4 million of his own money to win election in 1992—over $41 per vote!

And Huffington was far from the only candidate who dipped into deep pockets. Candidates for the House and Senate in 1994 contributed more than $60 million to their own campaigns, with fifty-one of them coming up with $100,000 or more. Political action committees, those controversial offshoots of special interest groups, kicked in another $200 million. In all, the 1994 House and Senate candidates spent over $700 million on their campaigns.

These numbers capture our attention because they are so enormous. But the truth is that Congressional campaigns are the bizarre exception in American politics, not the rule, representing just one-tenth of 1 percent of all elections. "Who runs for office?" and "Who runs for Congress?" are two entirely different questions, and the answer to the first question is the one that overwhelmingly concerns you and me.

## WHO RUNS FOR OFFICE?

Almost one million Americans run for public office in the typical election year, hardly any of them millionaires. Who are they and why do they run? Although there are probably as many sets of reasons as there are candidates, let's look at one real-life story.

Bill lives with his wife and son on a large lake in upstate New York. He and the other "lakers," as the shoreline homeowners are known, make up about 20 percent of the population of the town in which they live. Although he's always been interested in politics, he was never actively involved until an issue arose that directly affected his family—the water supply to his home.

The lakers had always drawn their water directly from the lake. But recently the lake had become increasingly infected with small shellfish known as zebra mussels. They clogged intake screens and caused severe damage to plumbing systems if they slipped by the filters. The town council, which included no lakers, had voted to connect the lakefront homes to the town water supply system, which would permanently solve the problem. But the approval of several state agencies was also needed, producing a very lengthy delay.

If their homes were not hooked to the water supply in the near future, Bill and his neighbors would have to spend several thousand dollars each for elaborate filtering systems to protect their home plumbing systems, then they would have to pay another $2,000 to $3,000 when public water was finally put in. Believing that the town was not doing all it could to push state agencies for quick approval, Bill decided that he would run for a seat on the town council. If elected, he could urge action on the water problem and give the lakers a say in future issues that could affect them. He didn't win, but the water installation became a major campaign issue and all candidates publicly pledged to do everything they could to speed the process. Although he was a bit discouraged at his defeat, Bill enjoyed the process of running for office and felt a sense of satisfaction at the impact his candidacy had.

PRESIDENTIAL ELECTION 25

# 1884
## GROVER CLEVELAND

Although Chester A. Arthur, as Postmaster of New York, had been linked to corrupt machine politics, he turned out to be a surprisingly independent and effective President. However, he had no deep political support, and the kidney disease that would take his life in 1886 left him with too little energy to make an all-out effort to obtain the Republican nomination in 1884. Perhaps it was just as well, because the time had come for Maine Senator James Blaine, the most prominent and popular Republican political figure. Ties to the railroad scandals had prevented Blaine from winning the nomination in 1876 and 1880, but a majority of Republicans let their hearts rule and nominated him for President and Gen. John A. Logan of Illinois (who also had been linked to the railroad scandals) for Vice-President. Reform-minded Republicans were outraged, storming out of the convention. These dissidents, or "mugwumps" as they came to be called, vowed to support the Democratic nominee.

Sensing an opportunity to win the Oval Office for the first time since 1856, the Democrats turned to a man whose political career had exemplified his motto, "a public office is a public trust." That man was Governor Grover Cleveland of New York, who had waged all-out war against the Tammany Hall machine during his two terms. According to the *New York World*, Cleveland had four major assets: "1. He is an honest man. 2. He is an honest man. 3. He is an honest man. 4. He is an honest man." Cleveland, who was very acceptable to the mugwumps, was the overwhelming choice of the convention, which also named Thomas Hendricks of Indiana as its vice-presidential candidate.

Blaine, who stumped the country making speeches in town after town, was the early favorite, but he was soon crippled by the release of some embarrassing letters that once again tied him to railroad scandals. However, Republicans soon found a skeleton in Cleveland's closet that became the first major sex scandal in a presidential election. Although his behavior as a public servant had been impeccable, the young Grover Cleveland had had an affair with an older widow and had fathered a child with her out of wedlock. Cleveland had provided financial support for the child, but the Republicans branded him a "moral leper."

The extremely close race hinged on the vote in New York. Even though Cleveland was the governor, Blaine led until slurs against Roman Catholics uttered by a Protestant clergyman at one of his rallies cost him vital support among Irish New Yorkers. Blaine lost New York by just 1,000 votes, and the Empire State's electoral votes gave Cleveland the presidency.

| Electoral votes: | | Popular vote: | |
|---|---|---|---|
| Cleveland | 219 | Cleveland | 4,911,017 |
| Blaine | 182 | Blaine | 4,848,334 |

PRESIDENTIAL ELECTION 26

# 1888

# BENJAMIN HARRISON

In 1832, it was the issue of tariffs, not slavery, that led to the first effort by a Southern state to secede. Northern industrialists wanted high tariffs to prevent competition from foreign-made goods, while Southern plantation owners wanted free trade to make it easier to sell their raw materials overseas. The North won the war, and high tariffs had been in place ever since. However, in late 1887, President Cleveland urged Congress to lower tariffs to stimulate the economy and reduce the costs of manufactured goods.

Republicans, and the Northern industrialists who bankrolled the party, were outraged. To center the campaign around the issue rather than around personalities, the party refused to nominate James Blaine again and turned instead to former Indiana Senator Benjamin Harrison, grandson of former president William Henry Harrison. Harrison was a strong supporter of the high tariffs, and so was his running mate, Levi Morton, a wealthy New York banker. Entering the ring against the Republicans was Cleveland, who was renominated without opposition, and his vice-presidential running mate, seventy-five-year-old Senator Allen G. Thurman of Ohio.

Although Cleveland had been an effective President, the Republicans had two advantages: a huge $3 million campaign war chest eagerly provided by their wealthy supporters and an issue that let them wave the flag. Harrison argued that his candidacy was a crusade based on a "great principle." Tariffs were essential to protect our American way of life and lowering the tariffs was tantamount to handing control of our land to greedy foreign powers. Although the former senator was a very stiff, even "cold" person who totally lacked charisma, other Republicans including James Blaine took to the stump to bring the message to both large and small towns throughout the country. Industrialists reinforced the message by warning workers of huge layoffs if Cleveland was reelected.

The Democratic response was nearly inaudible. Cleveland's view of campaigns was as oldfashioned as his morality. He believed that it was unseemly for a President to campaign at all, and he also prohibited his cabinet members from making speeches for him. Although the Democratic party did its best to portray Harrison as an antilabor stooge whose policies would lower wages and raise prices, they didn't have nearly enough money to purchase the exposure that Harrison enjoyed.

Despite the disparity in campaign funding, Cleveland actually won the popular vote. But Harrison captured more of the major industrial states and significant majority in the Electoral College.

| Electoral votes: | | Popular vote: | |
|---|---|---|---|
| Harrison | 233 | Harrison | 5,444,337 |
| Cleveland | 168 | Cleveland | 5,540,050 |

Like the vast majority of the people who compete for the 537,000 elective offices in our country, Bill didn't consider himself a politician, nor did he have any special education or training for the position he pursued. His campaign costs totaled a few hundred dollars, almost all of which were paid for by the local Democratic organization. Although a specific issue provided the impetus for him to run, he would not have committed himself to something that required so much time and energy if he hadn't had a genuine desire to make government work more effectively.

Is Bill typical? Let's take a briefer look at the motivations of other candidates.

- Victor, an attorney, retired from the Coast Guard after twenty years and decided to set up a legal practice in a small town. He decided that politics was a good way to meet prospective clients. He joined the Republican party, was nominated as a candidate for the town tax commission, and won the seat in the general election.
- Barbara had been a full-time mother for seven years when she became involved in a campaign to turn an unused auditorium into a community arts center. Although the proposal generated enthusiastic public support, the town council refused to allow a referendum on the issue. She came to believe that the town's long-term mayor had resisted innovate proposals in several areas, so she sought and received the Democratic nomination for mayor. Although she lost the general election, her surprisingly strong showing led her to decide to try again.
- Allen made a living as an insurance agent, but his passion was politics. For years he had attended every county board meeting and every public hearing, gaining a reputation as a gadfly who was not shy about expressing his opposition to what he considered wasteful spending and unnecessary attempts to limit public participation in those meetings. Shunned as too eccentric by the two major parties, Allen and eleven friends formed their own independent party and ran a slate of candidates in the next election. To the astonishment of every politician, Allen's party won a seat on the county board and got 23 percent of the vote for county executive.
- For over two decades, Sue had channeled her considerable energy into volunteer efforts involving her children. She had served as PTA president, girl scout leader, MADD coordinator, town soccer league registrar, etc. When her youngest child went off to college, she found herself with nothing to do. Because she realized that she had both an interest in politics and the time to spend weeks or months in the state capitol, she decided to run for a seat in the state general assembly. Because she was so well known in her community, she won a seat on her first try.
- Vinnie founded a small but very successful investment management firm, but the pressure and the eighteen-hour days finally led him to sell out to a larger firm. The money he received and his wife's income as a physician meant that he didn't have to work, so he was content to spend his days taking care of his two children and playing golf. However, when his youngest child entered elementary school, he was bored and decided to get involved in pol-

itics. After serving as campaign finance manager for a congressional candidate, he entered the primary election for his party's nomination for state treasurer. On his second try, he won the primary and the general election.

## SO WHO RUNS FOR OFFICE?

Today, the answer truly is, "people like you and me." I personally couldn't say that twenty-five years ago, when there were less than 1,500 African-Americans holding elected offices at any level throughout the United States. If you are a woman, you probably couldn't say that, either, because twenty-five years ago women held less than 4 percent of political offices at the state and national level. But there have been some dramatic changes in the last quarter century, as we'll explain.

### Women running for office

Here's a fact that I guarantee will surprise you: A study of 50,563 candidates who ran for the U.S. Senate, the U.S. House of Representatives, state governorships, and state legislatures from 1986 to 1992 showed that women had exactly the same chances of being elected to these major political offices as men! For example, women made up 20 percent of the candidates for state legislatures and won 21 percent of the seats. Why are there fewer women in office than men? Because, as the previous statistic shows, fewer women run for office.

This study, which was conducted by the National Women's Political Caucus, revealed that two-thirds of all voters, including those who say they would be more likely to vote for a woman, believe that men are much more likely to win elections. This misconception is widely held, despite the fact that women make up 51 percent of the population and 53 percent of all voters.

What does this study mean? Politics is an area of tremendous opportunity for women.

### Minorities running for office

Since 1970, the number of African-Americans holding elective office has soared 430 percent, to slightly over 8,000. Personally, I felt a strong sense of pride when my friend Douglas Wilder became the first black governor. He was elected chief executive of my home state of Virginia in 1989. Carol Mosley Braun became the first black female senator when she was elected from the state of Illinois in 1992.

However, I believe that we still have a long way to go before race is no longer a factor in elections. I know that many African-Americans have become discouraged or even alienated from the political process. But history has proven that the best way to defeat prejudice is to directly confront it. The number of elected officials from all minorities will increase only if more minority candidates try for office.

## Should you run for office?

If you've taken the time to read this book, it's a good bet that you're the type of person who's interested in the quality of our government. Having read the first two sections, you're also a lot more knowledgeable about the structure of government at all levels and the nature of our political system than the vast majority of voters. So now comes a big question: should your interest and your knowledge lead you to take the next step—running for political office yourself?

I hope the short profiles of candidates in this chapter has convinced you that few of the million Americans who run for office in the average election year are professional politicians or have specific educational backgrounds in government. In fact, a government that is truly "of the people" must elect officials with the widest variety of backgrounds and experience. If you feel qualified to volunteer your time to a wide variety of activities from the PTA to scouting, you're probably qualified for some elective office.

There are, however, a few practical questions you have to answer before making this decision:

1. **Do I have the time?** As I've said, as much as I'd like to run for office, the demands of my job make it impossible. In the next chapter, we'll explore the research you need to do before deciding to run for a specific office. Part of that research is finding out exactly how much of your time the position demands. Although you can be expected to make some sacrifices, your job and your family must come first.

2. **Do you have the support of your family?** Much of the time you'll spend running for office and fulfilling your duties as an elected official must be subtracted from the time you spend with your family. If your family isn't enthusiastic and supportive from the start, conflicts may arise in the future.

3. **Am I comfortable meeting and talking with people?** If you've ever watched C-Span for any length of time, you've discovered that few congressmen are great orators. The truth is that most elected officials never or rarely have to give public speeches at all. However, every candidate and every elected official has to interact with a wide variety of people—voters, lobbyists, constituents, government employees, other elected officials, etc. If you're not a people person, you'd probably be better off behind the scenes rather than running yourself.

4. **Can you handle rejection and criticism?** Exactly half of all candidates who run for office lose; if you're running against an incumbent in your first campaign, your

## WHAT PERCENTAGE OF ELECTED POSITIONS DO WOMEN HOLD?

According to the National Women's Political Caucus, women represent:

7 percent of U.S. Senators
11 percent of U.S. Representatives

8 percent of U.S. Governors
21 percent of State Legislators

# WHO WAS GROVER CLEVELAND?

Grover Cleveland, the only President to be reelected after defeat and a man who was famous for his refusal to betray the public trust, was born the son of a country clergyman in Caldwell, New Jersey, on March 18, 1837. Prevented by his father's death from attending college, Cleveland moved to an uncle's home near Buffalo, New York, and clerked for a law firm. Studying by himself, he was admitted to the bar in 1859.

In a series of minor political offices, Cleveland won a reputation for scrupulous honesty. This earned him the Democratic nomination for mayor of Buffalo in 1881, and he won the office on a reform platform. In his inaugural address, he launched an attack on the notoriously corrupt board of aldermen, and in the ensuing battles to reduce graft and break the board's power, Cleveland earned the title of the Veto Mayor. With bipartisan support in Buffalo, he became the Democratic nominee for governor in 1882 and achieved an enormous victory. Because he pursued reform, however, much of his legislative agenda was opposed by the New York City Democratic machine.

In 1884 Cleveland's supporters proposed that he run for president. The Republican convention had chosen as its candidate James G. Blaine, whose political career had been marred by suggestions of corruption in aiding the railroad industry years before. A sizable reform faction in the Republican party, however, opposed Blaine's nomination, and they seceded, earning the label "mugwumps." They promised to vote for the yet unchosen Democratic candidate if he supported reform. Cleveland's past public service therefore made him the ideal candidate despite Tammany's opposition, and he won the election.

Taking office in 1885, he resisted the petitions of thousands of party members and supporters for jobs and continued the civil service reforms begun by his predecessor, Chester A. Arthur. This disappointed many Democrats who were hoping for lucrative jobs after twenty-four years of Republican rule. In 1887 Cleveland persuaded Congress to repeal the Tenure of Office Act, which had restricted the President's right to dismiss federal officeholders without the consent of the Senate. This left him free to remove officials appointed by the previous administration before their terms expired, to carry out reforms in government agencies, and to reassert the independence of the president's powers. In two other controversial moves, he vetoed a general pension bill that would have allowed American Civil War veterans to collect pensions for disabilities suffered after they had left the army, and he opposed protective tariffs on imported goods.

Cleveland narrowly lost the election of 1888 to the Republican Benjamin Harrison despite winning a majority of the popular vote. He was returned to the White House in 1892, but economic crises prevented him from concentrating on additional reform. Cleveland's opposition to the Sherman Act of 1890, which required the U.S. to purchase 4.3 million ounces of silver every month, and his use of federal troops to quell violence in a strike by railroad workers against the Pullman Company cost him the support of Northern Democrats who supported unions and Western and Southern Democrats who favored silver interests. As a result, he lost the 1896 nomination to William Jennings Bryan.

In 1897, Cleveland returned with his family to Princeton, New Jersey, where he pursued private life, occasionally giving lectures at universities. He died at Princeton, on June 24, 1908.

odds of losing are even greater. It's more common than not to lose an election or two before winning office. If losing is going to devastate you, you shouldn't run. There has never been a political figure at any level who could please all of the people all of the time. No matter what position you take on any issue, some people are going to disagree with you, and sometimes that disagreement may escalate into personal attacks. Politics is not for the thin-skinned.

5. **Am I running for office primarily to serve others?** There's no doubt that being elected to office is personally gratifying, and no honest candidate wouldn't admit that ego enhancement was part of his or her reason for stepping into the public limelight—just as I would be dishonest if I didn't admit that I enjoyed whatever fame being on national television has afforded me. Also, there's nothing wrong seeking office partially because being elected would benefit you professionally. However, I believe no one should seek office unless their primary motivation is to make government work more effectively.

Let's compare running for office to other volunteer work. I've devoted a lot of time over the years to literacy programs for adults and children. Although I've gotten some publicity and received some honors, my main reason for spending so much of my time on the activity is that I believe the ability to read and write effectively is essential to being a productive member of society. It's the cause that's important, not any side benefits. The same thing holds true for government positions—if you run for a seat on the local zoning board, you must be committed to making that body more effective. If you're not committed, you're cheating the government and yourself.

## If you've answered yes to all the questions

Read on to discover how you should proceed. If you've answered no, you will still find the inside information on the elective process very interesting.

# 1892

# GROVER CLEVELAND

Grover Cleveland was not the kind of man to give up a fight, so it's not surprising that the 1892 campaign was a rematch of the one in 1888. Although neither Harrison nor Cleveland encountered any serious opposition in winning their respective party nominations, neither inspired a great deal of affection. Harrison's icy demeanor and Cleveland's rigid idealism offended many people. Said one observer, "One of them had no friends, the other only enemies." Both parties balanced the ticket slightly by nominating more charismatic figures for Vice-President. The Republicans named *New York Tribune* publisher Whitelaw Reid, while the Democrats picked Senator Adlai E. Stevenson of Illinois.

The Republicans and Democrats once again squared off on the issue of protectionism, but both faced criticism from a third party, the Populist party, which drew its support from Southern and Western farmers. The farmers were caught in a major economic squeeze because of falling prices for their raw materials and the crushing burden of meeting payments for increasingly expensive farm machinery. The Populist party solution was to essentially devalue the dollar by coining silver and issuing more paper currency. They also called for other reforms such as a graduated income tax and popular election of senators. To carry their flag in the election, they chose James B. Weaver for President and James G. Field for Vice-President.

Cleveland was a self-proclaimed "hard money" man who detested the idea of moving away from the gold standard. His stand won him the financial support of bankers and investors, who gave him a war chest that matched or exceeded that of his major opponent. The funds were spent on rallies and advertising, because neither candidate participated. Harrison's wife was very ill, and she died two weeks before the election. Cleveland severely restricted his activities out of respect for the President and First Lady. The contest might have been a replay of 1888. If the steelworkers union hadn't engaged in a bitter labor negation with the Carnegie Steel Corporation.

Huge profits had made Andrew Carnegie one of the world's wealthiest men, but rather than share those profits with his employees, he instructed his manager, Henry Clay Fricke, to try to break the union by offering a contract that slashed wages by 22 percent. When the union rejected the agreement, Fricke locked them out, hired scabs, and then brought in Pinkerton detectives who waged such a bloody battle with picketers that the National Guard had to be brought in.

This incident shattered the Republican contention thatthe tariffs that protected American industries also brought about higher wages. So many voters defected to the Democrats that Cleveland was elected by a comfortable margin, becoming the first and only President ever to win a second term after suffering a defeat.

| Electoral votes: | | Popular vote: | |
|---|---|---|---|
| Cleveland | 277 | Cleveland | 5,554,414 |
| Harrison | 145 | Harrison | 5,190,802 |
| Weaver | 22 | Weaver | 1,027,329 |

# A Step-by-Step Guide for Getting on the Ballot

"DEMOCRACY'S CEREMONIAL, ITS FEAST, ITS GREAT FUNCTION, IS THE ELECTION."
—H. G. WELLS

Because everyone knows that I broadcast from a remote location on the average of one day per week, I get an enormous number of invitations from the organizers of every conceivable kind of event from county fairs to conventions. I'm grateful that it's primarily the job of our *Good Morning America* producers to work out my travel schedule, because the vast majority of the events sound interesting and a lot of fun. That's because the organizers almost always make sure to send us a presentation that highlights the features of their events that are unique and special.

One of the main reasons that I wrote this book is to invite you—and every other American—to participate in those very special events called elections. While I can attend a fair or convention just by getting on an airplane, there are some procedures you have to follow to participate in an election. As we've already seen, to participate as a voter, you have to register. In this chapter, we'll move on to another set of procedures that allow you to participate as a candidate.

But before we do, I want to play my part as pitchman for American democracy and give you a little background so you can appreciate just how rare our open election system has been in human history.

## A SHORT HISTORY OF ELECTIONS

From the beginning of history until the last two hundred years, few human beings were given the opportunity to participate in the selection of their government in any other way than serving in an army. Although the word *democracy* dates back to the time of ancient Greece, the members of the council of state for the various city-states were chosen by lot from a list of candidates selected by the *demes*, or local governments. The citizens of ancient Rome elected important public officials and voted on public matters, but citizenship was sharply restricted to Romans of substance.

After the fall of Rome, elections were virtually unknown. The early Teutonic tribes elected their kings, but heredity soon became the basis for kingship. From the mid-thirteenth century until the beginning of the nineteenth century, the German monarchs and the emperors of the Holy Roman Empire were elected by the princes of the realm, who were called electors. Medieval Venice chose its doges, or chief magistrates, by a complicated system of indirect elections involving an intermediate electoral body selected by lottery.

In England, the method of selecting the members of Parliament was not defined by law in the early history of that institution. The statesman Simon de Montfort summoned a parliament in 1265, calling for representatives of counties and boroughs. Subsequently, an informal and irregular system of electing parliamentary representatives developed with procedures varying from county to county. Many elections took place at mass meetings following a reading by the sheriff of a writ of election. It wasn't until the mid-to-late 1800s that an organized system of popular elections was firmly established.

As we've discussed, the U.S. Constitution provided for the election of the chief executive in Article II, Section 1, and the members of the national legislature in Article I, Section 2. But the early elections weren't anything like our elections today. Candidates were selected by caucuses and the selection of presidents and senators was made by state legislatures. The number of Americans eligible to cast votes was less than 5 percent of the population.

A number of election reforms were gradually adopted in the nineteenth century—expansion of eligibility to vote, selection of presidential candidates by election, registration of voters, the use of the secret ballot, and the establishment of a system of primary elections to select candidates for general elections. It wasn't until the twentieth century that women and African-Americans obtained the right to freely participate in elections. Although our nation is more than two hundred years old, our system of elections has been constantly evolving. In this chapter, we'll take a look at how candidates—including you—can get on the ballot.

## Why can't just anyone sign up to be a candidate?

In a pure democracy, everyone would vote and everyone would be eligible to be selected. But there are basically three reasons why every unit of government has established procedures and restrictions designed to limit the number of candidates on the ballot:

> • Candidates must meet legal requirements for each specific office. The most basic requirements are that every candidate be a U.S. citizen, be eligible to vote (e.g., convicted felons can't vote), and be a legal resident of the geographic district in which he or she is running. Because it makes sense that someone has to live in a town or county for a while to become familiar with its people and problems, there is often a length of residency requirement. Federal offices, and some state

# WHAT DOES IT MEAN?
## BALLOT

The word *ballot* comes from a Germanic word related to the English word *ball* and *balloon*. Small balls, variously marked or colored, have often been used in secret voting. In ancient Athens, jurors in trial voted with one kind of ball for acquittal and with another for condemnation. Even today, some clubs accept or reject candidates for membership on the basis of a vote taken with white and black balls, hence our word *blackball*. Renaissance Venice, a republic from the eleventh century, used this same kind of secret vote. A Venetian, being Italian, called the ball he voted with a *ballotta*, or "little ball." The English borrowed this name to use for a ball, or any other object, used in casting a secret vote. In modern times, the most common form of ballot has been the written or printed ticket.

offices, have age requirements—no one under age thirty can run for the Senate, for example. The specific duties of a job sometimes require that candidates have specific training or experience—for example, a coroner may have to be a licensed physician, a judge or prosecuting attorney may have to be a member of the bar of that state, etc. And in some cases, some people are prohibited from running for positions that may occasion a conflict of interest—for example, in some districts teachers or administrators can't run for a seat on the school board.

• Candidates have to demonstrate that they are serious about running for office. If just anyone could get on the ballot by making a phone call or filling out a form, you might have twenty or thirty people running for mayor instead of two or three. This could result in an enormous amount of voter confusion and could even lead to the election of candidates who were running primarily for publicity rather than a sincere desire to serve.

That's why it makes sense to require candidates go through a process that requires some effort on their part. For example, they have to fill out a series of long forms and meet a rigid schedule of filing deadlines. They may have to obtain a certain number of signatures of registered voters on nominating petitions, establish a formal campaign committee, and name a campaign finance manager to compile detailed lists of contributions and expenditures.

• The incumbents who write election laws have an interest in making it difficult for certain individuals or groups to run against them. Because state legislatures pass election laws, the two major political parties sometimes make it difficult for third-party or independent candidates to run. For example, in New York State, an independent candidate must submit petitions signed by 5 percent of the registered voters—this can mean tens of thousands of signatures in some election districts.

# 1896

## WILLIAM MCKINLEY

Grover Cleveland strongly believed that the gold standard was the key to prosperity, but he lost the support of the majority in his own party when the Panic of 1893 was followed by a severe economic depression. Hard times were worst for the farmers and small businessmen who had big mortgage and other debt payments to make. Desperate, they embraced in growing numbers what had been the primary issue of the tiny Populist Party in 1892—the devaluation of the currency through the free and unlimited coinage of silver. Because the majority of the people most affected by the depression were Democrats, it was no surprise when the "free silver" movement took over the Democratic convention. To carry their banner, they selected 36 year-old Nebraska Congressman William Jennings Bryan, a fiery, spellbinding orator who was the youngest man ever to run for the presidency. In the debate over the currency plank in the Democratic platform, Bryan gave an impassioned speech in which he warned the wealthy bankers, "You shall not press down upon the brow of labor this crown of thorns, you shall not crucify mankind on a cross of gold." This "Cross of Gold" oration, one of the most famous speeches in American political history, touched off a riotous demonstration. Bryan's nomination and fierce opposition to the gold standard led some party members to walk out of the convention and form the National Democratic Party, which ran John Palmer for president. The rest of the delegates balanced the ticket slightly by nominating the wealthy shipbuilder Arthur Sewall of Maine for vice-president. After a brief debate, the Populist Party decided to endorse Bryan, too.

The Republicans had their dissidents, too—twenty "silver Republicans" from Western states walked out of the convention. But the rest of the party was solidly on the side of gold in what was called the "Battle of the Standards." To lead their campaign, they chose Ohio Governor William McKinley, a favorite of the influential Republican industrialist Mark Hanna. Although McKinley had demonstrated more moderate positions on the tariff and on gold when he was a congressman, he was now a staunch supporter of both high tariffs and hard money. For vice-president the Republicans named Garrett A. Hobart of New Jersey.

In the campaign, Bryan traveled more than 18,000 miles and gave more than 600 speeches, and his energy gave the Democrats an early lead. However, the economy began to improve dramatically in the fall of 1896, shifting enough support back to the Republicans to give McKinley a 600,000 popular vote majority and a comfortable victory in the Electoral College.

Electoral votes:

McKinley.................................271
Bryan .........................................176

Popular vote:

McKinley.........................7,035,638
Bryan ..............................6,467,946
Palmer ..............................133,148

• In the past, restrictions have also been used to discriminate against certain classes of voters or ethnic groups. For example, poll taxes, literacy requirements, and citizenship tests were used to prevent poor or minority candidates from registering to vote and from running for office.

## How do you find out the rules in your area?

Most elections are conducted under rules established by state legislatures, and each state has an election commission that supervises elections and enforces these rules. We've listed the addresses of each state election commission in this chapter. The first thing you should do the minute you become interested in running for office is to contact the commission and ask them to provide you with:

• Complete information on that state's election laws, procedures, and deadlines.

• The name of any local government agency that establishes additional rules, procedures, and deadlines for local offices.

If there is a local office, you should stop by in person to meet the staff and pick up any pamphlets or other printed material.
BEFORE WE GO ON....

---

## DISCLAIMER!

Every state's laws and regulations are different. These general descriptions are great background information, but you shouldn't rely solely on anything in this book if you're actually planning to run for office. Instead, pore over the material you receive from state and local election officials.

---

## Decide what office to run for

I'd be willing to wager that very, very few people could list every elective office in their local government. Although we'd all like to start at the top (I think President Christian has a nice ring to it, don't you?), it's often more practical to set your sights on an office you actually have a chance of achieving, in which you're interested, and for which you feel qualified. Here are some steps you can follow:

• Obtain a complete list of local elective offices from your local government. I'll bet there are several that will surprise you, especially seats on boards or commissions other than school boards, and town or county councils.

• Do some research on specific offices. If you're interested in what members of a board or commission do, the best way to find out is to attend a few meetings. You should also make a point of talking to someone who is serving on or has served on that elected body—preferably someone you won't be running against. You should also talk to people who are served by a specific board or official—for example, talk to individual parents and the officers of parent

organizations if you're considering running for the school board. Finally, the duties of most officials are spelled out in great detail in each state's legal code. You can find a copy of the state code in almost any public library or you can contact the state election commission.

- Match the demands of a position with your specific circumstances. Some elective bodies meet as infrequently as once a month, while others require as much as twenty hours per week. Many state legislators have to spend several weeks or months per year in the state capitol. Don't run for any office that will jeopardize your job or family life.

- Obtain the results of past elections. Your library or your local election office will help you get a copy of the results of recent elections. You'll see that some offices attract so few candidates that the elections are virtually uncontested. You'll also be able to determine if certain incumbents or the candidates from a certain party routinely roll up large majorities, or if the elections tend to be closely contested.

- Look for "open seats," or offices for which incumbents are not running. Incumbents win, on the average, 92 percent of congressional elections and a similarly high percentage of state and local elections.

- Follow your heart as well as your head. A friend of mine served as campaign manager for woman who seemed to be playing Don Quixote. She was for running against a four-term incumbent major from a political party that had a three-to-one edge in voter registrations in her suburban town. However, the woman decided to run because she felt passionately about certain issues that the incumbent was ignoring. That passion attracted so many voters that the incumbent only eked out a narrow victory and gave the challenger the name recognition that could propel her to victory on her second try. This case study shows that politics is about issues and principles as well as statistics. That's why running a losing campaign can also be rewarding.

## Before you try to get on the ballot

The process you'll follow to get on the ballot is determined by the answer to one question: Is the election nonpartisan or partisan? All congressional elections and most state elections (New Hampshire is an exception) are partisan elections, meaning that candidates run with a political party affiliation that they have to win or they have to run as independents. However, it's also common for elections to school boards, commissions, and other bodies to be conducted on a nonpartisan basis. This means that each candidate is individually responsible for following the steps necessary to get on the ballot.

## Getting on the ballot for a partisan election

In a partisan election, you either have to be nominated by a political party or decide to run for office as an independent. As we've discussed, it is much easier to win election

with the support of a political party, so most candidates choose to seek a party nomination. There are two basic ways in which a candidate can be nominated by a political party for a specific office: through winning a primary election or through a caucus or convention. Most states have established a system of primary elections for candidates seeking nominations for Congress, major state offices, the state legislature, and major local offices. To participate in a primary, each candidate must be registered as a member of that political party and must submit a certain number of required signatures on nominating petitions. There are two types of primary elections:

• A closed primary is one in which only voters registered as members of a specific party can sign petitions or vote for candidates from that party.
• An open primary is one in which any registered voter can sign a petition or cast a vote. In other words, a registered Democrat can choose to vote for a candidate in the Republican primary.

## WHAT DOES IT MEAN?
## DARK HORSE

It's no surprise that the phrase "dark horse" came from thoroughbred racing. It was first used around 1831 to identify an unlikely contender that unexpectedly won a race. It gradually came to mean any little-known or widely unregarded person who captured an honor, such as the nomination or election to political office. The major "dark horse" candidates who have captured the presidency were James Polk, Franklin Pierce, James Garfield, Rutherford B. Hayes, Warren Harding, and Jimmy Carter.

Candidates for many local offices and some major offices in some states are nominated by a caucus or convention. The party files the paperwork to get the candidate on the ballot, and no nominating petitions are required to be filed. In some states, however, primary elections must be held if one candidate fails to get a clear majority of the votes in the state.

Running as an independent in a partisan election normally requires filling a nominating petition with a significant number of signatures—in many states, up to ten times as many signatures as a candidate running for a party nomination. That's why there are relatively few independents who run for state or federal offices.

## Getting on the ballot for a non-partisan election
In the vast majority of nonpartisan elections, each candidate must submit a nominating petition with a required number of signatures from registered voters. In many such elections, political parties throw their weight behind specific candidates, even though party affiliation is not listed on the ballot. If this is the case, you might want to seek the endorsement of a party in such elections.

## STATE ELECTION OFFICERS

**ALABAMA**
Administrator of Elections
State House, Room 21
Montgomery, AL 36130

**ALASKA**
Director of Elections
P.O. Box AF
Juneau, AK 99811

**ARKANSAS**
Supervisor of Elections
State Capital
Room 206
Little Rock, AR 72201

**ARIZONA**
State Election Officer
1700 W. Washington
Phoenix, AZ 85007

**CALIFORNIA**
Chief, Elections and
Political Reform
1230 J Street
Sacramento, CA 95814

**COLORADO**
Elections Officer
Department of State
1560 Broadway
Suite 200
Denver, CO 80202

**CONNECTICUT**
Manager Election Services
30 Trinity St.
Hartford, CT 06106

**DELAWARE**
State Election
Commissioner
32 Loockerman Square
Suite 203
Dover, DE 19901

**DISTRICT OF COLUMBIA**
Executive Director
Board of Elections
and Ethics
350 Pennsylvania Ave., NW
Washington, DC 20004

**FLORIDA**
Director, Division
of Elections
The Capitol, Room 1801
Tallahassee, FL 32399

**GEORGIA**
Director, Elections Division
State Capitol, Room 110
Atlanta, GA 30334

**HAWAII**
Director of Elections
Office of Lt. Governor
State Capitol, Fifth Floor.
Honolulu, HI 96813

**IDAHO**
Chief Deputy Secretary
of State for Elections
203 State House
Boise, ID 83720

**ILLINOIS**
Executive Director
State Board of Elections
1020 S. Spring St.
P.O. Box 4187
Springfield, IL 62708
Asst. to the
Executive Director
State Board of Elections
State of Illinois Center
100 W. Randolph
Suite 14-100
Chicago, IL 60601

**INDIANA**
Executive Director
State Board of Elections
302 W. Washington,
Room C032
Indianapolis, IN 46204

**IOWA**
Director of Elections
Office of the
Secretary of State
Hoover Building
Des Moines, IA 50319

**KANSAS**
Deputy Assistant for
Elections and
Legislative Matters
Capitol Building
Topeka, KS 66612

**KENTUCKY**
Executive Director
State Board of Elections
State Capitol, Room 71
Frankfort, KY 40601

**LOUISIANA**
Administrator,
Election Division
State Capitol,
19th floor
P.O. Box 94215
Baton Rouge, LA 70804
Executive Director
Dept. of Elections
and Registration
P.O. Box 231
Baton Rouge, LA 70898

**MAINE**
Director of Elections
State House Station 101
Augusta, ME 04333

**MARYLAND**
Deputy Administrator
State Admissions
Board of Elections
P.O. Box 231
Annapolis, MD 21404

**MASSACHUSETTS**
Director of Elections
Election Division,
Room 1705
One Ashburton Place
Boston, MA 02108

**MICHIGAN**
Director of Elections
Department of State
Mutual Building
208 N. Capitol Ave.
Lansing, MI 48918

**MINNESOTA**
Director
Election Division
180 State Office building
St. Paul, MN 55125

**MISSISSIPPI**
Asst. Secretary of State
P.O. Box 136
Jackson, MS 39025

**MISSOURI**
Dep. Secretary of State
Election Services
Truman Office Building
Room 780
Jefferson City, MO 65102

# STATE ELECTION OFFICERS

**MONTANA**
Election Bureau Chief
Office of the
Secretary of State
State Capitol,
Room 225
Helena, MT 59620

**NEBRASKA**
Director of Elections
State Capitol
Room 2300
Lincoln, NE 68509

**NEVADA**
Deputy Secretary of
State for Elections
Capitol Complex
Carson City, NV 89710

**NEW HAMPSHIRE**
Secretary of State
State House, Room 204
Concord, NH 03304

**NEW JERSEY**
Director
Election Division
Department of State
Trenton, NJ 08625

**NEW MEXICO**
Director
Bureau of Elections
State Capitol
Building, 4th Fl.
Santa Fe, NM 87503

**NEW YORK**
Executive Director
State Board of Elections
Swan Street Building,
Core 1
Empire State Plaza
Albany, NY 12260

**NORTH CAROLINA**
Executive
Secretary/Director
State Board of Elections
P.O. Box 1166
Raleigh, NC 27602

**NORTH DAKOTA**
This state has no
office

**OHIO**
Elections Administrator
Office of the
Secretary of State
30 E. Broad St., 14th Floor
Columbus, OH 43266

**OKLAHOMA**
Secretary, State
Election Board
3-B State Capitol Building
Oklahoma City, OK 73152

**OREGON**
Director of Elections
Office of the
Secretary of State
141 State Capitol
Salem, OR 97310

**PENNSYLVANIA**
Commissioner of Elections
305 North Office building
Harrisburg, PA 17120

**RHODE ISLAND**
Chairman
State Board of Elections
50 Branch St.
Providence, RI 09204

**SOUTH CAROLINA**
Executive Director
State Election Commission
P.O. Box 5987
Columbia, SC 29250

**SOUTH DAKOTA**
Supervisor of Elections
500 E. Capitol
Pierre, SD 57201

**TENNESSEE**
Coordinator of Elections
James K. Polk Bldg.,
Suite 500
Nashville, TN 37219

**TEXAS**
Special Assistant for
Elections
P.O. Box 12060
Austin, TX 78711

**UTAH**
Lt. Governor's Office
State Capitol Bldg.,
Room 203
Salt Lake City, UT 84114

**VERMONT**
Director of Elections
Office of the
Secretary of State
Montpelier, VT 05602

**VIRGINIA**
Secretary
State Board of Elections
Ninth Street Office
Bldg. Room 101
Richmond, VA 23219

**WASHINGTON**
Election Director
Office of the
Secretary of State
Olympia, WA 98504

**WEST VIRGINIA**
Deputy Secretary of State
State Capitol, Room 157-K
Charleston, WV 25305

**WISCONSIN**
Executive Director
State Elections Board
132 E. Wilson St., 3rd Floor
Madison, WI 53702

**WYOMING**
Deputy Secretary of State
Capitol Bldg., Room 106
Cheyenne, WY 82002

Presidential Election 29

# 1900

## WILLIAM MCKINLEY

The turn-of-the-century election was a rematch of the 1896 presidential candidates, but the contest lacked the fierce intensity with which the prior campaign had been waged. "Free silver" was still a major issue for William Jennings Bryan and the Democrats, but not for much of the rest of the country. Huge deposits of gold had been discovered in South Africa, and the flood of the precious metal onto the market had effectively devalued the currency in the same way that free coinage of silver would have. So they needed a new issue, and they found one: U.S. imperialism.

One result of the victory in the Spanish-American War, Spain ceded to the U.S. huge territories in the Caribbean and the Pacific, especially the Philippine Islands. Although the U.S. Senate in 1899 had ratified the Treaty of Paris that made the Philippines an American possession, there was still enough anti-colonial feeling left over from our war of independence to make U.S. colonialism an issue. After the Democratic convention nominated Bryan for president and Adlai E. Stevenson of Illinois (vice-president during Cleveland's second administration) for vice-president, the team head to the campaign trail.

The Republican convention had an easy time naming McKinley to run for reelection, but a fierce battle developed over vice-presidential nomination. The popular choice was the charismatic New York Governor Teddy Roosevelt, who had become a national hero when he led his Rough Riders in a famous charge up San Juan Hill in the Spanish-American War. Roosevelt, who had overcome numerous childhood ailments through vigorous exercise that included a stint as a cowboy, was particularly loved by delegates from Western states. However, the party establishment, especially chairman Mark Hanna, considered him a "madman" who was too unpredictable. In the end, the power brokers found enough value to getting Roosevelt out of New York and into an essentially powerless position in Washington, so they permitted his nomination for Vice-President.

The campaign itself was dull. Although Bryan campaigned with his usual feverish intensity, economic prosperity had made his audience too complaisant to respond with enthusiasm. McKinley didn't bother to campaign at all, leaving Roosevelt to go barnstorming. The former New York City police commissioner proved to be nearly Bryan's equal as an orator.

The results on election day were no surprise, as McKinley coasted to an easy victory. Ironically, Mark Hanna, in his concern about Roosevelt, had said to him, "Your duty to the country is to live for four years from next March." Tragically, six months after his inauguration, McKinley was assassinated by an anarchist in Buffalo, New York. The Rough Rider, Teddy Roosevelt, became president.

| Electoral votes: | | Popular vote: | |
|---|---|---|---|
| McKinley | 292 | McKinley | 7,219,530 |
| Bryan | 155 | Bryan | 6,358,071 |

Many potential candidates have learned the extremely painful lesson that all the *i*'s have to be dotted and *t*'s crossed in every election document. For example, in many states, one illegible signature on a nominating petition can cause the entire petition to be thrown out. In many cases, your political opponents will go over your material with a fine tooth comb to discover any reason why you should be taken off the ballot. If you're not a meticulous person, you should recruit a friend who's into details to double and triple check all paperwork and verify all deadlines.

Off course, the system works both ways. As a responsible candidate, you should make sure that your opponent's paperwork is completely in order—who knows, you might get lucky.

---

# CAUTION

Follow election rules and restrictions to the letter!

---

## Let's Review

How does a candidate get on the ballot? The major steps are:
- Get a copy of state and local election laws
- Research the offices for which you're eligible
- Decide what office to run for
- Find out if the election is partisan or non-partisan
- If the election is partisan, seek the nomination through a primary or caucus
- If you don't get a party nomination, decide whether to try to get on the ballot as an independent
- If the election is nonpartisan, follow the steps for filing petitions to get on the ballot
- Pay meticulous attention to all rules and requirements.

There is, of course, one more element in seeking a nomination or election that we haven't discussed—campaign funding. We'll get to that in the next chapter.

PRESIDENTIAL ELECTION 30

# 1904

## THEODORE ROOSEVELT

Teddy Roosevelt may have become president by accident, but the public embraced him with the kind of passion they hadn't accorded a chief executive in nearly a century. Even though he had been elected from the party of big business, his legislative agenda, which he called the "Square Deal," included environmental protection, increased regulation of corporations, and a new focus on issues of benefit to workers. A "Square Deal" was a concept most voters could identify with, and they also loved Roosevelt's youthful energy and enthusiasm(he was only forty-five).

The only Republicans who didn't share the public's affection for the president were the old guard, such as Mark Hanna. But they had enough sense to get out of the way of a political steamroller. After inserting such basic issues as the tariff and the gold standard in the party platform, they sat quietly as the convention renominated Teddy and added Indiana Senator Charles W. Fairbanks as his running mate.

William Jennings Bryan wanted a third chance at the Oval Office, but free silver was a tired issue. After casting about for a suitable candidate, the Democrats turned to a man who couldn't have been more different from Bryan, Judge Alton B. Parker of the New York Court of Appeals. Parker was taciturn, passionless, and most amazingly, a strong supporter of the gold standard. And instead of pairing Parker with a vigorous campaigner, the Democrats nominated little known eighty-two-year-old Henry B. Davis of West Virginia. Neither candidate hit the campaign trail; Roosevelt thought it unseemly for a sitting President and Parker didn't have the appetite for pressing the flesh. The only zest in the contest was injected by the New York newspaper owner Joseph Pulitizer, who charged that the Republican national chairman appointed by Roosevelt had been bought and paid for by wealthy industrialists. Roosevelt, furious, responded with personal outrage, and his denial made the charges a dead issue.

Soon after, the former Rough Rider was elected by the largest margin since Andrew Jackson defeated Henry Clay in 1832. Teddy Roosevelt carried every single Northern state in a candidacy that had, at least temporarily, healed a lot of political wounds. And, as he proudly told his wife, he was no longer President by accident.

| Electoral votes: | | Popular vote: | |
|---|---|---|---|
| Roosevelt | 336 | Roosevelt | 7,679,006 |
| Parker | 140 | Parker | 5,084,491 |

# How Are Campaigns Financed?

"THERE ARE TWO THINGS THAT ARE IMPORTANT IN POLITICS.
THE FIRST ONE IS MONEY, AND I CAN'T REMEMBER WHAT THE SECOND ONE IS."
     —MARK HANNA
"I JUST RECEIVED THE FOLLOWING WIRE FROM MY GENEROUS DADDY:
'DEAR JACK—DON'T BUY A SINGLE VOTE MORE THAN NECESSARY....
I'LL BE DAMNED IF I'M GOING TO PAY FOR A LANDSLIDE.'"
     —JOHN F. KENNEDY

I doubt that J.F.K was confessing that he literally purchased votes in his 1960 presidential campaign. Rather, he's acknowledging that his father's wealth may have been the crucial factor in his victory over Richard M. Nixon by the narrowest popular vote percentage in history. The money paid for an intense media blitz in major industrial states in the critical last few days of the election.

Extensive use of television is the rule instead of the exception in major elections these days, which has lifted the cost of campaigning for major office to a level that must be making Joseph Kennedy turn over in his grave. But even though the dollar figures are higher today, Mark Hanna's observation has been true since the founding of our country. Candidates with more money to spend have had a significant advantage over less well-funded opponents. As far back as 1758, a candidate for the Virginia House of Burgesses named George Washington treated 391 voters to a staggering (literally!) 160 gallons of rum, beer, and hard cider on election day. Today, campaign money is not poured down our throats, but into our homes through television, radio, telephone campaigns, and direct mail. In an ideal world, there would be nothing wrong with bringing more and more information about candidates and issues to the attention of the voters. The problem is the source of the money. Candidates for major offices either have to be independently wealthy or they have to devote a substantial portion of their time and energy soliciting contributions from political action committees and wealthy individuals. Despite a number of reforms, the relationship between campaign funding and good government is hotly debated.

PRESIDENTIAL ELECTION 31

# 1908
## WILLIAM HOWARD TAFT

Feeling that he had a popular mandate, President Roosevelt moved vigorously in his second term to institute a reform agenda, which included strengthening the Interstate Commerce Commission and establishing the Food and Drug Administration. Although the Republican old guard stymied other of his efforts to curb big business, Roosevelt remained immensely popular. He didn't want to go against tradition by seeking a third term, but he did have a strong interest in choosing the man who would succeed him as the Republican nominee.

That man was his close friend and his Secretary of the Navy, William Howard Taft. A huge burly man of nearly three hundred pounds, Taft had been an able attorney and was more interested in being a judge than in politics. But his wife and the enthusiastic Roosevelt persuaded him to seek the nomination. Although some dismissed Taft as Roosevelt's puppet (the President's ovation was twenty minutes longer than the nominee's), he was nominated on the first ballot, and New York Congressman James S. Sherman joined him on the ballot.

Roosevelt's progressive agenda moved his party closer to the Democrats. So it was fitting in a way that the standard bearer for the opposition, William Jennings Bryan, should once again be the man who injected progressivism into national politics. By 1908, Bryan had long left the issue of free silver behind. But he was a staunch advocate of the rights of working people and a crusader for fundamental reforms that would curb the still mighty power of the industrial and financial elite. He was nominated on the first ballot and was joined on the ticket by John W. Kern of Indiana, another compelling orator.

The issue in the election, according to Bryan, was "Shall the people rule?" He and his running mate took to the stump and brought their message to the growing number of middle-class Americans who saw some merit in the progressive message. To counter Bryan's appeal, Roosevelt convinced Taft to take more progressive positions on several issues. He also coached Taft on pubic speaking, and as the campaign neared the end, the Republican candidate was trading fiery barbs with his opponent as he, too, took to the stump.

Probably because of Roosevelt's popularity, Taft won an unexpectedly large victory, capturing a million more popular votes and doubling Bryan's electoral vote total. The three-time Democratic candidate was stunned by the margin of his loss, a greater margin than his loss in 1896. And the election was to be Bryan's last hurrah.

| Electoral votes: | Popular vote: |
|---|---|
| Taft ..............................321 | Taft ................................7,679,006 |
| Bryan .........................162 | Bryan ............................6,409,106 |

In this chapter, we'll take a quick look at the history of campaign funding reform, explain the current situation for major campaigns, then explain how campaign funding rules affect candidates for local office—including you!

## CAMPAIGN FUNDING REFORM

The patrician-politicians who founded our country believed that public service was a moral obligation, and they were almost unanimously fearful of what would happen to government if it were opened to the less educated and less wealthy "masses." That's why the right to vote in the early years of our country was limited to the small percentage of men who owned substantial property. Naturally, many Americans found that idea offensive, and the right to vote was dramatically expanded in the early 1800s.

Unfortunately, for the next fifty or sixty years, it appeared that our founding fathers' predictions were true. Beginning with the presidency of Andrew Jackson, nepotism, cronyism, and flagrant corruption became hallmarks of American government. Rock bottom was the administration of Ulysses.S. Grant (1868–1876), during which major financial scandals involving the Vice-President and several cabinet members were exposed.

Fortunately, the system survived. Outraged by practices that turned government into a cesspool, reformers from both parties seized control and began instituting reforms. The first significant legislation against electoral frauds was enacted in 1890 by New York State. It listed amounts that candidates for various offices might legally

---

## WHAT DOES IT MEAN?
### PAC

PAC stands for "political action committee," an organization established specifically to disperse campaign contributions to political candidates. The very first PAC was established by a labor union, the CIO (Congress of Industrial Organizations) in 1943, but they didn't proliferate until 1974, when amendments to the Federal Election Financing Law severely restricted the amount of money individuals or corporations could donate to candidates. Business and labor lobbyists succeeded in having a provision inserted into the law that allowed PACs to donate up to $5,000 per candidate. As a result, the number of PACs jumped from 113 in 1972 to 4,195 in 1993.

PACs now distribute more than $150 million in a national election year, the vast majority of which goes to incumbents. The top contributor is the PAC established by the National Association of Realtors, followed by the American Medical Association and the National Education Association. In 1992, senators running for reelection received an average of $1 million each from PACs.

spend and required candidates to file itemized accounts of campaign expenditures. Violations of the law were punishable by imprisonment and loss of office. Subsequently, the law was extended to include the treasurers of political committees as well as the candidates they sponsored. Illegal registration, the use of false naturalization papers, personation, and bribery were made punishable by jail sentences of up to five years. Bribe givers were also disqualified from holding office, and bribe takers were disenfranchised for five years. In 1909 New York State prohibited candidates from soliciting donations and forbade all corporations, except political organizations, from making campaign contributions or spending money for political ends. A one-year prison sentence and a $1,000 fine were established as punishment for the violation of this law. Other states also enacted electoral reform laws.

---

## WHAT DOES IT MEAN?

## SLUSH FUND

A slush fund is money siphoned from campaign contributions and used illegally by a candidate or elected official for personal expenses. In the early nineteenth century, slush was a nautical term used for the grease left over from cooking salt pork. The slush was sold when the ship returned to port and the money was put into a fund to purchase luxury items for the crew. In 1866, the term was used to describe a contingency fund set up by Congress, and it later came to mean a secret or illegal fund. Many politicians have gotten into trouble for slush funds, most notably Richard Nixon when he served as vice-president under Dwight D. Eisenhower. Nixon's response was the famous Checkers speech, in which he tearfully maintained the only gift he'd ever gotten was his little black dog.

---

A federal law enacted in 1925 provided that treasurers of political committees, operating in two or more states, had to file with the clerk of the House of Representatives sworn statements containing the names and addresses of all contributors of $100 or more, the names and addresses of all persons receiving $10 or more from the moneys collected by the committees, and the purposes for which the disbursements were made. Candidates for Congress were required to submit itemized accounts of contributions made to their campaign expenses both before and after election. Limits were placed on the amounts candidates were allowed to expend in campaigning. Candidates for public office, members of Congress, and federal employees were prohibited from soliciting campaign contributions among government workers. National banks and corporations organized under congressional charter were forbidden to make contributions to the campaign funds of candidates for congressional seats and for the Electoral College.

However, revelations from the Watergate scandal in the early 1970s—such as the discovery that milk producers had illegally contributed $680,000 to Richard

PRESIDENTIAL ELECTION 32

# 1912

## WOODROW WILSON

Teddy Roosevelt orchestrated Taft's victory in 1908; in 1912, he worked even harder in an attempt to bring about his defeat. The popular ex-president had embarked on a long African safari and tour of European capitals after leaving office, and when he returned to the United States in 1910, he discovered that Taft had apparently moved closer to the Republican old guard and away from the progressive reforms. He and Taft quickly became estranged, and Roosevelt launched a campaign to win the 1912 Republican nomination.

There is no doubt that Roosevelt was the overwhelming choice of the people. Nine states had instituted presidential primaries, and Roosevelt won all but one by impressive margins. But the Republican machine controlled the selection of delegates in the remaining states, and the party leadership made sure that Taft (and James Sherman) were renominated. The outraged Roosevelt charged that the nomination had been stolen from him, and he organized his own convention two months later. Calling themselves the Progressive party, the delegates anointed Teddy Roosevelt as their nominee (California Senator Hiram Johnson was the vice-presidential nominee).

With the Republican party split in two, the Democrats felt they had an excellent chance to recapture the White House. But the convention bogged down into a battle between the big-city machine Democrats, who favored Speaker of the House Champ Clarke of Missouri, and the reform Democrats, led by William Jennings Bryan, who favored liberal New Jersey Governor Woodrow Wilson. The struggle lasted 46 ballots before Wilson gained a majority. Thomas Marshall of Indiana was the vice-presidential nominee.

The campaign was the most vigorous and interesting in half a century. Roosevelt went after Taft with a vengeance, and it soon became apparent that the incumbent President couldn't win. Wilson, however, was an unexpectedly effective campaigner. His program, which he called "The New Freedom," promised much more substantial major reform than Roosevelt espoused.

But Teddy hadn't lost his flare for the dramatic. On October 14, Roosevelt was shot in the chest outside a Milwaukee arena. Although he was bleeding profusely, he insisted on delivering an hour-and-a-half speech before going to the hospital. It turned out that the bullet had broken a rib and had not reached the heart because the victim had such massive chest muscles. Afterwards, Teddy said that it was hard to stop an old bull moose, and his party became known as the Bull Moose party.

Roosevelt did succeed in beating Taft, but he couldn't overcome the Democratic vote. Even though he got just 41 percent of the popular vote, Wilson captured forty of the forty-eight states.

| Electoral votes: | | Popular vote: | |
|---|---|---|---|
| Wilson | 435 | Wilson | 6,286,214 |
| Roosevelt | 88 | Roosevelt | 4,126,020 |
| Taft | 8 | | |

Nixon's campaign—triggered a new wave of campaign financing reform. The Federal Election Campaign Act of 1972, which was amended in 1974, 1976, and 1979, established federal funding for presidential campaigns and established new controls on spending for other federal offices.

## CAMPAIGN FINANCING TODAY

The Federal Election Commission requires that all candidates for federal office and all national political committees file detailed reports. The current law prohibits contributions from corporations, labor unions, national banks, government contractors, foreign nationals, and persons contributing in the name of other persons. It establishes a limit of $1,000 per person per candidate per election and $5,000 per political action committee per candidate per election. However, there is no limit on how much money a candidate can contribute to his or her own campaign. Also, the law allows candidates to accumulate unspent contributions to form a nest egg for future campaigns.

The net result of the current laws gives an enormous advantage to incumbents and challengers with considerable personal wealth. Although both political parties have publicly expressed support for campaign financing reform, there is no specific legislation on the horizon.

### Campaign financing on the state and local level
Several states jumped on the campaign financing reform bandwagon after NewYork State's legislation of 1890. Massachusetts forbade the subsidizing of newspapers to support candidates, contributions by certain corporations to political parties, and payments by political committees of naturalization fees for prospective voters. Oregon established a maximum amount of money that candidates are legally permitted to spend in pursuit of election and arranged to pay a part of their campaign expenses. Kansas prohibited a candidate from spending more than 10 percent of the yearly salary of the office to which he or she sought election.

Today, almost all states now require publication by candidates of financial statements concerning their campaign expenses both before and after election day. The campaign financing laws and reporting requirements are published and administered by each state's election commission, the addresses of which are listed at the end of the previous chapter of this book.

### Campaign financing and you
Campaign financing laws apply to every single person running for office, no matter what the position. Violations of these laws have derailed many a campaign, so following the rules is one of the most important responsibilities of any candidate. Reporting of campaign contributions and expenditures is required of all candi-

dates who collect or spend over a certain amount of money—in some states, as little as $100. It's best to assume that the rules apply to you.

Almost all political professionals recommend that every candidate appoint another person as campaign treasurer, preferably someone with some accounting or financial background. The first thing this person has to do is become familiar with the dates on which financial reports are due. In most cases, reports are due both before and after the election. Being late by just a day can be punishable by

# HOW MUCH DID YOUR CONGRESSMAN SPEND TO GET ELECTED?

In 1992, voters elected 435 Congressmen and 33 senators. Interested in what the candidates spent to get a job that pays $33,600 per years? The answer is a whopping $677 million. Winning a Senate seat cost, on the average, $3.7 million; Al D'Amato's re-election campaign in New York topped the list with expenditures of $11,550,000. However, by far the most spent per vote was $24.01 by Kent Conrad in North Dakota. The average winning congressman spent $551,000; top spender was Michael Huffington of California, with $5.4 million ($41 per vote).

Campaign financing statistics dramatically show the advantage of being an incumbent when raising money. In House races, 227 incumbents raised $126 million, while 513 challengers could scrounge up just $34 million. One major reason was that contributions from political action groups went overwhelmingly to incumbents: in House races PACs gave $64 million to those running for reelection and just $7 million to their challengers.

Want to know what political action groups contributed to your congressman's campaign? Interested in how much of a war chest is being carried over to future years? Federal law requires that candidates submit detailed financial statements to the Federal Election Commission, and all of that information is available to you, toll-free. You can call:

Federal Election Commission
Public Records Information:
(202) 219-3420
Toll-free: (800) 424-9530

For a wealth of additional information
on campaign financing, contact:

National Library on Money and Politics
Center for Responsive Politics
Phone: (202) 857-0318

fines that may exceed the entire funding of the campaign.

The next step is detailed record keeping. How detailed? In some states, if you list an expenditure for newspaper advertising, you have to list the name of the paper, its address and telephone number, and the date on which the ad appears. Although the law may require that you keep receipts for expenditures of $25 or over, it's wise to keep all receipts.

It's also important to know that contributions of materials and services must be treated as if they were cash. Examples are free office space, photocopying services, transportation, use of office machines, etc. These contributions are governed by the same limit as cash. For example, you may not be able to accept services valued at more than $1,000 from any individual.

A final tip—at least three people should review the completed financial reporting forms before they are submitted. Although these requirements may seem like a pain, look on the bright side—candidates who learn how to take care of the details of their campaign finances may be more qualified to look after the details of public spending when they take office.

## How local campaign funds are raised

Most local candidates have to rely on many, many small contributions. That means that no candidate can be shy about asking for money. The best advice from professionals is to treat every event as a fundraising event. This can range from passing the hat at coffees in people's homes to taking names and passing out fundraising brochures when making a speech or participating in an event.

Party organizations can provide crucial assistance in raising money. One of the best resources is their lists of people who have contributed to previous elections. Many parties also hold events that raise money to be distributed to all of the party's candidates.

Although fundraising may be tedious and at times embarrassing, it is a necessity in a system in which anyone can run for political office.

# PRESIDENTIAL ELECTION 33

# 1916

## WOODROW WILSON

In his first term, Woodrow Wilson became the architect of an impressive list of reform legislation, including the Underwood-Simmons tariff, which lowered duties for the first time in forty years; the Federal Reserve Act, which set up a new system to back finance and banking; the Clayton Antitrust Act, which strengthened earlier laws limiting the power of large corporations; and the establishment of the Federal Trade Commission. In 1916 Wilson secured federal loans and marketing aid for farmers, an eight-hour day for railroad workers, and a law prohibiting child labor. However, domestic affairs were only a side issue in the 1916 presidential election. It was dwarfed by the question of whether or not the United States would be drawn into the terrible war in Europe that would later be called World War I.

Ironically, at a time when Bosnia has been in the headlines in recent years, the war began with shots fired in Sarajevo and escalated to a conflict between two factions, one headed by Germany and the other by Britain, France, and Russia. America was having a difficult time maintaining the neutrality of its shipping, particularly against German submarine attacks. After the Germans sunk the British liner *Lusitania* in 1915, killing 128 Americans, President Wilson had ordered an increased state of readiness for American armed forces. However, Wilson was determined to keep America out of the war, and the majority of Americans agreed with him. He was easily renominated, as was his Vice-President, Thomas Marshall.

Teddy Roosevelt wanted the Republican nomination, but his third-party candidacy had alienated too many Republicans. Instead, the party choose Supreme Court Justice and former New York Governor Charles Evans Hughes and added to the ticket Roosevelt's former Vice-President, Charles W. Fairbanks. Roosevelt was strongly in favor of U.S. intervention in the war, and an attack on Wilson's peace policy made its way into the Republican platform. The Progressive Party nominated Roosevelt, but he declined, having had enough of third-party politics.

Wilson pounded the peace theme during the campaign, while Hughes was faced with walking a narrow line between Republicans who favored peace and those who favored war, and those who were part of the old guard and those who sympathized with the progressives. Perhaps the entire election hinged on an incident in California in which Hughes failed to arrange a meeting with California's progressive Republican Governor Hiram Johnson, a snub that got national publicity.

On Election Day, Wilson swept the East and needed just 12 electoral votes from the entire West to become President. But he lost all the states, including California's 13 electoral votes by just 3,800 votes out of one million cast. Wilson squeaked back into the White House.

| Electoral votes: | | Popular vote: | |
|---|---|---|---|
| Wilson | 277 | Wilson | 9,129,606 |
| Hughes | 254 | Hughes | 8,538,221 |

PRESIDENTIAL ELECTION 34

# 1920

## WARREN G. HARDING

Despite Woodrow Wilson's best efforts and intentions, German submarine attacks on American shipping led the United States to declare war on April 6, 1917. Between June, 1917, when the first U.S. troops arrived in Europe, and the signing of the Armistice on November 11, 1918, 126,000 American troops were killed and 435,000 were wounded. Wartime controls and restrictions caused economic hardships and rising unemployment. Although President Wilson had been the driving force behind the creation of an international organization, the League of Nations, which he believed would help prevent world wars, a majority of the American people were reluctant to make any commitment that would draw the United States into a future conflict.

Wilson had suffered a stroke in 1919, hampering his efforts persuade the Senate to allow the United States to join the League of Nations. But the Democrats remained loyal to his vision. They had a difficult time settling on a candidate, but on the forty-fourth ballot the nomination went to Ohio Governor James M. Cox. For Vice-President, the Democrats nominated a cousin of a famous Republican president—Assistant Secretary of the Navy Franklin D. Roosevelt. Both promised to campaign for the League of Nations.

Illinois Governor Frank Lowden and General Leonard Wood were the top contenders for the Republican nomination, but after a few ballots the Republicans turned to a dark horse, Ohio Senator Warren G. Harding. Harding's public career had been completely undistinguished; his primary assets were that he was a successful small-businessman (he owned the *Marion Star* newspaper) and was from the heartland of America. In an election year in which the voters seemed angry at the Democrats, Harding seemed a safe choice and won nomination on the tenth ballot. Massachusetts Governor Calvin Coolidge was nominated for vice-president

Harding ran on a simple campaign slogan: "Return to Normalcy." His speeches emphasized "old-fashioned American values," a welcome relief to a public tired of messy involvement in foreign wars. But it's a good thing that Harding wasn't running today—in his personal life he was a card player, a heavy drinker (even though Prohibition had become law in 1919) and an adulterer with at least one out-of-wedlock child.

Cox campaigned diligently, but Harding won a landslide victory in a year in which less than half the voting-age public went to the polls. When Harding died of a heart attack in 1923, investigations revealed massive corruption in his administration, especially the Teapot Dome Scandal, in which the nation's oil reserves had been leased in exchange for bribes. While Harding wasn't personally implicated, a cloud remains over his presidency.

| Electoral votes: | | Popular vote: | |
|---|---|---|---|
| Harding | 404 | Harding | 16,152,200 |
| Cox | 127 | Cox | 9,147,353 |

# Billboards or Bumper Stickers?

**11**

## How Campaigns are Organized and Conducted

"AN ELECTED OFFICIAL IS ONE WHO GETS 51 PERCENT OF THE VOTE CAST
BY THE 40 PERCENT OF THE 60 PERCENT OF THE VOTERS WHO ARE REGISTERED."
—DAN BENNETT

I've always thought that an election campaign is a lot like a football game. The results that end up on the scoreboard depend upon carefully developed strategy, skilled execution of that strategy, and more than a little bit of plain old-fashioned luck.

Strategy begins with a comprehensive "scouting report" that evaluates an opponent's strengths and weaknesses and compares them to your strengths and weakness. Then a game plan is put together that's designed to maximize your strengths and minimize your weaknesses as both on offense and defense. The type of game plan a team—football or campaign—puts together depends on whether it's the favorite or the underdog. Underdogs have to be more aggressive, while favorites may opt for a more conservative approach. Once the "game" begins, both the candidate and his "coaches"—the campaign manager and staff—have to constantly revise the game plan to counter an opponent's moves, take advantage of opportunities that arise, and institute damage control when the inevitable errors and problems arise.

## RUNNING FOR OFFICE

Now, if you're running for office and aren't a football fan, don't worry. In this chapter, we're going abandon our metaphor and provide an outline of the steps necessary to run a successful campaign.

### Appoint a campaign manager

Like almost every on-air person on television, I am represented by an agent. When I first got into broadcasting, I thought it was very strange that a journalist would need representation like a movie star or football quarterback. But I soon discovered that having

someone to worry about business decisions in the incredibly competitive world of television freed me to concentrate my total energy on my real job—informing my viewers.

It's even more important that a candidate for any office have a campaign manager who establishes the candidate's schedule, helps make strategy decisions, recruits and supervises volunteers, and generally makes sure that everything that needs to get done actually does get done on time. That leaves you, the candidate, free to do what a candidate must do—get out and meet the voters. If you've never run for office before, you will probably seriously underestimate the time and energy you'll need to devote to the quest. Trying to wear two hats is a prescription for disaster.

How do you find a campaign manager? Your party may be able to help you find someone with experience who can help you out. If not, approach a friend whose management skills you admire. It's much better to choose a person with excellent management skills over a less skilled manager who has some political experience.

What if you're reluctant to ask someone to volunteer so much time? Asking for help from a lot of people is essential for running for office, so get used to it!

## Locate your district

Ohio Court of Appeals Judge Lawrence Grey, in his excellent book *How to Win a Local Election*, tells of pulling up to a remote farmhouse while he was campaigning for the job of county prosecutor. The elderly farmer sitting on the porch invited him to sit a spell and they had a very pleasant hour-long chat. Finally, Judge Grey got up to leave and asked the farmer if he had his vote. The farmer said, "Son, I think you're a fine man but I'm not going to vote for you." "Why not?" the stunned candidate asked. "Because," the old man said, "your county line ends at the beginning of my driveway."

Judge Grey goes on to make a crucial point: The first step in any campaign is to obtain detailed maps of the area—be it city, town, county, congressional district, state senate, or assembly district, precinct, ward, etc.—in which you're running. Don't assume you know the boundaries, because many districts change. By federal law, the number of seats a state is allocated in the House of Representatives is readjusted every ten years when the results of the official Census are known. The legislatures of the states that gain or lose seats have to redraw the state's congressional districts. Blatant gerrymandering, or the drawing of the lines of districts to give an advantage to one party, is largely a thing of the past. But the Supreme Court has allowed districts to be drawn so that minorities can be a majority. The result can be some very odd-looking districts.

The districts of state legislators and even some city and county governing bodies are occasionally redrawn to reflect population changes.

## Know your constituents

You're running for office to serve the people, so it stands to reason that you need comprehensive and accurate information on who the people in your district really

are. The place to start is with the data compiled by the U.S. Census Bureau, which should be in your local library. The Bureau divides the entire country into relatively small census tracts, and for each tract provides a wealth of information from median age of the population to average annual income to average number of bathrooms. Your library may also have information about your area from private market research firms, who delve into such issues as lifestyles and quality of life concerns. If you're on-line or have a friend who is, both U.S. Census Bureau statistics and market research information is available on the Internet.

## Compute a target vote total

The quote that begins this chapter may sound a bit cryptic on first reading, but it deals with one of the single most important issues in any campaign—figuring out how many votes you actually will need to win and election. Without this computation, it's difficult to formulate a workable campaign strategy.

To explain what I mean, I'm going to use the figures compiled by a friend of mine who worked as campaign manager for a woman running for mayor in a small

# HOW MANY VOTES DOES IT TAKE TO WIN ELECTION TO THE U.S. HOUSE OF REPRESENTATIVES?

The answer is, it depends where you live. Although each congressional district has an average population of 500,000, the actual numbers go as high as 800,000 (Montana's population, which has only one House member.) As a result, Montana residents cast about 344,000 votes on Election Day, 1994, the most of any election district.

Barely 10 percent of that total were cast in California's Thirty-Third District, and Democratic Representative Lucille Roybal-Allard's 30,350 votes (81 percent of total) represented the lowest winning total in the United States. At the other extreme was Democratic Rep. Tim Johnson of South Dakota, who won reelection with 183,038 votes, 60 percent of the total.

Then there's Republican Cy Jamison of Montana, who outpolled all but a dozen House winners nationwide but still lost to Democratic Rep. Pat Williams. Jamison drew 145,312 votes to Williams' 167,178 votes.

Voter turnout was low in many majority-minority districts, which could have been part of the reason Democrats did so poorly on November 8th. Fourteen of the twenty-five districts where candidates won with the fewest votes were majority-minority. That included ten Hispanic-majority districts, where many residents are not U.S. citizens and therefore are ineligible to vote.

## WHAT DOES IT MEAN?
# GERRYMANDER

It is perhaps ironic that a man who signed the Declaration of Independence and attained the Vice-Presidency of the United States should be chiefly remembered for a notorious bit of political flimflam. Gerrymandering, the now universal term for drawing the boundaries of electoral districts in such a way as to give one party an unfair advantage over its rivals, "honors" the name of Elbridge Gerry (1744–1814). Gerry was a Massachusetts delegate to the second Continental Congress and one of the signers of the Declaration of Independence. As a Democratic-Republican he was elected to the governorship of Massachusetts in 1810 and reelected in 1811.

His second administration achieved lasting notoriety because of a measure of February 11, 1812 that has since become known as the "Gerrymander Bill." The purpose of the bill was to redistrict the state in such a way as to give the Democratic-Republicans a majority in the state senate. Gerry's home territory of Essex County, in the northeast corner of Massachusetts, was subdivided into strangely shaped senatorial districts. During the campaign a map of Essex County was displayed at a meeting of the Federalist Party, the opposition. Onto an outline of the grotesquely configured district, one of the Federalists—perhaps the noted painter Gilbert Stuart himself—sketched an animal's head, wings, and claws. Upon completing his handiwork, the artist proclaimed, "That will do for a salamander!" Another party member quickly rejoined, "Gerrymander!" The caricature of the district as a winged monster—with Gerry's profile superimposed upon its back—was widely reproduced, and the coinage "gerrymander" immediately caught on, at first applied to the caricature itself and then to the actual act of redistricting. With equal alacrity "gerrymander" was turned into a verb. In its December 28, 1812 issue, the *New York Post* reported an attempt "to Gerrymander the State [of New Hampshire] for the choice of Representatives to Congress."

As far as the Democratic-Republicans of Massachusetts were concerned, the act of 1812 worked exactly as intended: in the election of April 1812, the Federalist candidates for the state senate received 51,766 votes to 50,164 for the Democratic-Republicans, but the Federalists won only 11 seats and the Republicans won 29. Their victory was neither complete nor enduring, however. Gerry himself was defeated in his reelection bid, and the Gerrymander Bill of 1812 was repealed on June 16, 1813. A few weeks after his defeat for reelection, he was nominated by the Republicans for the U.S. Vice-Presidency on a ticket headed by James Madison. However, he died eighteen months into his term.

## AFRICAN–AMERICANS IN CONGRESS

In the first 204 years of congressional history, eighty-nine African-Americans have served in Congress: eighty-five in the House and four in the Senate. The first wave came during Reconstruction after the Civil War. Mississippi Republican Hiram R. Revels broke the color barrier when he was seated in the Senate on February 25, 1870, shortly after his state was readmitted to the Union. The first Representative was Joseph H. Rainey, a South Carolina Republican, who served from December 12, 1870 to March 3, 1879. The largest number of new black members were the seventeen who were elected in 1992.

Connecticut town. The town's population is about 23,000 people, of which approximately 16,600 are of voting age and approximately 13,000 are registered voters. Looking back at turnout in previous nonpresidential election years, my friend discovered that an average of 7,000 people actually voted—52 percent of the registered voters and 42 percent of the residents of voting age.

The next calculations involved looking at voting patterns. There were three candidates in the race: the incumbent Republican mayor, a candidate from an established third party, and the Democratic challenger my friend worked for. In past elections, the

## WHY DOES THE HOUSE OF REPRESENTATIVES HAVE 435 MEMBERS?

The Constitution does not mandate that the House of Representatives have a certain number of members, only that the number of members from each state should be apportioned according to the population. The first House had seventy-three members, and the number grew until it reached 435 in 1910. In 1911, worried that future increases would make the House so big that it would become unwieldy, Congress passed legislation permanently freezing the number of representatives. At that time, the average size of a congressional district was 235,223; today it is 572,466.

third party, which advocated slashing spending and property taxes, had consistently gathered about 1,500 votes. In her previous four races, the Republican incumbent averaged 3,700 votes, while the Democratic candidates averaged just 2,000 votes.

From these statistics, my friend the campaign manager concluded that his candidate started from a solid base of 2,000 votes. From his knowledge of the town, he knew that the third-party voters, who were almost exclusively older residents concerned about property taxes, were nearly impossible to sway. Therefore, the goal of the entire campaign was to find a strategy that would win over 851 of the voters who had traditionally supported the Republican incumbent.

Breaking the statistics down like this makes the process of winning an election seem much more manageable. The disparity between Democratic and Republican voters in my friends town is unusually large—more commonly, the difference between winning and losing an election comes down to swaying 200, 300, or 400 voters.

---

## WHAT DOES IT MEAN?
### SLOGAN

The Celts had a word *sluagh* meaning "host, crowd, multitude" that is involved in a couple of modern English words. It was combined with the Gaelic *gairm* meaning "shout, cry." The resulting compound, meaning "war cry," first appeared in Scottish English in such spellings as *slughorne*, *sloghorne*, and *slogurn*.

By the seventeenth century its modern spelling *slogan* began to appear. The war cry itself usually consisted simply of a clan or family name or a place name—not very bloodthirsty, but it seems to have been effective. By the eighteenth century slogan was being used in violent (at least physically violent) pursuits; it referred to a word or phrase used by a person or group to stand for an attitude, position, or goal—not very different from the use of *motto*. Extension to politics and advertising was to be expected, and by the time of World War I slogan was in everyday use by all sorts of organized groups.

---

## Develop a campaign strategy

Many political observers believe that Bill Clinton unseated the incumbent George Bush in 1992 primarily because his entire campaign was focused on a message summed up in four words: "It's the economy, stupid." He never used that phrase in talking to the public, but it was taped to the podium every single time he gave a speech, participated in a debate, or answered questions. Although he had to give his opinions on many issues, the theme of his entire campaign was elegantly simple.

Because candidates for local office have many fewer opportunities to get the attention of the voters, it is even more important that you formulate a campaign

PRESIDENTIAL ELECTION 35

# 1924
## CALVIN COOLIDGE

In August 1923, Calvin Coolidge ascended to the presidency, but he was totally untainted by the Harding administration scandals. Assuming the reins of state was much easier for him because the country's economy was booming. Coolidge's nomination was a certainty, and in this era of Prohibition, the Republican convention was so dull that the humorist Will Rogers joked that they had to open the churches to liven things up. The Republicans named the incumbent President on the first ballot, and made Charles G. Dawes his running mate.

In stark contrast, the Democratic convention was the site of fierce nine-day struggle before a nominee emerged. The primary issue wasn't Coolidge or his administration, but rather the Ku Klux Klan, a viciously anti-Semitic, antiblack, anti-Roman Catholic organization that began to spread after World War I. The Klan was strong in the South, the Democratic stronghold; while a strong majority of the delegates condemned the violence of the Klan, the convention was almost evenly deadlocked over a resolution to condemn the organization. A mild anti-Klan statement passed by just 1 vote out of the 1083 cast. Then the delegates split between New York governor Al Smith, a Roman Catholic and strongly anti-Klan, and William G. McAdoo, the son-in-law of Woodrow Wilson who opposed a strong anti-Klan position. The convention remained deadlocked for 102 ballots before Smith and McAdoo finally released their exhausted delegates. On the next ballot—the most in U.S. political convention history—John W. Davis, a New York lawyer, was nominated for President and Charles Bryan (William Jennings's brother) was nominated for Vice-President.

The choice between the conservative Coolidge and a Wall Street lawyer didn't please progressives in either party, so they got together to nominate a third-party slate. Republican Wisconsin Senator Robert ("Fighting Bob") LaFollette was nominated for President and Democratic Montana Senator Burton K. Wheeler for Vice-President. The Progressives hoped to get enough votes to throw the election into the House of Representatives.

The strategy failed. Despite vigorous campaigning, neither Davis nor LaFollette was able to come up with an issue that captured the imagination of a largely contented, prosperous nation. On election day, Coolidge polled more popular votes than his two opponents combined. Commented William Allen White, "In a fat and happy world, Calvin Coolidge is the man of the hour."

| Electoral votes: | | Popular vote: | |
|---|---|---|---|
| Coolidge | 382 | Coolidge | 15,725,016 |
| Davis | 136 | Davis | 8,385,586 |
| LaFollette | 13 | LaFollette | 4,822,856 |

# 1928

## HERBERT HOOVER

Calvin Coolidge declined to seek reelection in 1928, and for a change there was no doubt about which two men would face off in the election to replace him. Even before the convention, the Republican favorite was clearly Herbert Hoover, the Secretary of Commerce under Coolidge. Born on a farm in Iowa, Hoover had earned an engineering degree, became a millionaire opening mines in China during the Boxer Rebellion, and supervised European relief efforts in World War I. A rather stiff and dignified man, Hoover was a strong believer in big business, small government, and Prohibition. He was nominated for President on the first ballot (Kansas Senator Charles Curtis was the vice-presidential nominee).

The Democratic nominee, who was also named on the first ballot, couldn't have had a more starkly contrasting background and personality from Hoover. Al Smith was born in New York City, dropped out of school at an early age, and made his living on the streets for several years until he was taken under the wing of Tammany Hall and given the first of a number of political jobs that eventually led to the governorship of New York. Smith was a charismatic man with a great sense of humor who ,as governor, had a reputation for being both compassionate and efficient. Smith, a Roman Catholic, was a "wet" (anti-Prohibition) who esposed the public position that states should have the authority to allow the sale of beer and wine. To balance the ticket, the Democrats nominated a "dry" for Vice-President, Arkansas Senator Joseph G. Robinson.

The campaign was unusually vicious, with Smith's religion the major target. The Klu Klux Klan burned crosses at Democratic rallies across the South and West. Millions of people were told that the Pope was packing his bags to move into the White House the moment Smith was elected, and that all Protestant religious ceremonies would be banned. Smith also came under heavy fire on the alcohol issue. He was portrayed as a drunk who would open the spigots and lead the country on a ruinous binge. Although Hoover also complained about mud-slinging, Smith received the worst of it by far.

These slanders no doubt cost Smith votes, but the high-flying economy would have insured a Republican victory no matter who the Democratic candidate had been. The public believed that Hoover was the "great engineer" who could keep the good times rolling, and the Republican candidate carried forty states in a convincing landslide victory.

| Electoral votes: | | Popular vote: | |
|---|---|---|---|
| Hoover | 444 | Hoover | 21,392,190 |
| Smith | 87 | Smith | 15,016,443 |

strategy based on a simple, comprehensible theme. You may be running for office because you have informed opinions on a wide variety of issues, but unless you have the money for unlimited television advertising, you'll only confuse the public if you

try to convey all those issues. You need a campaign theme that can be summarized in a sentence or phrase on the front of a brochure.

How do you find a focus? The answer lies in the small group of voters you identified when you defined your campaign goal. The issue or theme you pick should be designed to sway their votes, not the votes of the electorate at large. For example, in the mayoral campaign in which my friend participated, the swing voters turned out to be parents with young children. A surge in elementary school enrollment had taken the town by surprise, resulting in overcrowding and a reduction in services. The obvious campaign strategy for a challenger was to attack the incumbent mayor for poor planning and offer innovative new solutions to the problem. The strategy nearly worked—the challenger attracted 650 of the 850 voters she needed, losing by just 400 votes in the closest town election in two decades.

Obviously, your strategy will have to be crafted to the problems and interests of the voters in your district. Even if nothing comes to mind immediately, continue your research. No governmental unit at any level is able to cope effectively with all problems and concerns. With enough work, you'll find your strategy.

## Prepare a campaign budget

Budgeting and fundraising have sort of a chicken and egg relationship—it's harder to budget before you know how much you have to spend, but it's also hard to raise money and spend it effectively if you don't have a budget. Most experts recommend budgeting first so you have a target to shoot for and so you can ask specific people for specific types of contributions.

The best way to start preparing a budget is to obtain the campaign finance reports from previous campaigns for the office you're seeking. You'll see exactly how much the incumbents and challengers raised and spent, and what they spent their money on. You'll probably see such spending categories as:
- Phone
- Stationery and envelopes
- Postage
- Printing
- Office supplies
- Campaign materials design and artwork
- Copying expenses
- Computer costs
- Mailing lists
- Campaign and volunteer forms
- Media advertising

Most local candidates use their homes, places of business, or their party offices as campaign headquarters.

## Raise the funds to meet your budget

Asking for money is everyone's least favorite part of campaigning, but it's also one of the most essential. As with anything else in life, you'll get better at it with practice. And you'll get lots of practice, because the most effective way to obtain the money you need is to make fund-raising part of almost every campaign activity.

Candidates for Congress, for governor, and other major offices hire consultants to produce sophisticated direct mail and other fundraising programs. The fee of just one consultant would probably dwarf your entire campaign budget. You can probably obtain lots of good advice from the "old pros" in your political party. Here are a few suggestions we've developed:

- Always include your campaign theme in every written or spoken pitch. Don't say, "Please contribute," but say, "Please help us eliminate overcrowding and poor planning in our schools by making a donation."

- Get a list of people who've contributed to the campaigns of the previous candidates from your party who ran for the same office you're running for. Try to set up appointments with the large contributors and call everyone else.

- Use direct mail sparingly, because it is expensive. But always send a personal thank-you letter to everyone who contributes, no matter what the amount.

- The voters who sign your nominating petition are excellent prospects for campaign donations. Call them.

- Include a fundraising appeal in your brochure and in all other appropriate campaign literature.

- It's no secret that campaigns cost money, so there's no reason not to ask for money at such campaign events as coffees or teas. While it's not appropriate to ask for money when your shaking the hands of commuters outside a local train station or coffee shop, you should always bring the subject up when a voter stops you for a longer conversation.

- When you're asking for donations in person, always try to include information on what the money will be used for. For example, you might say "$5 allows us to send brochures to twenty homes, $10 is half the cost of a radio spot, and $50 pays half the cost of an ad in our weekly newspaper."

- You'll be surprised at the effectiveness of asking for contributions of equipment and services as well as cash. For example, a businessperson who may not want to give cash will let you use his copying machine, or a supporter will make campaign calls for you from home. Just remember, you have to report these contributions in the same way as you do cash.

- Be just as gracious and effusive about small contributions as you are about large contributions. Word of mouth is a powerful soliciting technique—you can never tell who will urge friends and relatives to give you money because you were so nice to them.

## Recruit campaign volunteers

Many political professionals believe that volunteers are at least as important as money. Every campaign needs people to:

* Distribute brochures, posters, lawn signs, and other material
* Fold literature and stuff envelopes
* Maintain mailing lists and campaign records
* Make calls to voters and answer the telephones
* Canvas door-to-door
* Host a coffee or tea
* Drive voters to the polls on election day.

Recruiting volunteers and soliciting campaign funds go hand and hand—whenever and wherever you ask for money, also ask for volunteers.

Of course, your work is only half done when you recruit a volunteer. The second and equally important part is making the experience rewarding for the person involved. This means scheduling volunteers only when you have meaningful work for them to do, making sure they are adequately informed and trained, and providing lots of encouragement. In larger campaigns, a volunteer coordinator is directly responsible for scheduling and training; in most others, the campaign manager wears this hat. But in all cases it's the responsibility of the candidate to make sure volunteers feel important and appreciated.

## Prepare and distribute campaign material

Designing and printing brochures, flyers, posters, and yard signs used to be difficult and expensive. But today's powerful personal computers, sophisticated word processing and graphics software, and inexpensive high-quality printers make it a much less daunting and a much less expensive task. If you're running a campaign, you may even be able to prepare the materials on your computer and go to a local copy shop to have them run off.

It is better, however, if you can recruit a volunteer with an advertising or graphic arts background to assist you. Polished, professional materials make you look like a polished, professional candidate. You will probably not be able to meet every voter in your district, but there's no doubt that every voter will see at least some of your campaign material. This is a great place to invest extra time and money.

Once you have the materials, you need the assistance of your volunteers to get them distributed. If you have the money, you'll probably want to do at least one mailing to voters. But most of the materials, from brochures to lawn signs, will be distributed person to person.

It's important to be careful and considerate when placing campaign material. A friend of mine who owns a large child-care center discovered that a campaign sticker for a school-board candidate was plastered right over her flyer and others on the

bulletin board of a local supermarket. The thoughtlessness of the candidate or volunteer cost him hundreds of votes.

## Get to know the local media

While it's unlikely Ted Koppel will be calling you to appear on *Nightline*, your local media (newspapers, radio, and television) will be covering your race. I don't have the space in this book to provide detailed information on how to take advantage of the opportunities to promote yourself and your campaign that the media can provide (there are many excellent books on public relations), but I do have a few tips:

- Always be courteous and polite. You may get angry if you're misquoted by a newspaper reporter or a television station doesn't cover one of your campaign events, but it is almost always counterproductive to give into the impulse to yell and scream. The overwhelming majority of journalists try to be fair and objective under great pressure. If you treat them like professionals even when they make a mistake or misjudgment, they are much more likely to give you the benefit of the doubt in the future.

- Always tell the truth. More campaigns are sabotaged by lying to the press than for any other reasons. It's much better to say "no comment" or "I'll have to look into that and get back to you" than to lie or make up an answer.

- In an interview, answer the question that's asked and try to be brief. Inexperienced candidates often try to make a speech every time they're asked a question, but that is just as rude in public as it is in private conversation. Thoughtful, responsive interviewees get more interviews.

- Don't try to please all of the voters with every answer. Remember your campaign strategy and stick rigidly to your theme. It may not win applause from the specific audience you're addressing, but changing the message could confuse your small group of target voters.

- Relax. I've been involved in thousands of interviews on both sides of the microphone, and I've found that most people do a terrific job. One of the perks of running for office is to become a little bit of a media star!

## Spend your advertising dollars wisely

Every candidate would like to have a spot running on TV during *ER* or *Seinfeld*, but the truth is that broadcast advertising is extremely expensive. Unless you're independently wealthy or have rich backers, plan your advertising carefully. In most districts, weekly newspapers are very well read and are a cost-effective way to reach the voters. Radio can also be effective, but picking the right station among many alternatives can be tricky. Make sure that you get accurate information about the listener demographics of a station and make sure it matches your target group of voters before you spend the money—your kids might get a kick out of hearing your ads on

a local rock station, but voters may never hear them. Because spots are inexpensive (as low as $5 to $10 in certain time slots on certain systems) cable television has become an increasingly popular choice. Many candidates choose to advertise on channels adults turn to frequently, such as CNN or the Weather Channel. Your local cable sales rep can give you the details. A final option is billboards, which can be effective on heavily traveled commuter routes.

Whatever media outlets you consider, always compare their cost and results with that of direct mail. At least you know everyone goes to their mailbox every day.

## Meet the people

Your final and most important job as a candidate is to meet the people. I pay attention to local politics when I read the paper, but what sticks in my mind most is the evening a couple years ago when the state assemblywoman for my district knocked at our door. She wasn't in the middle of a campaign; she just wanted to introduce herself and offer her help if we had any questions or problems with state government. I was impressed, and I'm sure I'll vote for her until she stops running.

You'll get your chance to make the same kind of impression if you get out to meet people. And going door-to-door isn't the only way. You should make it a policy to get invited to every kind of event in your community, from school concerts to parades to meet-the-candidate nights. Go early, stay late, and don't spend time talking to people you already know. The technique politicians call "pressing the flesh" is time-honored because it works.

Even if you don't have an event to go to, get out and meet the people in the course of their daily activities—outside coffee shops, grocery stores, movie theaters, etc. Always have your campaign material and a big smile on your face. You're guaranteed to make an impression.

## Be gracious on election night

It's easier to be gracious when you win, but it's most important to be gracious when you lose, no matter how badly you feel or how viciously your opponent attacked you during the campaign. Mending fences keeps your options open for another race.

PRESIDENTIAL ELECTION 37

# 1932

# FRANKLIN D. ROOSEVELT

In the Roaring Twenties, it seemed, everyone was getting rich, especially in the stock market. Because the election of the "Great Engineer" in 1928 seemed to insure that prosperity would continue indefinitely, investment in stocks became a national frenzy. Millions of Americans took borrowed money against their homes and liquidated other savings to play the market, and every week stock averages reached record highs—until October, 1929, when the bubble burst. The stock market lost an incredible $15 billion in value in just one month, bringing millions of people to financial ruin. Soon the nation was plunged into the worst depression in its history.

Americans needed someone to blame, and the President was the logical target. Although Hoover did institute a number of welfare programs that would have appalled Republicans in more prosperous times, it was too little, too late. By 1932, one-quarter of the work force was unemployed, thousands of banks and tens of thousands of companies had gone bankrupt, and hundreds of thousands of people were forced out of their homes into shantytowns that the residents sarcastically called "Hoovervilles."

But dire economic times didn't prevent Hoover from seeking reelection, and the Republicans had no choice but to give him the nomination. Shunning the incumbent would be as good as admitting blame for the Great Depression. Hoover and his Vice-President, Charles Curtis, were renominated on the first ballot at a convention so restrained that there were no demonstrations or posted pictures of the candidates.

Because Hoover seemed doomed to defeat, the contest for the Democratic nomination was fiercely fought. Al Smith sought a rematch and had significant support in the party, as did Speaker of the House John Nance Garner. But the front-runner was New York Governor Franklin D. Roosevelt. Roosevelt had given the nominating speech for Al Smith in both 1924 and 1928, but in 1932 sought the top spot for himself. Although many professionals considered him a lightweight, Roosevelt shrewdly orchestrated a deal that won him the nomination when, after failing to win a majority on the first few ballots, he persuaded John Nance Garner to support him in exchange for the vice-presidential nomination.

Despite his handicap (he had been crippled by polio in 1921), Roosevelt proved a tireless campaigner. In his acceptance speech, he said, "I pledge you, I pledge myself, to a new deal for the American people." "New Deal" became the name of his program of reforms, and it captured the imagination of the voters. Hoover captured just six states as he went down to defeat.

| Electoral votes: | Popular vote: |
|---|---|
| Roosevelt....................................472 | Roosevelt......................22,821,857 |
| Hoover .......................................59 | Hoover ........................15,761,841 |

# 1936

## FRANKLIN D. ROOSEVELT

Riding into office on FDR's coattails were large Democratic majorities in both houses of Congress. During the first three months the administration, known as the Hundred Days, that same Congress passed many pieces of innovative legislation originating in the executive branch. The Roosevelt Administration moved to subsidize agricultural prices, prevent wage and price gouging by big business, create a huge public works program, provide liquidity for financial institutions, establish the Tennessee Valley Authority, and, finally, abandon the gold standard, which devalued the dollar and helped U.S. exports. Even after the Hundred Days, FDR continued to offer legislation that reshaped the relationship between government and its citizens.

That's why it's no mystery that the 1936 election was essentially a referendum on Franklin D. Roosevelt. The Democratic convention was an emotional rally for the President; both FDR and Vice-President John Nance Garner were renominated by acclamation. In his acceptance speech, Roosevelt promised an expansion of the New Deal, proclaiming that Americans had a "rendezvous with destiny."

But one man's meat is another man's poison, and many wealthy businessmen loathed FDR, arguing that he was really a Socialist or Communist in disguise. These businessmen approved of the Republican nominee, Kansas Governor Alfred M. Landon, because he was a fiscal conservative who had balanced the budget in his state (Frank Knox was the vice-presidential nominee). However, Landon also had some progressive roots, and he favored some New Deal measures such as unemployment relief and subsidies for agriculture. Although the Republican platform lambasted FDR, it waffled on the whole package of New Deal legislation. The passions produced by the Great Depression also spawned a number of minor parties, including the Socialists, Communists, Prohibitionists, and the new Union party, formed by an odd combination of extremist groups. None, however, made any headway with the electorate.

FDR campaigned very little in the early fall, giving the Republicans the opportunity to go on the attack. Although it seems strange at a time when attacking Social Security was political suicide, many in Landon's camp made the brand-new legislation (which would take effect in 1937) their prime target. The Republicans vilified the program as a new tax that would give the government control over working people's hard earned money. This attack finally goaded FDR into a series of speeches in which he lambasted his opponents as the voices of selfishness and greed. He asked his fellow Americans if they'd like to go back to the conditions in 1932 or if they thought they were better off after four years of the New Deal.

The resounding answer was that a huge majority of Americans felt they were better off. FDR won all but two states in a landslide victory that gave the New Deal four more years of life.

| Electoral votes: | | Popular vote: | |
|---|---|---|---|
| Roosevelt | 523 | Roosevelt | 27,751,597 |
| Landon | 28 | Landon | 16,679,583 |

# Do You Really Want to Be President?——

**12**

## A Step-by-Step Explanation of the Most Expensive and Grueling Process in American Life

"ANY AMERICAN WHO IS PREPARED TO RUN FOR PRESIDENT SHOULD AUTOMATICALLY, BY DEFINITION, BE DISQUALIFIED FROM EVER DOING SO."
  —GORE VIDAL

"RUNNING FOR PRESIDENT DEMANDS A SINGLE MINDED OBSESSION THAT CAN DISTORT PEOPLE. THAT'S ALL YOU THINK ABOUT. THAT'S ALL YOU TALK ABOUT. THAT'S WHO YOU'RE AROUND. THAT'S YOUR SCHEDULE. THAT'S YOUR LEISURE. THAT'S YOUR LUXURY. THAT'S YOUR READING. I TOLD SOMEONE, 'THE QUESTION IS NOT WHETHER I CAN GET ELECTED. THE QUESTION IS CAN I GET ELECTED AND NOT BE NUTS WHEN I GET THERE.' IT CAN TWIST PEOPLE."
  —WALTER MONDALE

Bill Clinton took the oath of office as president of the United States on January 20, 1993, an inauguration that marked the end of the 1992 election campaign. Less than one month later, Senator Phil Gramm of Texas made an appearance in the crucial primary state of New Hampshire in another ritual that kicked off the 1996 presidential campaign. And if you think Senator Gramm was jumping the gun a bit with the election forty-four months away, ponder the fact that three of his competitors for the GOP presidential nomination also found a reason to visit the Granite State in the next six months.

It's a fact of American political life that a person who wants to seek our nation's highest office today must be willing to devote, at the minimum, two to three years to campaigning. Because most presidential candidates are senators, congressmen, or governors—positions that carry significant duties and responsibilities—politics consumes their lives twenty-four hours a day, seven days a week. They travel hundreds of thousands of miles, place tens of thousands of telephone calls, make thousands of appearances, and give hundreds of speeches. Every part of their public and private lives is open to intense scrutiny by the media. And they operate

under the pressure of knowing that any slip of the tongue they may make could be a torpedo that sinks their entire campaign.

So why would sensible people want to subject themselves to this process? The best answer I've ever heard was supplied by former New York Governor Nelson Rockefeller: "We're politicians, and like in any profession, we want to reach the top, which in America means only one thing." That "thing" is the presidency. Throughout American history, the race for the presidency has attracted most of the major political figures in each generation.

However, the race for the Oval Office has become so grueling and so expensive that there are legitimate fears that physical endurance and access to big money have replaced talent as the most important qualifications for the American presidency. Certainly, our present system for choosing candidates for the White House would shock the founders of our country.

## A SHORT HISTORY OF PRESIDENTIAL CAMPAIGNING

As we've seen earlier in this book, the first presidential election was more like a coronation than a contest—the country appealed to George Washington to take the reigns of power, and he consented. The idea of asking people to vote for him would have been as appalling to the Father of Our Country as taking off his wig and taking out his teeth in public. Although elections were contested after Washington stepped down in 1796, the early presidential candidate held just as firmly to the belief that it was improper and undignified to campaign. The approximately 4 percent of American citizens eligible to vote were gentlemen, property owners of the same class as the candidates. Appealing to their support would seem like begging.

That attitude changed dramatically in 1828, when the number of people eligible to vote was dramatically expanded to include most adult males. John Quincy Adams, who was seeking reelection, was the last of the patrician presidents who believed, in his words, that "if my country wants my services, she should ask for them." Andrew Jackson, on the other hand, was a general who commanded armies made up of working people, and he had no qualms about asking for their support. Although Jackson made no public campaign appearances, he privately organized the nation's first sophisticated political campaign that organized demonstrations and meetings across the country. It's no surprise that Jackson won a landslide victory.

Subsequent campaigns were much better organized, but candidates restricted themselves to what was called "front porch campaigning," that is, delegations from all over the country traveled to the candidate's homes, where they would meet the presidential aspirant and perhaps hear a short speech. Finally, in 1860, in an election that was to determine whether the nation would have war or peace, Stephen Douglas became the first presidential candidate to make a nationwide tour to promote his candidacy.

Another losing candidate, William Jennings Bryan, became the first candidate to spend months on a nonstop barnstorming tour. Bryan traveled 18,000 miles, gave 600 speeches, and appeared before nearly five million people. Over the next half century, many other candidates followed his example of touring the country by train to give speeches at every stop. Franklin Roosevelt was a master of the technique, and his successor, Harry Truman, produced one of the great upsets in American political history by "giving 'em hell" during his exhaustive whirlwind tour.

It's ironic that perhaps the most successful barnstormer of them all should also have been the last to participate in an "old-fashioned campaign." By the next election in 1952, candidates had a much more effective way to reach American voters—television. In a series of brilliant ads, the Republicans showcased Dwight Eisenhower, a national hero, as the leader America needed. The technique worked brilliantly, and by 1956, television advertising was the dominant campaign technique.

But television advertising is extremely expensive, so candidates were forced to take to the road again—not to talk to the public, but to appeal to the fraction of the electorate who could make major contributions. After the Watergate investigations revealed huge, secret contributions made to Richard Nixon, federal law was changed to provide federal financing for the campaign between the nominees of the two major parties.

However, that didn't solve the problem of raising money to get the nomination in the first place. Today, three-quarters of the convention delegates from both parties are selected in presidential primary elections. In 1996, 70 percent of the delegates were chosen over a forty-four day period. Expensive saturation television advertising is the only way to reach so many voters in such a short period of time.

Presidential campaigning today couldn't be more different from the process in which the founders of our country participated. Let's take a look at the long and arduous work that has to be done before the very first presidential primary or caucus takes place.

## Money, money, money

January 1 of any presidential election year is a magic date for aspirants to the nation's highest office. On New Year's Day, candidates for the nomination of the two major parties who have met certain requirements become eligible to receive federal funds. Although the amount of money they receive is computed according to a complex formula (the federal government matches 100 percent of smaller contributions but a smaller percentage of larger contributions), the amount they receive represents, on the average, 36 percent of the money they have raised in the preceding year. Candidates can continue to receive matching funds if they run strongly in the primary elections.

How much money does a candidate have to raise before January 1 to become a serious contender in the primaries? You'd better sit down. The answer is at least $20 million, and preferably, $30 million. The campaign manager for one 1996 contender said that staying in the race requires raising $1 million every ten days for the entire preprimary season.

# 1940

# FRANKLIN D. ROOSEVELT

Although America had still not recovered fully from the Great Depression, the economy and the New Deal were only minor issues in the 1940 elections. Instead, the focus was on Europe, where Hitler's ruthless military machine had conquered Norway, Denmark, Holland, Belgium, and France and was threatening Great Britain, America's closest ally. The issue of whether or not the United States should enter the war dominated the headlines, private debate, and, naturally, the 1940 political conventions.

The Republican convention quickly adopted the moderate position that the United States should remain at peace but provide assistance to Great Britain and other allies. In this light nominating a candidate was not so easy. In early 1940, the clear favorites were New York District Attorney Thomas Dewey and Ohio Senator Robert Taft, son of President William Howard Taft, two veteran Republican politicians. Then, out of the blue, came a third candidate who had never run for public office and who had been a Democrat until 1939. Wendell Willkie, a native of Indiana, was a Wall Street lawyer and the head of a large utility holding company. Willkie was very intelligent and had an engaging manner that first attracted support among "amateur" politicians all across the country. Even though he didn't enter a single presidential primary, Willkie had generated considerable enthusiasm by the time of the convention. When neither Dewey nor Taft were able to win a majority on the first five ballots, the delegates turned to the political neophyte, nominating him on the sixth ballot. The convention balanced the ticket by adding Senate Minority Leader Charles McNary as the vice-presidential candidate.

If war hadn't threatened, FDR would most probably have retired after his two full terms. But he disliked the idea of living office in the midst of a crisis, especially since there was no outstanding successor in the Democratic ranks. The only problem was the long-standing custom that no president should seek a third term. Roosevelt finally decided he would run again—if he was drafted by the convention. Sure enough, he was, on the first ballot. Secretary of Agriculture Henry B. Wallace got the vice-presidential nod.

Early in the campaign, Willkie attacked Roosevelt for seeking a third term, but few voters cared. Increased defense spending gave the economy a large boost. Desperate for an issue, Willkie ended up attacking Roosevelt for waffling on peace, charging that the Democrats would lead the country into war. Roosevelt countered by pledging that he would not lead America into war unless we were attacked. His credibility, and the reluctance of voters to change horses in midstream, gave him a third term by a substantial margin.

| Electoral votes: | | Popular vote: | |
|---|---|---|---|
| Roosevelt | 449 | Roosevelt | 27,243,466 |
| Willkie | 82 | Willkie | 22,304,755 |

What does this money go for? An average budget would be:
- $5 million for setting up an organization and travel expenses
- $3 million for accounting and legal fees
- $4 million for fund-raising
- $8 million left over for the first primaries.

The prize for the candidate who reaches the $20 goal is an average of $7.2 million in matching federal funds on January 1.

## Successful fundraising strategy

Federal law sets a limit of $1,000 on the amount any individual can contribute to any presidential candidate. That means that to raise $20 million, a candidate must successfully solicit funds from a minimum of 20,000 people. In practice, since everyone doesn't give the maximum, the number of contributors is at least double that figure.

Now, I'm a personable sort of guy, and I hope you'd enjoy talking with me if I showed up on your doorstep one day. But I doubt very much if you'd finish the visit by opening your checkbook and making a contribution to my presidential campaign. There would be three very good reasons (other than the fact that I'm not running!):

1. You wouldn't have any idea if you agree with my stands on major political issues.
2. You would have no reason to believe I actually had a chance to capture a presidential nomination.
3. Most important, the odds are you wouldn't be among the tiny fraction of the population who contribute $500 or $1,000 to a single political candidate.

That's why there are three important qualifications for successful fundraising:

1. Having a constituency that understands and identifies with a candidate's record and positions on major issues.
2. Convincing potential contributors that the campaign can be successful.
3. Identifying and reaching likely political contributors.

## The importance of a constituency

Since 1924, the successful candidates for the presidency have included:
- five former governors
- four former Vice-Presidents (three of whom had also served in the Senate)
- one former senator
- one former Cabinet member
- one national hero

While some of these men were not well known nationally (for example, Jimmy Carter and Bill Clinton), all had a political constituency from which they could solicit the money to get them started. You'll notice the list includes no members of the House of Representatives—a congressional district is not a large enough base for fund raising, and very few congressmen get the exposure necessary to build a

national or regional constituency. Although the 1996 presidential primaries are months away as I write this, I'd be willing to place a wager that the Republican nominee is a man who has been either a senator or governor.

## The secret of becoming a serious contender

Since no one wants to give money to a loser, presidential candidates have to appear to have a reasonable chance to capture their party's nomination. Before the primaries, however, it's not necessary to convince the general public that the candidate is a potential winner—if fact, some successful fundraisers do poorly in public opinion polls. Rather, the important group to convince is the small minority of people who regularly make large contributions. And these people are often swayed not by

### WHO WAS...

Franklin Delano Roosevelt was one of the twentieth century's most skillful political leaders. His New Deal program, a response to the Great Depression, utilized the federal government as an instrument of social and economic change in contrast to its traditionally passive role. Then, in World War II, he led the Allies in their defeat of the Axis powers.

Roosevelt was born at Hyde Park, New York, on January 30, 1882, the only child of James Roosevelt (a cousin of Theodore Roosevelt) and Sara Delano Roosevelt.

After graduation from Harvard University in 1904, Roosevelt attended Columbia University Law School. In 1905, despite his widowed mother's objections, he married a distant cousin, Eleanor Roosevelt, in a gala society wedding at which President Theodore Roosevelt gave the bride away.

Franklin Roosevelt's political career began with his election to the New York State Senate as a Democrat in 1910. His support of Woodrow Wilson's candidacy as the Democratic presidential nominee in 1912 resulted in his appointment to the post of assistant secretary of the navy, which he held during World War I. James M. Cox of Ohio, the party's 1920 nominee for the presidency, chose Roosevelt as his running mate.

Roosevelt faced the greatest personal crisis of his life when he was stricken by poliomyelitis at his Canadian summer home on Campobello Island, New Brunswick, in 1921. He veiled his deep physical agony with a cheerful demeanor and rejected his mother's advice that he abandon politics and become a country squire at Hyde Park. Encouraged by Eleanor and his dedicated political mentor, Louis McHenry Howe (1871–1936), he resumed his career by nominating Alfred E. Smith for the presidency at the Democratic convention in 1924 and again in 1928, when Smith won the party's nomination. At Smith's urging, Roosevelt successfully campaigned for the governorship of New York that same year. During two terms as governor of New York (1928-32), Roosevelt established a reputation as a reforming progressive in the Theodore Roosevelt tradition and as a champion of relief for impoverished upstate farmers. With the aid of a progressive Southern Democratic coalition in 1932, Roosevelt won the party's presidential nomination, then easily defeated Hoover in the national election.

His first three months in office, known as the Hundred Days, were marked by innovative legislation originating in the executive branch. Although Roosevelt's ties to

who the candidate is, but by who the candidate's campaign professionals are.

What campaign professionals am I talking about? The answer is, individuals who have worked in a number of successful campaigns and have developed personal relationships with large numbers of potential donors. Candidates compete fiercely for the services of the best of these men and women, and their personal recruiting success directly affects the success of their candidacy.

These professionals are important because they provide the candidate credibility where it counts. For example, one of the lesser known candidates for the 1996 Republican nomination became a major contender when he recruited Ronald Reagan's former campaign finance manager as his finance manager. This man not only provided the names of thousands of potential donors, but also told those donors, "I

## FRANKLIN DELANO ROOSEVELT?

the city and organized labor were never strong, many New Deal measures alienated the business community at the same time they attracted the urban minorities and the labor movement into the orbit of the Democratic party. This constituency led to his landslide victory over Alfred M. Landon in the 1936 presidential election.

In the late 1930s, spurred by Adolf Hitler's aggression in Europe and Japanese expansionism in the Pacific, Roosevelt moved the United States back toward engagement in world affairs. He was restrained, however, by the persistence of strong isolationist sentiment among the voters and by congressional passage of a series of neutrality laws intended to prevent American involvement in a second world war. Roosevelt won the contest when, alarmed by Germany's defeat of France in 1940, Congress passed his lend-lease legislation to help Great Britain's continued resistance to the Germans. The Japanese attack on Pearl Harbor on December 7, 1941, brought the United States into the worldwide contest on the side of Britain and the Soviet Union.

Roosevelt framed his diplomatic objectives as wartime leader in a series of wartime conferences. In collaboration with Winston Churchill he explained Anglo-American war aims in August 1941 in the form of the Atlantic Charter. It denied territorial ambitions, favored self-government and liberal international trade arrangements, and pledged freedom from want and permanent security against aggression. At Casablanca, Morocco, in January 1943, Roosevelt and Churchill insisted on Germany's unconditional surrender as a means of preventing the enemy's future military resurgence. The Quebec Conference (August 1943) planned the Normandy invasion. At Moscow (October 1943) the Allied foreign ministers approved in principle a postwar organization for world security. Military strategy and the problem of postwar Germany came under discussion at Cairo (November-December 1943) and Quebec (September 1944). Finally, at Yalta in the USSR (February 1945), Roosevelt, Churchill, and Joseph Stalin broached their plans for a postwar world. In the process, Roosevelt pressed for admission of China to the Allied councils as a major power, liberalization of international trade as a means of preventing future wars, and the creation of a United Nations organization as a mechanism for preserving peace. He did not, however, see the end of the war. He died of a cerebral hemorrhage at Warm Springs, Georgia, on April 12, 1945.

PRESIDENTIAL ELECTION 40

# 1944

## FRANKLIN D. ROOSEVELT

By the time campaigning began for America's first wartime election since 1864, the tide had turned to favor the Allies in both the Pacific and European theaters. In an attempt to take advantage of public pride in this accomplishment, the Republicans tried to recruit a military hero, Gen. Douglas MacArthur, as their candidate. But MacArthur turned them down. When Wendell Willkie faltered in the primaries, the logical choice became New York Governor Thomas A. Dewey. Dewey got all but one delegate vote in an overwhelming first ballot victory, and was joined on the ticket by Ohio Governor John Bricker.

In the interests of party and national unity, President Roosevelt had agreed to run for a fourth term, and he was nominated on the first ballot. However, the vice-presidential nomination was a subject of great controversy. Henry Wallace wanted a second term as Vice-President, but many delegates thought that his views were too radical to take a chance that he might have to step into the presidency. After failing to get a consensus on a couple of other candidates, Roosevelt's advisors settled on Missouri Senator Harry S. Truman, who had won praise for his investigations of wartime corruption. Truman loved the Senate and was extremely reluctant to take what he considered a powerless position, but he yielded to Roosevelt's argument that he was needed.

The Republicans generally endorsed the current administration's handling of the war, and Dewey strongly believed that foreign policy should not become a campaign issue when American lives were on the line. While Dewey believed that the Democrats went too far in intervening in the economy, he had no quarrel with the major New Deal programs. Instead, he focused on one stated and one unstated issue. The stated issue was that the Democrats had been in power too long and had become inefficient and complacent. The unstated issue was that Roosevelt was in poor health and could not devote his full energy to running the country.

Roosevelt had decided to stay aloof from the campaign and spend all his time on the war effort. However, rumors about his health finally drove him to the campaign trail. He made a number of speeches in which he vigorously defended the record of his administration and reassured the public that he was just as much in control as ever. Roosevelt's message was the one that got through, and he defeated Dewey by a slightly smaller margin than his victory over Willkie in 1940. But after only two-and-a-half months in office, FDR died from a massive cerebral hemorrhage, and Harry Truman became President.

| Electoral votes: | Popular vote: |
|---|---|
| Roosevelt..................................432 | Roosevelt.....................25,602,505 |
| Dewey...........................................99 | Dewey..........................22,006,278 |

wouldn't be working for this candidate if he didn't have a chance to win, just like Ronald Reagan." In stark contrast, well-known candidates who failed to recruit top-level campaign professionals quickly fell by the wayside.

## Identifying and reaching potential contributors

Campaign professionals bring lists of potential donors; longer lists are culled from public records of contributors to other campaigns and lists of wealthy professionals such as physicians, attorneys, and business executives. The best-known candidates who are considered front-runners generally have some success in appealing to these people through direct mail campaigns.

However, direct mail is expensive (costs can be 30 percent of contributions or greater) and the average campaign contribution tends to be small ($100 or under). That's why the staple of most candidates' fundraising efforts are personal appeals by the candidate, a time-consuming and grueling process.

One activity is familiar to anyone who's sold magazine subscriptions—cold-calling. Although it may seem demeaning, most candidates devote two to four hours per day, every day, calling potential donors on the telephone. One 1996 candidate, a senator, admitted, "It makes me feel like a dog," but the process is essential and brings in funds.

The second approach is organizing fund-raisers. One staple technique is the house-party. A wealthy supporter is persuaded to invite twenty-five to one hundred friends capable of giving $1,000 to a cocktail party or reception (the costs of such entertainment are exempt by federal law from the $1,000 campaign limit). At these events, the candidate shakes hands, makes a general speech, then turns the meeting over to a fundraiser who actually asks for the money.

A second technique is major fundraising dinners. A $1,000-a-plate dinner that attracts 2,000 people grosses $2,000,000, which is reduced by an average of only $150,000 in expenses.

How much time does fund-raising take in the year before the primaries begin? The average candidate appears at between 300 and 400 fundraisers and makes between 5,000 and 10,000 telephone calls seeking money. And all this takes place before a single vote has been cast for a single candidate.

PRESIDENTIAL ELECTION 41

# 1948

# HARRY S. TRUMAN

War means sacrifice, and after the conflict is over voters tend to want a change in government. In 1920, after World War I, the mood of the nation led to a landslide Republican victory; in 1946, after World War II, the Republicans captured control of Congress for the first time since 1932 and most political observers believed that the Grand Old Party would capture the White House in 1948.

Both parties wooed Gen. Dwight D. Eisenhower, Commander-in-Chief of Allied forces in Europe, but he declined to enter politics so soon after the war. So the Republicans turned again to the articulate and popular Thomas Dewey. Nominated on the first ballot, Dewey ran on a platform of stopping communism in Europe and rooting out communism at home. For Vice-President, the Republicans nominated Earl Warren from California, an important state.

The Democrats unenthusiastically nominated Truman for President and Kentucky Senator Alben W. Barkley for Vice-President. And it was not just the political strength of the Republicans that made the party so gloomy. Dissident Democrats had broken from the party to form not one, but two splinter parties. The Progressives blamed Truman for the Cold War, and they nominated Henry Wallace for President. Southern Democrats were incensed that Truman had proposed a series of measures to protect the civil rights of African-Americans, and they formed the States' Rights Democratic party with South Carolina Governor Strom Thurmond as their presidential candidate. It's no wonder that the polls showed Dewey leading Truman by a wide margin.

However, the pollsters and the pundits didn't take into account one factor—Harry Truman's fiery personality. Truman shrewdly decided not to run against Dewey, but against the Republican Congress that had refused to pass any of the social reform programs he had proposed. Truman told his vice-presidential candidate, "I'm going to give them hell," and in a 22,000 mile campaign train tour, he did just that. He called the Congress the "worst in history" and labeled the Republicans "bloodsuckers with offices on Wall Street." At every campaign stop, the crowd roared with approval, shouting "Give 'em hell, Harry."

Dewey refused to take off the gloves and defend the Congress, believing that remaining more "presidential" would protect his lead. With the polls showing him comfortably ahead, he spent the last days of the campaign planning his inauguration. So confident were political observers of his victory that the *Chicago Tribune* printed a postelection day headline that read "Dewey Beats Truman." The actual results made half of America eat crow, as Truman recorded a comfortable victory over his "unbeatable" opponent.

| Electoral votes: | | Popular vote: | |
|---|---|---|---|
| Truman | 303 | Truman | 24,105,812 |
| Dewey | 189 | Dewey | 21,970,065 |
| Thurmond | 39 | Thurmond | 1,169,021 |
| | | Wallace | 1,157,172 |

# Primaries and Caucuses—

13

## Weeding out the Contenders

> "THERE THEY SMOKE TOBACCO TILL YOU CANNOT SEE FROM ONE END OF THE
> GAMUT TO THE OTHER. THERE THEY DRINK FLIP, I SUPPOSE, AND THERE THEY
> CHOOSE A MODERATOR—WHO PUTS QUESTIONS TO THE VOTE REGULARLY; AND
> SELECTMEN, ASSESSORS, WARDENS AND REPRESENTATIVES ARE REGULARLY CHO-
> SEN BEFORE THEY ARE CHOSEN BY THE TOWN."
> —JOHN ADAMS

In this passage from his 1753 diary, the future second president of the United States provided a vivid description of the caucus club, which met in the attic of an influential Bostonian to choose candidates for local office. For most of the history of our country, it was in such "smoke-filled rooms," in meetings controlled by party bosses, that presidential candidates were chosen. However, early in this century, the winds of change began to blow away the smoke. Today, almost three-quarters of the delegates to the convention are chosen in primary elections; the caucuses in other states aren't closed door meetings, but mini-elections open to the public. The result is that our political system requires that a successful candidate for President wage not one, but two campaigns: The first, and probably the most grueling, is the fight to sway enough voters in enough states to win the party's nomination.

A lot of political observers, myself included, find the primary season much more fascinating than the postelection campaign. Upsets and the unexpected have become the rule, rather than the exception. The crucial New Hampshire primary has been so unpredictable that the state is known as the Bermuda Triangle of pollster reputations. The primaries have toppled incumbent Presidents, humbled front runners, and propelled virtual unknowns to the nomination, then to the presidency. In this chapter, we'll take a close look at the crucial part of our system for electing a President.

## A SHORT HISTORY OF PRESIDENTIAL CANDIDATE SELECTION

In America's first two elections, there were no caucuses, nominating conventions, speeches, or campaigns—the electors in each state simply met and voted for George Washington. But by 1792, when Washington retired, there were two parties (the

Federalists and the Democratic-Republicans), so party leaders (mostly congressmen) met informally to choose candidates. By 1804, the parties held formal "nomination caucuses" in Washington, at which candidates were selected by the congressmen and senators from the two parties. The system worked because the members of Congress adequately represented the small percentage of wealthy Americans who were eligible to vote.

By 1824, however, suffrage had been greatly expanded, and the legion of new voters across the country resented Washington dictating the choice of candidates. The Democratic-Republican national caucus nominated William H. Crawford for the presidency, but that nomination was virtually ignored. Without a system, three major candidates emerged (John Quincy Adams, Andrew Jackson, and Henry Clay) in an election so close that it was decided in the House of Representatives.

In 1828, the national caucuses were replaced by conventions or caucuses in each state. Although there was a general consensus that produced a two-man race, no one was happy with that system. It was a third party, the Anti-Masonic party, that introduced the concept of the national convention in 1831, and the two major parties (the Democratic-Republicans and the National Republicans) followed suit in 1832. National conventions have been held every year since.

The delegates to the convention, however, were chosen by state conventions or caucuses controlled by party leaders. This system gradually came under attack in the late-nineteenth century, at the same time that civil service reform and antitrust legislation emerged. Wisconsin established the first primary system in 1903, and by 1912, ten states selected delegates by presidential primary. The number of states holding primaries grew slowly, as the country became preoccupied with a series of major crises—World War I, the Great Depression, the World War II. But by 1952, primary elections had become the predominant method of choosing presidential candidates. Today, primaries are held in forty states and the District of Columbia. For the last three decades, one presidential candidate from each party has gone into the convention with enough delegates to win nomination on the first ballot.

## THE MODERN POLITICAL CAUCUS

The smoke-filled rooms of yore are long gone; today's presidential selection caucuses are really mini-elections in which voters who have registered as members of a party are allowed to participate. Although the procedures vary, the very important Iowa caucuses typify the procedure. Party members from a specific town or district meet to select delegates to a district or county convention. These delegates meet to select delegates to the state convention. The state convention then elects delegates to the national party convention.

Campaigning in a caucus state is very different from campaigning in a primary, where the total popular vote determines a winner. Success in a caucus requires a

large and well-organized organization that concentrates on identifying party members who are likely to vote for a specific candidate, then making sure they attend their town or precinct caucus. The system strongly favors candidates from that specific state (e.g., Iowa Senator Tom Harkin easily emerged with the most delegates from the 1992 Democratic caucuses in that state) and candidates who declare early and have the time to establish a large organization.

## THE MODERN PRIMARY ELECTION

Primaries have become the main method of selecting delegates to the national conventions. However, the structure of primaries varies from state to state. Some states have what is called presidential preference primaries in which votes are tallied for individual candidates. The state's delegates, which are chosen either by ballot or by convention, are normally bound to vote for the winner of the primary on the first ballot at the convention. In other states, the voters elect delegates or a slate of delegates who are pledged to a specific candidate. In some states, the primaries are "winner take all," while in others the delegates are apportioned according to the percentage of votes received by each candidate.

While this sounds confusing (and it is!), the results are not. The candidate who wins the majority of the primaries traditionally has gone on to win the party's nomination. However, that candidate is often not the preprimary favorite. In many elections, the fortunes of candidates have risen or fallen practically overnight; the primaries are so close together that candidates who have been doing well may drop out of the race a week later.

Most candidates who drop out are forced to do so because of lack of funds, particularly matching federal funds. A presidential hopeful from either party who fails to get at least 10 percent of the vote in two successive primaries becomes ineligible for federal funds. The only way the candidate can regain eligibility to win at least 20 percent of the vote in a future primary, a difficult task without sufficient funds for an adequate television advertising program. Candidates who lose eligibility for federal funds also have a much more difficult time obtaining private campaign contributions.

### The primary season

Although the caucuses and primaries span a four-and-a-half-month period from late January through early June, thirty-five primaries are packed into a twenty-nine-day period in February and March. This intense schedule provides little time to regroup, reformulate campaign strategy, or recover from a campaign error. Let's take a closer look at the gauntlet of presidential politics.

# THE SPECTATOR'S GUIDE TO THE PRIMARY SEASON

In terms of political importance, all primaries are not created equal. Traditionally, certain primaries have served as bellwether or turning points for most candidates seeking the nomination. We'll discuss some of these highlights, using the 1996 primary dates:

## February 12: Iowa caucuses

Although Iowa has just 2.8 million residents, the Farm State is divided into ninety-nine counties. And each election season, more presidential hopefuls visit more of those counties in Iowa than in any other state in the Union. From late summer through February, voters run into candidates at every conceivable location from country fairs to coffee shops. Although three states hold caucuses before the Hawkeye State, Iowa is traditionally seen as the first major test. The prize isn't the

## WHO WAS...

Dwight David Eisenhower was a general whose great popularity as Allied supreme commander during World War II secured him election as the Thirty-Fourth President of the United States. He was born in Denison, Texas, on October 14, 1890 and grew up on a small farm in Abilene, Kansas. He went to West Point for the free education, was an infantry officer upon graduation in 1915, and married Mamie Doud (1896–1979) the following year. They had two sons, one of whom died in childhood.

Eisenhower did not see combat duty during World War I, but he was decorated and promoted to lieutenant colonel for his administrative skills in commanding a tank corps training center. In the postwar years, he was recognized as a promising leader at the Command and General Staff School and served as an industrial mobilization planner, and as an aide to the army chief of staff and later military adviser to General Douglas MacArthur.

Called to the War Department as a Philippines expert a few days after the attacks on Pearl Harbor and the Philippines, Eisenhower won further promotion to major general and was named chief of the newly organized Operations Division of the General Staff three months later. By this time the army's top planner, he then prepared plans for the European theater of operations, and in June 1942 he was given command of U.S. forces in Europe by Army Chief of Staff George C. Marshall. Subsequently as Allied commander in the invasions of North Africa, Sicily, and Italy, Eisenhower demonstrated outstanding skill in forging the allies into an effective fighting force and managing the large-scale operations.

Appointed supreme commander of the Allied Expeditionary Force for the invasion of France, Eisenhower, by then a full general, began his new assignment in January 1944. In the months prior to the invasion, on June 6, 1944, he supervised the preparation of air, sea, and land forces and all other strategic

number of delegates (just twenty-five Republican delegates in 1996), but the label of "front-runner" going into the New Hampshire primary.

## February 20: New Hampshire primary

Generations of presidential candidates have been shocked to discover that some of the most probing questioning they will encounter during the entire campaign comes from students at the many New Hampshire high schools that hold presidential candidate forums before America's most famous primary. Citizen participation in government is a hallmark of the Granite State—New Hampshire has 424 state legislators, by far the most of any state. It's residents are politically sophisticated, and take the presidential primary very seriously.

Of course, it would be hard not to, given the fact that in January and early February it's hard to walk ten feet without running into a candidate, campaign worker, or mem-

## DWIGHT DAVID EISENHOWER?

planning and made the crucial decision on the date of the assault. During the fighting that ensued until the end of the war in Europe, Eisenhower, who became General of the Army in December 1944, had the overall responsibility of strategic and administrative control of an Allied force that eventually numbered more than 4,500,000. In the fall of 1945, Eisenhower became army chief of staff. Although he accepted the presidency of Columbia University in 1948, he still served as a military adviser, and, some three years later, he returned to Europe as supreme commander for the North Atlantic Treaty Organization.

Although he had previously rejected numerous overtures from members of both parties to run for the presidency, Eisenhower yielded to the appeal of liberal Republicans in 1952. As a war hero of enormous popularity, he appealed to many Democrats as well, and he handily defeated Adlai Stevenson by more than 6.6 million votes. When he ran again in 1956, the margin was 9.5 million. Eisenhower pursued a moderate course in domestic affairs to the evident satisfaction of most Americans. Throughout all but the first two years of his administration, his power was limited by the Democrats' control of Congress. He did trim some government activities but also expanded the Social Security program, aid to education, and the Interstate Highway System. In foreign affairs, he invigorated the National Security Council, brought a quick end (July 27, 1953) to the stalemated war in Korea, and reduced the strength of the conventional forces. Eisenhower supported the strong moralistic, anti-Communist stance of his secretary of state, John Foster Dulles.

In retirement, the former president wrote several volumes of memoirs and enjoyed his hobbies of golf and painting. He remained a popular elder statesman, and presidents John F. Kennedy and Lyndon B. Johnson consulted with him during their administrations. He died on March 28, 1969, in Washington, D.C..

ber of the media. Candidates spend more money per capita in New Hampshire for one reason: Since 1952, the results of the primary have been crucial in the quest for the nomination. New Hampshire primary results have felled incumbent presidents: Harry Truman decided not to run in 1952 after Estes Kefauver won here, as did Lyndon Johnson after Eugene McCarthy's strong showing in 1968. New Hampshire allowed Ronald Reagan to recover from an Iowa caucus loss to George Bush in 1980, and Bush to recover from an Iowa loss to Bob Dole in 1988. Bush's unexpectedly narrow victory over Pat Buchanan in 1992 pointed out a lack of enthusiasm in the electorate that cost him reelection, while Bill Clinton's strong secondplace finish showed that he was recovering from charges of extramarital affairs.

With a huge field seeking the Republican nomination in 1996, there is no doubt

# 1996 Schedule of Primaries and Caucuses

The following is the calendar of principal Republican party presidential nominating events in 1996. Democratic party nominating dates are usually, but not always, the same. Although the dates change every four years, the general order and timing of the primaries and caucuses are usually the same.

Jan. 26-29: Alaska causcuses.
Jan. 25-31: Hawaii caucuses.
Feb. 6: Louisiana caucuses.
Feb. 12: Iowa caucuses.
Feb. 20: New Hampshire primary.
Feb. 24: Delaware primary.
Feb. 27: Arizona, North Dakota, South Dakota primaries.
March 2: South Carolina primary.
March 3: Puerto Rico primary.
March 5: Colorado, Connecticut, Georgia, Maine, Maryland, Massachusetts, Rhode Island, and Vermont primaries; Minnesota caucuses.
March 7: New York primary.
March 9: Missouri caucuses.
March 10: Nevada caucuses.
March 12: Florida, Mississippi, Oklahoma, Oregon, Tennessee, Texas.
March 19: Illinois, Michigan, Ohio, Wisconsin primaries.
March 25: Utah caucuses.
March 26: California, Washington primaries.
April 2: Kansas primary.
April 23: Pennsylvania primary.
May 7: Washington, D.C., Indiana, North Carolina primaries.
May 14: Nebraska, West Virginia primaries.
May 21: Arkansas primary.
May 28: Idaho caucuses, Kentucky primary.
June 4: Alabama, Montana, New Jersey, New Mexico primaries.

PRESIDENTIAL ELECTION 42

# 1952
## DWIGHT D. EISENHOWER

By 1952, the Democratic momentum had totally bogged down in yet another war, the bloody stalemate in Korea. The conflict gave the Republicans the perfect campaign issues—the Democrats were too soft to win in Korea and too soft on communism at home and abroad. They blamed the Truman administration for the Communists taking control in China and Stalin taking control over Eastern Europe, and they charged the corruption in Washington resulted from too many Communist sympathizers in government. And as their flag bearer, they had probably the most popular of all Americans, Gen. Dwight D. Eisenhower.

Eisenhower became the favorite for the nomination when he declared himself a Republican in early 1952. That pleased the party members, but not the party leaders; they favored Ohio Senator Robert Taft, who was called "Mr. Republican" because of his conservatism. Taft and Eisenhower supporters clashed at the convention, but Eisenhower was so overwhelmingly popular that he easily won the nomination. For vice-president, the convention chose California Senator Richard M. Nixon.

The Twenty-First Amendment, ratified in 1951, prohibited a president from serving more than two terms; although Truman was exempt, he chose to retire. The party then turned to one of the most intelligent, witty, and well-spoken men in American politics, Senator Adlai E. Stevenson of Illinois, grandson of Grover Cleveland's vice-president. The only problem was, Stevenson was adamant about not wanting to run. However, he was nominated despite his objections, and he eventually agreed to accept the honor. Senator John Sparkman of Alabama joined him on the ticket.

Eisenhower took a much more moderate position on domestic affairs than many Republicans, and he believed that the United States should exercise its leadership in world affairs. To avoid alienating the party faithful, the Republicans staged a television campaign that emphasized the general's leadership and integrity. It was left to Richard Nixon to press the communism issue that had made national figures of such politicians as Senator Joseph McCarthy of Wisconsin. Nixon nearly lost his place on the ticket when his secret political slush fund was exposed, but he rescued himself with an emotional television appearance known as the "Checkers speech."

Stevenson campaigned hard, and his speeches were widely admired for their clarity of thought and their humor. However, he never captured the imagination of the American voters. When Eisenhower made headlines by promising that he would end the Korean War when he became president, the election was decided. However, Eisenhower's landslide victory was largely personal—the Republicans managed only an eight seat majority in the House and a tie with the Democrats in the Senate.

| Electoral votes: | | Popular vote: | |
|---|---|---|---|
| Eisenhower | 442 | Eisenhower | 33,936,252 |
| Stevenson | 89 | Stevenson | 27,314,992 |

that New Hampshire will considerably narrow the field and point out the serious contenders once again.

## March 5 and 12: Super Tuesdays

A whopping nineteen primaries and six caucuses were held on March 8, the second Tuesday of the month, a day which has been called Super Tuesday. This scheduling terrified candidates and produced months of sleepless nights for campaign managers who were forced to make the difficult decisions about which states to visit and how to allocate television advertising dollars. Super Tuesday favored strong front-runners and the candidates with the biggest warchests.

# THE ORIGINS OF PUBLIC OPINION POLLS

Although occasionally opinion polls were conducted before the 1930s, they were generally neither systematic nor scientific. They dealt with unrepresentative samples or used methods that made certain people far more likely to be included in the poll than others. For example, in "straw polls" the only people counted were those who volunteered to take part. Public opinion polling improved vastly in the 1930s when business and educational organizations began to develop methods that allowed the relatively unbiased selection of respondents and the systematic gathering of data from a wide cross-section of the public. By present-day standards these polls were crude, but their results were useful in some ways. Among the pioneers were George H. Gallup, Elmo Roper (1900–71), and Archibald M. Crossley (1896–1985).

Two embarrassing disasters encouraged polling agencies to further refine their methods. In 1936 a poll conducted by the *Literary Digest* determined that the Republican candidate, Alf Landon, would win the U.S. presidential election, but the magazine was humiliated when Roosevelt defeated Landon by the biggest margin in American history. The error arose largely because most of the magazine's subscribers were wealthy people who tended to vote Republican. In the 1948 election, most polls mistakenly predicted a victory for the Republican candidate, Thomas E. Dewey, over President Harry S. Truman, again because poor people were underrepresented, and also because the polling agencies missed last-minute changes of attitude among the voting public.

Since 1948 techniques of public opinion research and polling have improved considerably. Efforts are now made to select respondents without bias, to improve the quality of questionnaires, and to train able and reliable interviewers.

PRESIDENTIAL ELECTION 43

# 1956

## DWIGHT D. EISENHOWER

The 1950s were a time of great prosperity for middle-class and wealthy Americans, and Dwight D. Eisenhower was an extremely popular President. But his political coattails were very short, and the Democrats regained control of the Senate in the 1954 midterm elections. After the censure of Joseph McCarthy by the Senate in 1954, witch-hunts for communists were discredited, and the Republicans lacked a compelling central issue. They needed Eisenhower to run again to retain control of the White House.

The main obstacle to a second term for Eisenhower was his health. He had a heart attack in September, 1955, and the next year he had colon surgery. But his doctors gave him permission to resume a modified work schedule, and Eisenhower sent word to the convention that he wanted to run. He was nominated by acclamation and Richard Nixon was again nominated for Vice-President.

The Democratic nomination came down to a race between Adlai Stevenson and Tennessee Senator Estes Kefauver. After a number of closely contested primaries, Stevenson won a convincing victory in California and Kefauver dropped out of the race. Stevenson was nominated on the first ballot, and the convention chose Kefauver over Massachusetts Senator John F. Kennedy for the vice-presidential nomination on the second ballot.

Stevenson campaigned on his vision for what he called a "New America," which included specific proposals ranging from a nuclear testing ban to health programs for low-income Americans. While not touching the subject of Eisenhower's health directly, he maintained an exhausting schedule to demonstrate his fitness for the job. Stevenson's eloquence and his insight into issues gained him international attention.

Eisenhower's campaign consisted primarily of television advertising. He focused his energy on being President, and during the campaign two major foreign policy crises arose. Soviet tanks rolled into Hungary to squash protesters and then the Egyptian government seized control of the Suez Canal. Although the Eisenhower administration's handling of these situations created some controversy, the American people seemed to have more confidence with the general at the country's helm.

Therefore, it was no surprise when Eisenhower won the most one-sided victory since 1936. While the President declared that the vote was a mandate for "modern Republicanism," the Democrats retained control of the Senate and captured control of the House. The win was very much a personal triumph instead of a party victory.

| Electoral votes: | | Popular vote: | |
|---|---|---|---|
| Eisenhower | 457 | Eisenhower | 35,585,316 |
| Stevenson | 73 | Stevenson | 26,031,322 |

PRESIDENTIAL ELECTION 44

# 1960

# JOHN F. KENNEDY

The election of 1960 was not only one of the most dramatic in American history, but it also brought to office a President that inspired an entire generation to get involved in politics. The result was a decade of dramatic social change that included some of the most moving, most important, and most wrenchingly violent events in our history.

Without a constitutional amendment prohibiting a third term, Dwight Eisenhower might have taken all the drama out of the 1960 race by running again. Instead, he passed the baton to his vice-president, Richard Nixon. No longer the anticommunist firebrand, Nixon worked hard to establish a new image as a sober, responsible statesman who provided the experience vital to maintaining our national prestige in difficult times. The Republican convention nominated him on the first ballot, and named former Massachusetts Senator Henry Cabot Lodge for Vice-President.

Two men had contested for the Democratic nomination: Senator Hubert Humphrey of Minnesota and the charismatic young Massachusetts Senator John F. Kennedy. Kennedy had some political liabilities: His wealthy father had been a controversial Ambassador to Great Britain in the early 1940s, he was only forty-three years old, and, most significantly, he was a Roman Catholic. But Kennedy overcame his handicaps to pull away from Humphrey in the later primaries and win the nomination on the first ballot. Kennedy chose Senate Majority Leader Lyndon Johnson of Texas as his Vice-President.

For the first time, Americans got the opportunity to compare the candidates as they engaged in a series of nationally televised debates. Although both men had spent hundreds of hours in preparation, the format of the debate (more like a press conference than a traditional debate) favored Kennedy, who was succinct in his answers, witty, and more comfortable in front of the cameras. Although Nixon tried to emphasize the contrast between his experience and Kennedy's youth, the Democratic candidate came across as extremely knowledgeable and mature. The first debate propelled Kennedy into the position of front-runner.

But if his age didn't prove to be an albatross for Kennedy, his religion did. His candidacy evoked much of the same religious bigotry that had crippled Al Smith in 1928. Kennedy addressed the issue head on, declaring that he believed unequivocally in the complete separation of church and state and vowed that his duties to his country would always come first. But observers predicted that the anti-Catholic vote would hurt the Democratic candidate and that the election would be close.

For once, the pundits were right—the popular vote was the closest in history in terms of percentage of votes cast. Razor-thin margins of victory in Illinois and Texas gave America its youngest-elected president.

| Electoral votes: | | Popular vote: | |
|---|---|---|---|
| Kennedy | 303 | Kennedy | 34,227,096 |
| Nixon | 219 | Nixon | 34,108,546 |

In 1996, SuperTuesday becomes SuperTuesdays, with fifteen states choosing their delegates. Sandwiched in the middle is the vital NewYork primary, which can win a candidate more than 10% of the delegates needed for the nomination. On the first of the Tuesdays, Georgia's results can be an indicator the candidates' strength in the South, as can Colorado's in the West. A candidate who captures both Florida and Texas on the secondTuesday is well on the way to nomination.

## March 26: California
The nation's largest state will have 163 delegates to the 1996 Republican convention, ten times New Hampshire's total. If the race is close after the Super Tuesdays, the results of the California primary can be crucial. If a strong front-runner has emerged, a win in California practically guarantees the nomination.

## June 4: Alabama, Montana, New Jersey, New Mexico Primaries
There are more than two months between California and the last of the primaries, and in that time even a strong front-runner could make an error that erodes vital support. In a close contest, these last primaries could make the difference.

## THE PRIMARY SEASON IS NORMALLY CONCLUSIVE

Since 1956, every presidential candidate from both major parties has won enough delegates in the primaries and caucuses to be nominated on the first ballot. However, if no candidate should receive a majority, the fight would be taken to the convention floor.

## Should our primary system be changed?
There is no doubt that our current primary system is much more democratic than the old system that allowed a handful of party bosses to select a candidate. In fact, it is the most democratic system of choosing candidates of any nation in the world. However, the hodgepodge of primaries is very exhausting to the candidates, and it somewhat favors candidates who have a strong appeal in the important early primary states.

Some people have suggested that the state primaries and caucuses be replaced by a single nationwide primary held in late May or early June, which would give the candidates more time to debate and present their positions on the issues. Another suggestion is to have the national conventions narrow the field down to two or three candidates, who would then compete in a national primary. However, both parties are reluctant to have the final say in choosing their candidate taken away from their national conventions. Also, the national primary system would tend to work against lesser-known candidates who demonstrate their strength in early primaries in smaller states.

For the foreseeable future, our current system is likely to remain in place—a boon to fans of politics.

PRESIDENTIAL ELECTION 45

# 1964

## LYNDON B. JOHNSON

It seems every generation has its "where were you when..." question, from the stock market crash of 1929 to Pearl Harbor Day to the Challenger space shuttle disaster. The most unforgettable day for my generation was November 22, 1963, the day John F. Kennedy was assassinated. The entire nation came to a standstill, glued to television sets that portrayed images that ranged from shocking (Jack Ruby's murder of Lee Harvey Oswald) to heartwrenching (little John-John Kennedy saluting his father's casket.) Also chief among those images was a photograph of Lyndon Johnson taking the oath of office on a plane bound back to Washington, with a blood-stained Jackie Kennedy standing next to him.

A little less than one year later, a nation that wanted to heal was to go to the polls again. Lyndon Johnson, after stepping into the presidency, vowed to continue JFK's legacy, building on the legislation offered as part of Kennedy's New Frontier to fashion a "Great Society" that would feature compassion and justice for all. Johnson, a formidable, experienced politician and campaigner, was quickly nominated on the first ballot and he chose Minnesota Senator Hubert Humphrey as his running mate.

Given the mood of the country, Johnson's reelection looked inevitable, so prominent Republicans stayed on the sidelines. Into this leadership vacuum came a coalition of extremely conservative Republicans who were violently opposed to almost everything government had done since the Great Depression, from welfare and civil rights to diplomatic relations with Russia. Standard-bearer for this dissatisfied but energetic minority was Arizona Senator Barry Goldwater. Before moderate Republicans appreciated what was happening, Goldwater's supporters grabbed control of the convention and nominated their candidate on the first ballot. Goldwater selected a virtually unknown upstate New York congressman named William Miller for Vice-President.

Lyndon Johnson was euphoric when Goldwater became his opponent, and his delight continued nearly every time the Republican candidate opened his mouth. Goldwater told farmers lower prices would be good for them, attacked the Tennessee Valley Authority in Knoxville, and suggested social security be made voluntary in St. Petersburg, Florida. Even more astounding were his positions on foreign affairs; he wanted to break off diplomatic relations with Communist countries, pull out of the United Nations, and use nuclear weapons in Vietnam.

Goldwater frightened a good many Americans, Republicans as well as Democrats. The Johnson campaign took advantage of this fear in a famous television ad that portrayed a little girl plucking daisies during a nuclear countdown, which ended in a mushroom cloud filling the screen. Johnson, as expected, captured a record 61.1 percent of the popular vote on the way to a landslide victory.

| Electoral votes: | | Popular vote: | |
|---|---|---|---|
| Johnson | 486 | Johnson | 43,126,506 |
| Goldwater | 52 | Goldwater | 27,176,799 |

# The National Conventions—
## A Behind-the-Scenes Look

14

> "IN SEVERAL WAYS THE CONVENTION IS A PECULIAR INSTITUTION. LIKE AN IMPA-
> TIENT BRIGADOON IT COMES TO LIFE EVERY FOUR YEARS; IT IS MASTER OF ITS
> OWN RULES, AND ITS DECISIONS ARE AS IRRECOVABLE AS A HAIRCUT. YET, THE
> CONVENTION ISN'T EVEN MENTIONED IN THE CONSTITUTION OR IN ANY LAW
> PASSED BY CONGRESS. IN THIS SENSE, IT MIGHT BE DESCRIBED AS THE MOST UNOF-
> FICIAL OFFICIAL (OR MOST OFFICIAL UNOFFICIAL) GATHERING IN POLITICS."
> —DAVID BRINKLEY

> "THE CONVENTION IS THE VOICE, THE BONE AND SINEWS OF A POLITICAL
> PARTY—AND SOMETIMES IT EVEN NOMINATES AN ABRAHAM LINCOLN."
> —FLETCHER KNEBEL

When I was young, the national political conventions were the great television spectacle of politics. All of the networks provided gavel-to-gavel coverage that stretched from the morning well into the night. The most skilled and energetic of all television journalists prowled the floor of the conventions like tigers on the hunt, pushing, shoving, and clawing to be the first on the scene if any news broke. From the aeries high above the convention floor, the network news anchors and commentators explained what and why things were happening. David Brinkley, Chet Huntley, Walter Cronkite, and Eric Sevareid were fascinating to listen to even if nothing interesting was happening on the podium or floor of the convention. The spectacle made me want to be a journalist even more, and I dreamed of someday anchoring a convention myself.

Today, gavel-to-gavel coverage of conventions on the major networks is a thing of the past, and public interest in conventions has waned. As I discussed in the previous chapter, there has even been some discussion by political commentators about whether conventions are necessary at a time when every candidate since 1952 has amassed a delegate majority during the primary and caucus season.

However, the national conventions are still very important to the parties, for a number of reasons:

- The conventions serve as a vital kick-off for the presidential campaign. Such highlights as the keynote speech, the nominating speeches, the delegate polling, and the acceptance speeches by the candidates still draw national television coverage, giving the party's nominees and major campaign themes the kind of exposure unavailable in any other way.
- The conventions help to hold the party together. As we discussed earlier in this book, the party structure is decentralized, with the state and local units having great autonomy. Conventions bring the party together and remind the delegates and alternates that they have common bonds. The delegates meet the party's candidates, important elected officials, and national officers and get a chance to socialize with each other.
- The conventions write the party platform, an expression of the positions and principles upon which the party stands. Although the nominees have been predetermined over the last three decades, both parties have had frequent vociferous, even bitter contests over planks in the party platform. Even though most delegates don't agree with every party position, they at least have the satisfaction of knowing that it was approved in a democratic process in which they participated.
- There is no guarantee that the primary system will always continue to give one candidate a first ballot majority. As I write this chapter, seventeen people are still in the race for the 1996 Republican nomination. It is possible, even probable, that the delegates will be split among two or more candidates in some future convention.

Personally, I'm glad that political conventions are with us, not only because they are an American political tradition that dates back to 1832, but because they provide a unique insight into the strengths and weaknesses of the major parties and their candidates.

## Who are the convention delegates?

Although the delegations include almost every major elected official, state chairmen, and other party leaders, the vast majority of the delegates comes from the rank-and-file of the party. Their trip to the convention is a reward for providing the volunteer time and the money that makes the parties work.

And there are a lot of them; in 1996, the Republicans will send about 2,000 delegates (plus alternates) to their convention, while the Democrats will send over 4,000. These delegates spend a lot of money, which is why the nation's big cities vigorously compete for the honor of hosting national conventions.

## How are delegates apportioned?

Unlike congressional seats, convention delegates are not apportioned solely on population, although a certain number of delegates are assigned for every congressional district a state contains—for example, the Republicans award three delegates for every district. But in addition, both parties award additional delegates based on the

success each state party has had in electing state and local officials and in turning out the vote for the parties' presidential candidates. The Republicans, for example, award extra delegates if a state:

- Gave its electoral votes to the Republican candidate in the last presidential election
- Has a Republican governor
- Has one or two Republican senators
- Has one or more Republican congressmen
- Has a Republican majority in one or both state legislatures

The total number of delegates can rise or fall with the party's success at the polls—for example, because George Bush lost the 1992 election, there will be fewer total delegates at the 1996 Republican convention than there were at the 1992 convention.

The Democrats have gone a step further and created a category called "superdelegates." These are governors, big city mayors, congressmen and senators, and state

| STATE | REPUBLICAN | DEMOCRAT | STATE | REPUBLICAN | DEMOCRAT |
|-------|-----------|----------|-------|-----------|----------|
| Alabama | 40 | 62 | Montana | 14 | 22 |
| Alaska | 19 | 18 | Nebraska | 24 | 31 |
| Am. Samoa | 4 | 10 | Nevada | 14 | 23 |
| Arizona | 39 | 47 | New Hampshire | 16 | 24 |
| Arkansas | 20 | 43 | New Jersey | 48 | 117 |
| California | 163 | 382 | New Mexico | 18 | 33 |
| Colorado | 27 | 54 | New York | 102 | 268 |
| Connecticut | 27 | 61 | North Carolina | 58 | 93 |
| Delaware | 12 | 19 | North Dakota | 18 | 20 |
| D.C. | 14 | 29 | Ohio | 67 | 167 |
| Florida | 98 | 160 | Oklahoma | 38 | 52 |
| Georgia | 42 | 88 | Oregon | 23 | 53 |
| Guam | 4 | 10 | Pennsylvania | 31 | 88 |
| Hawaii | 14 | 26 | Puerto Rico | 14 | 57 |
| Idaho | 23 | 24 | Rhode Island | 16 | 28 |
| Illinois | 18 | 3 | South Carolina | 37 | 50 |
| Indiana | 52 | 86 | South Dakota | 12 | 0 |
| Iowa | 25 | 57 | Tennessee | 37 | 77 |
| Kansas | 31 | 42 | Texas | 123 | 214 |
| Kentucky | 26 | 62 | Utah | 28 | 28 |
| Louisiana | 28 | 69 | Vermont | 12 | 19 |
| Maine | 15 | 30 | Virgin Islands | 4 | 10 |
| Maryland | 32 | 80 | Virginia | 53 | 92 |
| Massachusetts | 37 | 107 | Washington | 36 | 80 |
| Michigan | 57 | 148 | West Virginia | 183 | 8 |
| Minnesota | 33 | 87 | Wisconsin | 36 | 91 |
| Mississippi | 32 | 45 | Wyoming | 20 | 19 |
| Missouri | 36 | 86 | TOTAL | 1,984 | 4,313 |

party chairmen who are not pledged to any specific candidate. In a close race for the nomination, the unpledged superdelegates could hold the balance of power.

As an example, the tentative list of the number of delegates each state will send to the 1996 Republican and Democratic conventions is located on the pervious page.

## When are the conventions held?

Traditionally, the party that doesn't control the White House holds its convention in mid-July, while the other party holds its convention in mid-August. Chicago has hosted twenty-four conventions, by far the most of any city.

## What is the structure of the conventions?

The business of a political convention is basically divided into four parts:
- Checking credentials and seating the delegates
- Writing and approving the party platform
- Nominating a presidential candidate
- Nominating a vice-presidential candidate

## The emotional highlights of the convention are:
- The keynote address
- The nominating speeches
- The acceptance speeches of the presidential and vice-presidential candidates

We'll take a look at all these aspects of the convention.

## The business of seating delegates

The first act of business of a political convention is to elect a temporary chairman, who takes on the responsibility of formally checking and accepting the credentials of the delegates. Although this is a largely a pro-forma process today, it was the subject of great controversy at many nineteenth century conventions in which the delegates waged fierce battles over the nomination.

Each state's delegation has a chairman, whose responsibilities are organizing state caucuses and polling the state's delegates when formal votes are taken.

## The keynote speech

Today, campaign oratory has largely been replaced by the thirty or sixty second sound bite. The conventions provide almost the last forum for the old fashioned, riproaring political speech that extols the virtues of the party and rips into the programs and policies of the other party. The keynote speaker is normally the best public speaker among the party's major elected officials.

By far the most famous keynote speech in recent years was delivered to the 1984 Democratic Convention in San Francisco by then New York Governor Mario

## WHAT DOES IT MEAN?
# PLATFORM

*Platform* comes from the Middle French term *plate-forme*—literally, "flat form"—which was first used in 1535 as a term for a diagram or map. It later came to refer to a declaration of principles upon which a group of persons stands, especially the principles and policies of a political party. Although American political conventions and caucuses issued resolutions stating their parties' positions earlier, the first formal platforms were adopted by the conventions of 1848.

Cuomo. His affirmation of American values and the Democratic commitment to justice for all touched a far larger audience than just the party faithful. Other keynote speakers have been less brilliant, but all attempt to set the tone for the upcoming convention and campaign.

## The party platform

Over the course of the last two hundred years, convention battles over the party's position on major issues have been far more rancorous than the battles over the party's nominations. These issues have included every important matter faced by our country, from states' rights to slavery to war to civil rights. Delegates have frequently walked out of conventions over platform issues: For example, Southern delegates split from the Republican party in 1860, and a civil rights plank lead Southern Democrats to walk out in 1948. In 1968, a fierce debate between pro-Vietnam War and anti-Vietnam War delegates at the Democratic convention helped fuel the violence in the streets.

Contrary to popular belief, presidential candidates and party professionals take the platform very seriously. In recent years, party leaders and staff members of the prospective presidential nominee have collaborated in writing the draft of the platform that is presented to the convention. However, because the delegates are not legally bound to vote in a certain way on any issue, there are often fierce floor fights in which the nominee is forced to compromise. For example, in 1976, Jimmy Carter accepted a plank calling for wage and price controls under pressure from the supporters of Senator Edward Kennedy. In other years, the delegates have insisted on positions much more extreme than the candidates would like. For example, the supporters of Barry Goldwater pushed through such an extremely conservative platform in 1964 that it alienated many mainstream Republicans; similarly, the extremely liberal platform approved by McGovern supporters in 1972 alienated many mainstream Democrats. In the most recent conventions, the most divisive platform fights have been waged over the highly charged issue of abortion at Republican conventions.

## The nominating speeches

One of the consolation prizes for presidential candidates who don't emerge victorious from the primaries has been having their names placed in nomination at the convention and enjoying the subsequent demonstrations by their supporters. The nominating speeches are good oldfashioned politics, and they allow the delegates to discharge all the built-up emotions from the campaigns. The demonstrations that follow, however, are far from spontaneous. They are carefully organized, and go on for a predetermined length of time. The inflexible rule is that no losing candidate's demonstration can last as long as the outpouring of support for the candidate who will be the party's nominee.

## The presidential nomination

"Mr. Chairman, the great state of "......" proudly casts its fifty-three votes for the next President of the United States!" Although the polling of the state delegations has been

## MAJOR CONVENTION FIRSTS AND EVENTS

**1831**  The Anti-Masons hold the very first national presidential nominating convention in Baltimore.

**1832**  The Democratic party holds its first national nominating convention in May in Baltimore, with 334 delegates representing every state except Missouri.

**1856**  The Republican party, then only two years old, holds its first national nominating convention in Philadelphia to select a presidential ticket.

**1860**  Delegates from eight Southern states walk out of the Democratic convention in Charleston, South Carolina, protesting the party's stand on slavery. The convention is unable to agree on a candidate and has to adjourn. The party meets again in Baltimore two months later.

**1868**  Delegates at the Republican convention give Ulysses S. Grant 100 percent of the vote on the first ballot, the first time in GOP history.

**1880**  After thirty-six ballots, the all-time record for the Republican Party, James Garfield receives the nomination for president over former President Grant and Maine Senator James G. Blaine.

**1888**  Frederick Douglas receives one vote on the fourth ballot, and becomes the first black to receive a vote in presidential balloting at a national convention.

**1892**  The Democrats nominate Grover Cleveland, who becomes the first candidate nominated for three successive elections and the first defeated Democratic candidate to be renominated.

**1904**  Theodore Roosevelt becomes the first Vice-President to receive the nomination after succeeding a president who died in office (William McKinley).

**1912**  Republicans renominate a presidential ticket for the first time (President William H. Taft and Vice-President James S. Sherman).

largely ceremonial since 1952, it is still fun to watch. The vote of each state's delegates is announced by the chairman of that delegation. Should there be a question as to the accuracy of the count, any delegate can ask the convention chairman to poll the individual delegates. The vast majority of the delegates in both conventions are legally bound to vote for a specific candidate on the first ballot. When the balloting is completed, the losing candidates often formally withdraw from the race and release their delegates so that a unanimous vote can be officially recorded.

Of course, the drama intensifies when no candidate gets a majority on the first ballot. Some state delegates are no longer legally bound to vote for the state primary winner after the first ballot; others are bound for a second ballot or longer. In the past, when the conventions are deadlocked, negotiations between the campaign staffs of the major candidates begin. Sometimes, one has dropped out in exchange for concessions that range from the vice-presidential nomination to

**1920** Women serve as delegates to the Republican and Democratic conventions for the first time in significant numbers.

**1924** The Democrats nominate John Davis on the 103rd ballot on the ninth day of the convention, both all-time records.

**1924** Republican convention is the first to be broadcast over national radio.

**1940** Franklin Roosevelt becomes the first person ever nominated for a third term.

**1940** Republicans hold the first televised convention.

**1944** Thomas E. Dewey is the first GOP presidential candidate to accept the nomination in person at the convention.

**1948** Dewey becomes the first defeated GOP presidential candidate to be renominated.

**1952** Democratic candidate Adlai Stevenson is nominated on the third ballot, the last time the nomination wasn't decided on the first ballot.

**1960** Richard M. Nixon becomes the first Vice-President to be nominated to the presidency at the end of his eight-year term.

**1964** Maine Sen. Margaret Chase Smith, the first woman elected to both the House and Senate, is the first woman to be placed in nomination for the presidency by a major political party.

**1968** Rioting in the streets outside the Democratic convention in Chicago culminates in "Bloody Wednesday," when clashes between police and National Guardsmen and anti-Vietnam War demonstrators produces many injuries.

**1984** Congresswoman Geraldine Ferraro of New York becomes the Democratic nominee for Vice-President, the first woman ever to appear on a major party ticket.

PRESIDENTIAL ELECTION 46

# 1968

## RICHARD M. NIXON

After Johnson's election in 1964, the Congress passed an unprecedented array of social legislation in areas from civil rights to education, but it did not bring about any great society. Instead, violence and conflict seemed to be tearing our nation apart. There was rioting in the streets over civil rights, Dr. Martin Luther King and Robert Kennedy were assassinated, and an escalating number of American soldiers were dying halfway around the world in Vietnam.

It was the growing opposition to the war in Vietnam that brought down the President. Johnson was considering running for reelection until anti-war candidate Eugene McCarthy scored a stunning upset in the New Hampshire primary. Facing the possibility of an embarrassing defeat, the President announced he would not run and handed the reigns to his Vice-President, Hubert Humphrey. Humphrey easily won the nomination on the first ballot (Maine Senator Edmund Muskie was nominated for Vice-President), but the selection of the presidential candidate was not the main story of the convention. Inside the hall, hawks and doves waged a fierce fight over planks relating to the war; outside the hall, protests by antiwar demonstrators grew until Chicago Mayor Richard Daley ordered the police and the national guard to disperse the protesters. The resulting violence appeared on the nation's television sets on a night known as "Bloody Wednesday." Humphrey led a badly divided party into the election.

The Republicans, on the other hand, turned to an old war-horse—Richard M. Nixon, who had made a remarkable comeback since losing the 1960 presidential race and the 1962 California gubernatorial race. Nixon won nomination on the first ballot and selected Maryland governor Spiro Agnew as his running mate. Nixon promised a slow but steady decline in American involvement in Vietnam and stressed such bread-and-butter issues as law and order.

Both Nixon and Humphrey had to contend with a third-party candidate, Governor George Wallace of Alabama, who had made headlines defying court orders to desegregate his state's schools. Nixon was far ahead in the polls when the campaign began. But Wallace began to erode his support in the South and the outgoing Humphrey, an energetic speaker, began to win back the antiwar voters by distancing himself from Lyndon Johnson's policies. However, Humphrey ran out of time. Although Nixon managed a narrow popular vote victory, he captured a clear majority in the Electoral College. Wallace did unexpectedly well, capturing five Southern states.

| Electoral votes: | | Popular vote: | |
|---|---|---|---|
| Nixon | 301 | Nixon | 31,785,480 |
| Humphrey | 191 | Humphrey | 31,275,166 |
| Wallace | 45 | Wallace | 9,906,473 |

changes in the party platform; at other times, when compromise fails, a third candidate has stepped forward.

Party leaders prefer the certainty of knowing who their candidate is going to be. We fans of politics would love to see a rousing floor fight in a future convention.

## The vice-presidential nomination

The presidential nominee chooses the vice-presidential candidate, usually in consultation with party leaders. There are few legal requirements for the job. Like the presidential nominee, the vice-presidential nominee must be at least thirty-five years old and a native-born citizen of the United States. The presidential and vice-presidential candidates should also not be from the same state because the Constitution prevents electors from casting votes for two candidates from the same state.

Although vice-presidents from John Adams on have commented on the insignificant role they play in government (the vice-president has no official constitutional duties except breaking a tie in the Senate), the qualifications of the nominee have become increasingly important to voters who have seen one President assassinated and two others the victims of assassination attempts. The Vice-President is just "a heartbeat away" from the nation's top job, and voters expect nominees who are qualified for the position. For that reason, George Bush's choice of Dan Quayle was widely controversial and may have contributed to his inability to win reelection.

Politically, some presidential candidates try to choose a person who "balances the ticket." The classic example was liberal, Northern Catholic John F. Kennedy's choice of the more conservative, Southern Protestant Lyndon Johnson. Another was Walter Mondale's choice of a woman, Geraldine Ferraro, in 1984. Candidates also sometimes choose a popular political figure from an important state, as Michael Dukakis did in selecting Senator Lloyd Bensen of Texas in 1988. Finally, candidates sometimes consider the political compatibility of a vice-presidential nominee—one of the reasons Bill Clinton chose Al Gore in 1992.

## The acceptance speeches

Perhaps the single most important speech given by presidential nominees is the convention acceptance speech. It is the one time in the campaign when they have the undivided attention of the nation; the speech is carried live on prime-time television and highlights are repeated on network and local news reports. A stirring, emotional speech can set the tenor of the entire campaign, as it did for John F. Kennedy in 1960, Ronald Reagan in 1980, and Bill Clinton in 1992. On the other hand, blunders can be catastrophic, as it was for Jimmy Carter in 1980 when "Hubert Horatio Humphrey" came out as "Hubert Horatio Hornblower."

The acceptance speeches are followed by more demonstrations, and the campaign finally begins.

PRESIDENTIAL ELECTION 47

# 1972

## RICHARD M. NIXON

Richard Nixon did not prove to be a widely popular president. American participation in the Vietnam war escalated during his administration, and the Republicans did poorly in the 1970 elections. His approval rating in the polls sunk slowly, and he was gravely worried about his prospects for winning reelection.

However, he benefited greatly from a series of events that removed all of his major challengers from the race. In 1969, Senator Edward Kennedy had driven off a bridge on Cape Cod, and his female companion drowned in the accident. His presidential aspirations died with her. Senator Edmund Muskie dropped out of the race early, and Hubert Humphrey did poorly in the Democratic primaries. Finally, potential third party candidate George Wallace was crippled in an assassination attempt.

That left the Democratic nomination to a little known anti-war candidate, Senator George McGovern from the small state of South Dakota. McGovern, a former history professor, was an intelligent man who had a long record of support for civil rights, equal rights for women, and other liberal causes. His supporters, benefiting from new rules that opened the way for a broader spectrum of convention delegates, dominated the Democratic convention and nominated their candidate on the first ballot (Senator Thomas Eagleton of Missouri was his running mate). But just as Republican conservatives had alienated many voters through extremist positions in 1964, many Democrats were upset in 1972 when the convention called for immediate withdrawal from Vietnam, amnesty for draft evaders and deserters, and decriminalization of marijuana.

A gleeful Nixon and his vice-president, Spiro Agnew, were renominated, and embarked on a campaign that focused on McGovern's obvious weaknesses. Despite his commanding lead in the polls, however, Nixon was paranoid about his reelection, initiating a chain of events that led to an unsuccessful break-in at the Democratic headquarters in Washington's Watergate Apartments. McGovern never made adequate use of the issue, which faded away until media investigations brought it to light and toppled the president.

During the campaign however, the major scandal was the revelation that Senator Eagleton had undergone electric-shock therapy for treatment of severe depression in the past. Legitimate medical treatment shouldn't have been a major issue, but McGovern panicked and asked Eagleton to step down. He was embarrassed when several prominent Democrats turned down the opportunity to join him on the ticket; finally, his seventh choice, Kennedy in-law R. Sargeant Shriver, agreed to run for vice-president.

By then, the campaign was in shambles. Nixon went on to a landslide victory, capturing 49 of the 50 states.

# You Take the High Road, I'll Take the Low Road—
## The Changing Process of Presidential Campaigning

## 15

"A HEALTHY DEMOCRATIC POLITICAL SYSTEM RESTS ON THE ABILITY OF THE ELECTORATE TO KNOW, UNDERSTAND, AND JUDGE THE ATTITUDES, CHARACTERISTICS, OPINIONS AND QUALIFICATIONS OF CANDIDATES FOR PUBLIC OFFICE. CLEARLY, POLITICAL CAMPAIGNS ARE ESSENTIAL TO DEMOCRACY."
—JOHN F. KENNEDY

"BUT AS WE ALL KNOW, THE TRUTH IS A FREQUENT CASUALTY IN THE HEAT OF AN ELECTION CAMPAIGN."
—THOMAS P. (TIP) O'NEILL

In an ideal world, political campaigns would be conducted in a way that the goals President Kennedy expressed were adequately met. In our real world, as former Speaker of the House Tip O'Neill pointed out, campaigns are bitter struggles in which the facts are often twisted to score political points. Charges and counter-charges range from wasting money to coddling criminals to adultery. Sometimes it's easy to think that the only dirty word in a campaign is "ethics."

Having read this book, you know that negative campaigning is nothing new. No candidate has ever been accused of anything worse than Thomas Jefferson, who was accused of favoring "murder, robbery, rape, adultery, and incest" in addition to fathering children by forcing himself on a black slave. This doesn't excuse dirty tricks, personal innuendo, half-truths and other questionable campaign tactics. But it does show that candidates and their staffs want to win so badly that even the strongest of men have given in to temptations.

Of course, the vast majority of presidential candidates have been honorable men who have embarked on a quest for the nation's office for the most honorable reasons. They and their staffs, seasoned political professionals, plot a campaign strategy based

on the perfectly legitimate twin goals of putting forth their own positions and principles while attacking the weaknesses of the opposing parties. Let's take a look at how
campaigns are planned, conducted, and financed before examining how and why
things sometimes get out of hand. Before we do, though, it's important to understand
the Electoral College and the current system of financing presidential campaigns.

## WHAT IS THE ELECTORAL COLLEGE?

The President and the Vice-President of the United States are the only elective federal officials not elected by direct vote of the people. They are elected by the members of the Electoral College, an institution totally unique to the American political
system that has survived since the founding of the nation despite repeated attempts
in Congress to alter or abolish it.

Who are the members of the Electoral College? They are real people, delegates
pledged to support specific candidates. Delegate are usually nominated at each
party's state convention, and they cannot be a member of Congress or a federal official. Each state's electoral votes equal the sum of its senators and members of the
House of Representatives. That means that electoral votes range from a minimum of
3 (for the seven states that have only one congressional district) to California's 54.

Some states print the names of the candidates for President and Vice-President at the
top of the November ballot while others list only the names of the electors. In either case,
the electors of the party receiving the highest vote are elected. The entire slate, which
casts all of the state's electoral votes, goes to the candidate who gets the highest popular
vote total, even if the margin is only one vote. On the first Monday after the second
Tuesday in December, each state's electors meet in the state capitol to cast their votes. By
custom, the electors vote for the candidate who received the majority of that state's votes.
But legally they don't have to do so—nine times in U.S. history an elector has defied the
November election results and voted for a candidate who was not on the ballot.

Certified and sealed lists of the votes of the electors in each state are mailed to the
president of the U.S. Senate. He opens them in the presence of the members of the
Senate and House of Representatives in a joint session held on January 6 (the next day
if that falls on a Sunday), and the electoral votes of all the states are then counted. A candidate who receives 270 votes—one more than half of the 538 total votes—is elected.

One effect of the system is that three times in our nation's history—1824, 1876,
and 1888—the presidential candidate receiving the largest popular vote failed to
win a majority of the electoral votes. This can happen when a candidate wins the big
states by a small margin but loses other states by a large margin. A candidate can win
election by carrying just the eleven largest states.

If no candidate for President has a majority, the House of Representatives chooses a
President from among the three highest candidates, with all representatives from each

# WHO IS RONALD REAGAN?

Ronald Wilson Reagan, the fortieth president of the United States, was born February 6, 1911, in Tampico, Illinois, above the store where his Irish-American father sold shoes. In the depression year of 1932 he graduated from nearby Eureka College, a conservative Protestant institution, where he had been active in sports and drama. Hoping for a Hollywood career, he worked in radio as a sports announcer until a screen test won him a contract at Warner Brothers in 1937. During the next decade and a half he appeared in some fifty films.

As his acting career lost momentum in the post-World War II years, Ronald Reagan became more and more interested in politics. Originally a Democrat and an admirer of Franklin Roosevelt, he served as president of his union, the Screen Actors Guild, for several years. His move toward an ardent conservatism during the 1950s and his registration as a Republican in 1962 were apparently brought on by disillusionment with government bureaucracy and concern over Communist influence in his union. His conservatism was reinforced by his marriage (1952) to Nancy Davis (1923– ), a young actress who shared his developing conservative values, and by his employment for eight years as a public relations speaker for the General Electric Company.

In 1966 Reagan entered the California gubernatorial race and won. Very much a conservative ideologue and political amateur at first, he had difficulty working with the Democratic legislature. As governor he was able to order a hiring freeze on state jobs, but he was not able to obtain legislative support for lower taxes or for reducing the cost of government. After two years, however, he came to terms with the legislature, learning to listen and to compromise. He also learned how to use television to marshal popular support.

After he made halfhearted attempts in 1972 and 1976 to attain the Republican nomination for President, a conservative tide in 1980 swept Reagan into the race and on to an electoral victory that also gave him a Republican Senate and a House that could provide a bipartisan conservative majority. He emphasized a strong national defense and a hard line against the Soviet Union. On the domestic side Reagan promised to reduce the size and cost of government, except for defense, and to check inflation. Surviving an assassination attempt in March 1981, in which he was seriously wounded, Reagan was able to get Congress to support his economic plans, which cut spending for most domestic programs and provided for a tax reduction over a three-year period. The administration had assumed that the tax cut, by stimulating the economy, would produce increased federal revenues and a balanced budget, but this did not happen, and the national debt rose steeply during his first four years in office. Inflation and interest rates declined, however, and largely on the strength of the economic recovery, Reagan won a landslide reelection victory in 1984.

The President won passage of major tax-reform legislation in 1986, but charges that his administration had secretly sold arms to Iran and used profits from the sale to aid an insurgency in Nicaragua engulfed Reagan in the worst U.S. political scandal since Watergate (1972–74). But Reagan still left office with the affection of many American voters. He retired to California, and later retreated to a private life after he courageously revealed that he was suffering from Alzheimer's Disease.

PRESIDENTIAL ELECTION 48

# 1976

# JIMMY CARTER

On August 4, 1974, Gerald Ford became the first chief executive of our nation who was not elected either President or Vice-President. Ford was named Vice-President by Richard Nixon after Spiro Agnew, facing charges of tax evasion, resigned. He then became president when Richard Nixon stepped down when faced with the likelihood of impeachment. Gerald Ford, who had been a Congressman since 1948 and House minority leader since 1965, pledged to bring honesty back to government, but his unconditional pardon of Richard Nixon raised many questions about whether he was Presidential material because he struck a deal.

Ford was challenged in the Republican primaries by conservative California governor Ronald Reagan, who attacked the new President's leadership skills. The two battled neck-and-neck in the primaries, but a victory in his home state of Michigan gave Ford 1,187 delegates, 117 more than Reagan. After his narrow first ballot victory, Ford chose Kansas Senator Robert Dole as his running mate.

While the Republicans nominated an insider, the Democratic nomination was captured by an outsider, former Georgia governor Jimmy Carter. When he began is campaigning for the presidency in December, 1974, only 3 percent of the American people knew who he was. But as he traveled the country, the peanut farmer and born-again Christian attracted increasing attention to his simple message of bringing morality and honesty back to government. He went on to capture nineteeen of the thirty-one Democratic primaries and was nominated on the first ballot. Minnesota Senator Walter F. Mondale was nominated for Vice-President.

Carter's early lead in the polls was enhanced when Ford blundered in the second presidential debate, stating to the astonishment of the nation that there was "no Soviet dominance in Eastern Europe." The mistake enhanced Ford's image as a bumbler—his tendency to trip over his own feet became a running gag on *Saturday Night Live*. But Carter went on to make his own mistakes. In a long interview published in *Playboy*, Carter attempted to show that he was not a stiff, rigid Christian by admitting "I have committed adultery in my heart many times." The interview alienated many conservative Christians. Carter was also embarrassed later in the campaign when his Plains, Georgia church turned down a black man's request to become a parishioner.

By election day, it was apparent that neither candidate had managed to generate significant enthusiasm. By a margin of slightly under 2 million votes, the electorate opted for change, sending Jimmy Carter to the White House.

| Electoral votes: | | Popular vote: | |
|---|---|---|---|
| Carter | 297 | Carter | 40,828,929 |
| Ford | 240 | Ford | 39,148,940 |

state combining to cast one vote for that state. If no candidate for Vice-President has a majority, the Senate chooses from the top two, with the senators voting as individuals.

## THE PRESIDENTIAL CAMPAIGN

### Presidential campaign funding

At the top of your federal 1040 tax form are little boxes you and your spouse can check off to send $1 each of your tax payment to the federal presidential campaign. The federal government provides all the funding for presidential campaigns, and by law each candidate is limited to spending the amount of money received from the fund. This amount has grown from $23 million per candidate in 1988 to approximately $35-$38 million in 1996.

That sounds like a lot of money, but it goes fast when a thirty-second national television ad can cost $200,000. The money must also be budgeted to last the entire campaign—a campaign manager's nightmare is not having enough money left to counter last minute accusations or take advantage of an opponent's weakness or mistake.

### The length of the presidential campaign season

Traditionally, the presidential campaign lasts just two months, from right after Labor Day through the first Tuesday in November.

### Developing a campaign goal

It's somewhat ironic that the citizens of New Hampshire, who are bombarded with political advertising and besieged by candidates before their primary are virtually ignored during the actual presidential campaign. The reason is obvious—New Hampshire has just 4 electoral votes. When time and money are limited, candidates have to concentrate on the states with the largest number of electoral votes that they have a chance of winning.

In Chapter Eleven, we explained that candidates for office need to figure out how many votes they need to sway to win, which is one more than half the votes cast. When the number of voters who always vote for a specific party is subtracted, the amount of swing voters the campaign should target can be as low as a few hundred out of 15,000 eligible voters.

Presidential campaign managers make the same kind of calculations, only their target is 270 electoral votes. They try to decide which states their candidate is likely to carry and in which states their opponent is strong. After that, they make a list of the states that they need to carry to get to the magic number. Then they devise a campaign schedule and strategy aimed not at the country as a whole, but at those vital states.

### Creating a campaign theme

There have been times in American history when one important issue has dominated the presidential campaign—slavery in 1860, government reform in 1884, war or

# WHAT IS THE LEAGUE OF WOMEN VOTERS?

The presidential television debates are just one result of many voter education campaigns stimulated by the League of Women Voters of the United States. The organization, which was formerly the National League of Women Voters, is a nonpartisan women's political organization, which was founded in 1920 in Chicago for the purpose of educating women in the use of the newly won vote. The National League of Women Voters was an outgrowth of the National American Woman Suffrage Association, which was dissolved after its goal of women's suffrage had been achieved. Woman suffrage leader Carrie Chapman Catt was elected honorary president of the new group.

Today, the organization is concerned with political education and action on a wide variety of local, national, and international issues, including governmental reform, education, civil liberties, social welfare, and foreign trade. It conducts an intensive educational program designed to encourage the responsible participation by all citizens in government. The league publicizes the views and qualifications of political candidates of all parties and attempts to secure the passage of legislation in the public interest. Leagues exist in each state, the District of Columbia, Puerto Rico, and the Virgin Islands, with national headquarters in Washington, D.C.

peace in 1916, the Depression in 1932, war or peace in 1940, the Vietnam war in 1968. At other times, war or economic prosperity has made the incumbent President or party virtually impossible to beat—Coolidge in 1924, Roosevelt in 1936 and 1944, Eisenhower in 1956, and Reagan in 1984. But in most elections, success or failure has turned on a candidate's ability to focus in on a central issue or theme that captures the attention of the majority of the swing voters in the important states.

The wisdom of sticking to an issue was demonstrated in 1992, when the Clinton campaign came up with a phrase to remind themselves what the election was all about: "It's the economy, stupid!" In every ad, every speech, every debate, the candidate pounded away at that simple message while incumbent President George Bush failed to counter with an equally coherent theme, and lost the election. In 1976, after both the President and Vice-President were forced to resign, the nation elected an evangelical Christian, Jimmy Carter, whose theme was honesty and openness in government. In 1980, Ronald Reagan had great success promising less government and lower taxes.

Identifying and sticking to a central campaign theme sounds easier than it is. Presidential campaigns can be minefields. The best planning can break down in three areas: failing to counter an opponent's attacks, losing televised debates; and failing to adequately deal with unexpected events or issues.

## The high road and the low road

In 1988, the Bush campaign prepared a television ad that focused on a convicted criminal named Willie Horton, who had committed rapes and robberies while on a work-release program in Massachusetts during Michael Dukakis' tenure as governor. The message: Dukakis coddles criminals. Intellectually, blaming any elected official for the acts of any individual is ludicrous, but, emotionally, it was a turning point in the campaign. Although many observers felt the ad bordered on being unethical, the Dukakis campaign failed to deal with it quickly and effectively, and Dukakis lost the election.

Elections aren't fair and candidates don't always stick to the high ground. For example, while a candidate's personal life shouldn't be an issue in his or her fitness for office, indiscretions often are. Senator Edward Kennedy's presidential aspirations were permanently destroyed when he drove off a bridge on Cape Cod in 1969 in an accident that took the life of his female companion. For a time in 1992, Bill Clinton was crippled by charges from a woman who claimed to be his longtime mistress. Clinton, however, dealt with the charges immediately by appearing on national television with his wife, denying everything, then returning to hammer away at the central theme of his campaign.

## Presidential debates

Since 1960, when United States presidential candidates John F. Kennedy and Richard M. Nixon met in a series of televised debates, political debates have become commonplace in campaigns even between candidates for state and local offices. But these are not really debates in the formal sense. They are more like news conferences or panel discussions. Only on occasion do the candidates respond to each other's remarks, and such response is a key element of true debating.

The debates have frequently been turning points in presidential campaigns. Many observers tie Nixon's defeat to his performance in the debate with John F. Kennedy. In the second debate between Gerald Ford and Jimmy Carter in 1976, Ford responded to a question by stating that there was "no Soviet domination of Eastern Europe." The headlines the next day were horrendous, and Ford never recovered from the image of being a mistake-prone bumbler. Ronald Reagan, on the other hand, made maximum use of his decades of experience as a professional actor to appear presidential even when his knowledge of the details of domestic and foreign policy were fuzzy.

Preparing for debates is now a vital part of campaign preparation. The candidates hire professional consultants and undergo many hours of practice debates before the main events.

PRESIDENTIAL ELECTION 49

# 1980

## RONALD REAGAN

The role of outsider served Jimmy Carter well as a candidate, but not as President. The team of advisors that he brought to Washington quickly angered the Democratic congressional leadership, making it difficult for the administration to push through legislation. Carter appeared indecisive and his approval ratings plummeted as inflation soared. Carter's weakness brought a Democratic candidate into the race, Senator Edward Kennedy. Kennedy had a commanding lead in the polls in the preprimary year. But Chappaquiddick proved an albatross again—Kennedy did a poor job of explaining his actions in a television interview. And after November 4, 1979, when Iranian extremists seized control of their government and took hostages in the U.S. embassy in Teheran, the Democrats felt an obligation to rally around the President. Carter was renominated, as was his Vice-President, Walter Mondale.

Once again, the conservatives were after the Republican nomination, and this time they had a very attractive candidate in former movie star and California governor Ronald Reagan. Reagan's campaign had a simple, two-part theme: "get the government out of our lives" domestically while pursuing a hard line against communism abroad. Reagan promised to stop inflation and promote economic growth by lowering taxes. Even though his program was based on so many questionable assumptions that his chief opponent for the nomination, former CIA head George Bush, called it "voodoo economics," the voters bought the appeal. Reagan was nominated on the first ballot, and chose Bush to be his running mate. However, liberal Republicans established a third party, the National Unity party, which nominated Illinois Congressman John Anderson for President.

Reagan proved to be perhaps the best television candidate of all time. Although he often stuck his foot in his mouth (for example, by declaring that it was trees, not automobiles and factories, that caused air pollution), he had such an uncanny ability to joke himself out of the situation that he became known as the Teflon candidate. Reagan did especially well in the television debates, and his lead in the polls soared.

Carter, on the other hand, attacked Reagan with a passion that struck many voters as mean-spirited. Although Carter as President had proved to have an unusual skill in international negotiations (he brokered a Panama Canal treaty and a treaty between Egypt and Israel), he had no success with the Iranian extremists. When an attempted rescue mission by American special forces had to be aborted due to equipment failures, Carter's candidacy was doomed. Reagan went on to win a landslide victory.

| Electoral votes: | | Popular vote: | |
|---|---|---|---|
| Reagan | 489 | Reagan | 43,899,248 |
| Carter | 49 | Carter | 35,481,435 |
| | | Anderson | 5,719,437 |

## Dealing with the unexpected

In 1972, George McGovern was handed a perfect issue when people working for the Republicans were caught attempting to burglarize Democratic headquarters in the Watergate apartments. But the McGovern people didn't know what to do with the issue, and Richard Nixon was able to persuade the public that it was a minor misjudgment that happened in the heat of the campaign. McGovern lost by a landslide, and only later did the issue topple the President.

In 1980, on the other hand, Ronald Reagan benefited greatly when the Iranian government took American hostages while taking over our embassy in Teheran. While there was no evidence that any President could have prevented the Iranian extremists from exploiting the situation for propaganda purposes, the Reagan campaign used the issue to make President Jimmy Carter look ineffective and indecisive. Carter's inability to counter cost him reelection.

Many less dramatic events and issues have arisen during presidential campaigns, just as they do during a presidency. In many ways, the ability of a candidate to deal quickly and effectively with the unexpected during a campaign is a crucial test of his or her ability to deal with the unexpected during the presidency.

## Presidential campaigning then, now and in the future

To a great extent, barnstorming in presidential campaigns is a thing of the past. Campaign events are now created to generate sixty, ninety, or one-hundred twenty seconds of video on the evening news, and the major campaign money and energy goes into creating the perfect thirty and sixty-second television ads. Only during debates and in the nominee's acceptance speech at the convention do we get to listen to and evaluate the depth of a candidate's knowledge, personality, and positions and principles.

Many people feel that's not enough, but to date, other than increasing the number of debates and changing the format, there have been few comprehensive solutions to the problem. Perhaps, down the road, when most American households are linked to the information superhighway, home computers or televisions can provide more effective ways for voters to interact with the candidates. Until then, presidential campaigns will remain largely a spectator's sport for us voters.

PRESIDENTIAL ELECTION 50

# 1984
## RONALD REAGAN

Ronald Reagan looked pretty much unbeatable as the 1984 elections approached. His program of cutting taxes, particularly on the wealthy, and increasing defense spending had stimulated the economy and stopped the rampant inflation. Even though another result was a staggering increase in the budget deficit, voters ignored the future implications because they considered themselves better off. Reagan also showed signs of age (he would be seventy-eight at the end of a second term), such as falling asleep in cabinet meetings and demonstrating forgetfulness at times, though his jokes about his lapses prevented age from becoming an issue. He was easily renominated, as was his Vice-President, George Bush.

The Democratic primaries featured a race between Colorado Senator Gary Hart, former Vice-President Walter Mondale, and the first major black candidate, the Rev. Jesse Jackson. Hart was forced to drop out of the race after it was revealed he had taken a pleasure boat cruise with a woman who wasn't his wife. Although Jackson ran a spirited campaign, he was unable to extend his support far enough into the white community. Mondale won the nomination on the first ballot in what proved to be an interesting convention, for two reasons. First, New York Governor Mario Cuomo delivered a stirring keynote address on the need for family values and justice for all in America that became one of the most widely admired political speeches of all time. Second, the underdog Mondale took the unprecedented and historic step of choosing a woman, New York Congresswoman Geraldine Ferraro, as his vice-presidential candidate.

Mondale tried very hard to capitalize on weaknesses in the Reagan economic program. He warned of the dire consequences of the huge budget deficits, and decried the cuts in social programs for the poor and elderly. He also attacked Reagan's hawkishness in foreign policy, saying that it hampered the quest for true peace.

But the country had turned conservative, and Reagan found it easy to turn Mondale's attacks against him. He dismissed concern about the deficit and hammered home the concept that all Democrats wanted to do was "tax and spend." In foreign affairs, he called the Democrats the "blame-America-first party" while boasting that the Republicans were "America's party." Reagan's great skill as a television communicator brought his message home. He won one of the greatest landslide victories in history, capturing forty-nine states and all but 13 electoral votes. Commented Democratic Speaker of the House Tip O'Neill, "Reagan is the most popular figure in the history of the United States."

| Electoral votes: | Popular vote: |
|---|---|
| Reagan......................................525 | Reagan.........................54,281,858 |
| Mondale .....................................13 | Mondale ......................37,457,215 |

# An Armchair Companion to Election Night

## 16

## Key Facts to Watch for and a Scorecard to Track Winners and Losers

In this book, we've explored the history and structure of our political system, explained the history and function of political parties, provided a guide to running for political office at the state and local levels, and covered the fascinating spectacle of presidential elections. Along the way, we've included profiles of every presidential campaign in U.S. history along with brief biographies of some of our nation's greatest political figures.

In the process, we've never strayed from the central theme that the strength of our democracy rests on each of us exercising our right to vote. And once we've participated, we're entitled to sit back and watch the results unfold on Election Night, especially those nights every four years when the nation has voted for the next President. These evenings are among my favorite in television. Not only does great drama unfold, but the election results—and the commentary on them—provide a capsule view of what Americans are thinking, what issues they consider most important, and what direction they'd like the country to head in the future.

This entire book, of course, will help you better understand and enjoy what's going on. In this chapter, we've provided a scoresheet so you can keep track of the results at home. Also included are descriptions of the last five presidential elections, a list of how each state has voted in the last five years, background information on American presidents, their wives, and vice-presidents, and a list of which senators and governors are up for reelection in the near future.

I hope this material adds to your knowledge and appreciation of our political process. I have just one request—get to bed early enough on Election Night to get up and follow our comprehensive day-after coverage on *Good Morning America*!

PRESIDENTIAL ELECTION 51

# 1988

## GEORGE BUSH

Ronald Reagan retained his personal popularity throughout his second term; public affection increased after he courageously survived an assassination attempt that left him seriously wounded. But his administration often appeared to be leaderless and out of control. The worst scandal was the Iran-Contra affair, in which the Reagan administration secretly and illegally sold arms to Iran and illegally used the profits to aid the anti-government Contras in Nicaragua. The leading Republican contender for the nomination, Vice-President George Bush, vowed to end the excesses of the Administration while pursuing the popular Reagan goals. Bush had a mixed track record as a candidate, having twice been elected to Congress from Texas but twice losing senatorial races. He had been Ambassador to the United Nations, Republican National Chairman, and Director of the C.I.A. He won nomination on the first ballot, but created controversy by choosing as his running mate Indiana Senator Dan Quayle, widely considered unqualified to step into the presidency if something should happen to Bush.

On the Democratic side, once again a little known state governor became the leading candidate. Massachusetts Governor Michael Dukakis had been first elected in 1972, been defeated for reelection in 1978, then won again in 1982. His primary asset was the "Massachusetts Miracle," an economic boom in a New England state that had been crippled by the exodus of much of its manufacturing base. Dukakis ran a well-organized campaign in the primaries and was easily nominated on the first ballot. To balance his ticket, he chose Texas Senator Lloyd Bensten, one of the most powerful legislators in Congress, as his vice-presidential candidate.

Stung by charges that he had been a "wimp" in previous races, George Bush ran one of the most aggressive, and, in the eyes of some, one of the most vicious campaigns in recent history. He labeled Dukakis a "liberal," making the word into an epitaph that meant a person who favored high taxes, who coddled the unemployed and criminals, and who was weak in foreign affairs. His most controversial political ad featured Willy Horton, a career criminal who had committed rapes and robberies in Massachusetts while on a work-release program. The implication of the ad was that Dukakis was responsible for Horton's acts, and that Americans wouldn't be safe if he were elected.

Dukakis played into Bush's hands by staying on the defensive and failing to develop any effective campaign themes. He also made some serious public relations mistakes, such as having his picture taken driving a tank, which struck many voters as ridiculous. Although neither candidate generated much enthusiasm, voters decided to stick with the Reagan course and elected Bush by a wide margin.

| Electoral votes: | | Popular vote: | |
|---|---|---|---|
| Bush | 426 | Bush | 48,881,221 |
| Dukakis | 111 | Dukakis | 41,805,422 |

# Presidents of The United States

| No. | Name | Party | Born | In | Inaug. | At Age | Died | At Age |
|---|---|---|---|---|---|---|---|---|
| 1 | George Washington | Fed. | 2/22/1732 | Va | 1789 | 57 | 12/14/1799 | 67 |
| 2 | **John Adams** | **Fed.** | **10/30/1735** | **Mass** | **1797** | **61** | **7/4/1826** | **90** |
| 3 | Thomas Jefferson | Dem-Rep. | 4/13/1743 | Va | 1801 | 57 | 7/4/1826 | 83 |
| 4 | **James Madison** | **Dem-Rep.** | **3/16/1751** | **Va** | **1809** | **57** | **6/28/1836** | **85** |
| 5 | James Monroe | Dem-Rep. | 4/28/1758 | Va | 1817 | 58 | 7/4/1831 | 73 |
| 6 | **John Quincy Adams** | **Dem-Rep.** | **7/11/1767** | **Mass** | **1825** | **57** | **2/23/1848** | **80** |
| 7 | Andrew Jackson | Dem. | 3/15/1767 | SC | 1829 | 61 | 6/8/1845 | 78 |
| 8 | **Martin Van Buren** | **Dem.** | **12/5/1782** | **NY** | **1837** | **54** | **7/24/1862** | **79** |
| 9 | William H. Harrison | Whig | 2/9/1773 | Va. | 1841 | 68 | 4/4/1841 | 68 |
| 10 | **John Tyler** | **Whig** | **3/29/1790** | **Va** | **1841** | **51** | **1/18/1862** | **71** |
| 11 | James Knox Polk | Dem. | 11/2/1795 | NC | 1845 | 49 | 6/15/1849 | 53 |
| 12 | **Zachary Taylor** | **Whig** | **11/24/1784** | **Va** | **1849** | **64** | **7/9/1850** | **65** |
| 13 | Millard Fillmore | Whig | 1/7/1800 | NY | 1850 | 50 | 3/8/1874 | 74 |
| 14 | **Franklin Pierce** | **Dem.** | **11/23/1804** | **NH** | **1853** | **48** | **10/8/1869** | **64** |
| 15 | James Buchanan | Dem. | 4/23/1791 | Pa | 1857 | 65 | 6/1/1868 | 77 |
| 16 | **Abraham Lincoln** | **Rep.** | **2/12/1809** | **Ky** | **1861** | **52** | **4/15/1865** | **56** |
| 17 | Andrew Johnson | Rep. | 12/29/1808 | NC | 1865 | 56 | 7/31/1875 | 66 |
| 18 | **Ulysses S. Grant** | **Rep.** | **4/27/1822** | **Oh** | **1869** | **46** | **7/23/1885** | **63** |
| 19 | Rutherford B. Hayes | Rep. | 10/4/1822 | Oh | 1877 | 54 | 1/17/1893 | 70 |
| 20 | **James A. Garfield** | **Rep.** | **11/19/1831** | **Oh** | **1881** | **49** | **9/19/1881** | **49** |
| 21 | Chester Alan Arthur | Rep. | 10/5/1829 | Vt | 1881 | 51 | 11/18/1886 | 57 |
| 22 | **Grover Cleveland** | **Dem.** | **3/18/1837** | **NJ** | **1885** | **47** | **6/24/1908** | **71** |
| 23 | Benjamin Harrison | Rep. | 8/20/1833 | Oh | 1889 | 55 | 3/13/1901 | 67 |
| 24 | **Grover Cleveland** | **Dem.** | **3/18/1837** | **NJ** | **1893** | **55** | **6/24/1908** | **71** |
| 25 | William McKinley | Rep. | 1/29/1843 | Oh | 1897 | 54 | 9/14/1901 | 58 |
| 26 | **Theodore Roosevelt** | **Rep.** | **10/27/1858** | **NY** | **1901** | **42** | **1/6/1919** | **60** |
| 27 | William Howard Taft | Rep. | 9/15/1857 | Oh | 1909 | 51 | 3/8/1930 | 72 |
| 28 | **Woodrow Wilson** | **Dem.** | **12/28/1856** | **Va** | **1913** | **56** | **2/3/1924** | **67** |
| 29 | Warren G. Harding | Rep. | 11/2/1865 | Oh | 1921 | 55 | 8/2/1923 | 57 |
| 30 | **Calvin Coolidge** | **Rep.** | **7/4/1872** | **Vt** | **1923** | **51** | **1/5/1933** | **60** |
| 31 | Herbert C. Hoover | Rep. | 8/10/1874 | Ia | 1929 | 54 | 10/20/1964 | 90 |
| 32 | **Franklin D. Roosevelt** | **Dem.** | **1/30/1882** | **NY** | **1933** | **51** | **4/12/1945** | **63** |
| 33 | Harry S. Truman | Dem. | 5/8/1884 | Mo | 1945 | 60 | 12/26/1972 | 88 |
| 34 | **Dwight D. Eisenhower** | **Rep.** | **10/14/1890** | **Tex** | **1953** | **62** | **3/28/1969** | **78** |
| 35 | John F. Kennedy | Dem. | 5/29/1917 | Mass | 1961 | 43 | 11/22/1963 | 46 |
| 36 | **Lyndon B. Johnson** | **Dem.** | **8/27/1908** | **Tex** | **1963** | **55** | **1/22/1973** | **64** |
| 37 | Richard M. Nixon | Rep. | 1/9/1913 | Cal | 1969 | 56 | 4/22/1994 | 81 |
| 38 | **Gerald Rudolph Ford** | **Rep.** | **7/14/1913** | **Neb** | **1974** | **61** | | |
| 39 | Jimmy Carter | Dem. | 10/1/1924 | Ga | 1977 | 52 | | |
| 40 | **Ronald Reagan** | **Rep.** | **2/6/1911** | **Ill** | **1981** | **69** | | |
| 41 | George Bush | Rep. | 6/12/1924 | Mass | 1989 | 64 | | |
| 42 | **William J. Clinton** | **Dem.** | **8/19/1946** | **Ark** | **1993** | **46** | | |

# Vice-Presidents of the United States

The numerals given vice-presidents do not coincide with those given presidents, because some presidents had none and some had more than one.

| No. | Name | Birthplace | Year | Home |
|---|---|---|---|---|
| 1 | John Adams | Quincy, Mass. | 1735 | Mass. |
| 2 | **Thomas Jefferson** | **Shadwell, Va.** | **1743** | **Va.** |
| 3 | Aaron Burr | Newark, N.J. | 1756 | N.Y. |
| 4 | **George Clinton** | **Ulster Co., N.Y.** | **1739** | **N.Y.** |
| 5 | Elbridge Gerry | Marblehead, Mass. | 1744 | Mass. |
| 6 | **Daniel D. Tompkins** | **Scarsdale, N.Y.** | **1774** | **N.Y.** |
| 7 | John C. Calhoun 1 | Abbeville, S.C. | 1782 | S.C. |
| 8 | **Martin Van Buren** | **Kinderhook, N.Y.** | **1782** | **N.Y.** |
| 9 | Richard M. Johnson | Louisville, Ky. | 1780 | Ky. |
| 10 | **John Tyler** | **Greenway, Va.** | **1790** | **Va.** |
| 11 | George M. Dallas | Philadelphia, Pa. | 1792 | Pa. |
| 12 | **Millard Fillmore** | **Summerhill, N.Y.** | **1800** | **N.Y.** |
| 13 | William R. King | Sampson Co., N.C. | 1786 | Ala. |
| 14 | **John C. Breckinridge** | **Lexington, Ky.** | **1821** | **Ky.** |
| 15 | Hannibal Hamlin | Paris, Me. | 1809 | Me. |
| 16 | **Andrew Johnson** | **Raleigh, N.C.** | **1808** | **Tenn.** |
| 17 | Schuyler Colfax | New York, N.Y. | 1823 | Ind. |
| 18 | **Henry Wilson** | **Farmington, N.H.** | **1812** | **Mass.** |
| 19 | William A. Wheeler | Malone, N.Y. | 1819 | N.Y. |
| 20 | **Chester A. Arthur** | **Fairfield, Vt.** | **1829** | **N.Y.** |
| 21 | Thomas A. Hendricks | Muskingum Co., Oh. | 1819 | Ind. |
| 22 | **Levi P. Morton** | **Shoreham, Vt.** | **1824** | **N.Y.** |
| 23 | Adlai E. Stevenson III | Christian Co., Ky. | 1835 | Ill. |
| 24 | **Garret A. Hobart** | **Long Branch, N.J.** | **1844** | **N.J.** |
| 25 | Theodore Roosevelt | New York, N.Y. | 1858 | N.Y. |
| 26 | **Charles W. Fairbanks** | **Unionville Centre, Oh.** | **1852** | **Ind.** |
| 27 | James S. Sherman | Utica, N.Y. | 1855 | N.Y. |
| 28 | **Thomas R. Marshall** | **N. Manchester, Ind.** | **1854** | **Ind.** |
| 29 | Calvin Coolidge | Plymouth, Vt. | 1872 | Mass. |
| 30 | **Charles G. Dawes** | **Marietta, Oh.** | **1865** | **Ill.** |
| 31 | Charles Curtis | Topeka, Kan. | 1860 | Kan. |
| 32 | **John Nance Garner** | **Red River Co., Tex.** | **1868** | **Tex.** |
| 33 | Henry Agard Wallace | Adair County, Ia. | 1888 | Iowa |
| 34 | **Harry S. Truman** | **Lamar, Mo.** | **1884** | **Mo.** |
| 35 | Alben W. Barkley | Graves County, Ky. | 1877 | Ky. |
| 36 | **Richard M. Nixon** | **Yorba Linda, Cal.** | **1913** | **Cal.** |
| 37 | Lyndon B. Johnson | Johnson City, Tex. | 1908 | Tex. |
| 38 | **Hubert H. Humphrey** | **Wallace, S.D.** | **1911** | **Minn.** |
| 39 | Spiro T. Agnew IV | Baltimore, Md. | 1918 | Md. |
| 40 | **Gerald R. Ford** | **Omaha, Neb.** | **1913** | **Mich.** |
| 41 | Nelson A. Rockefeller | Bar Harbor, Me. | 1908 | N.Y. |
| 42 | **Walter F. Mondale** | **Ceylon, Minn.** | **1928** | **Minn.** |
| 43 | George Bush | Milton, Mass. | 1924 | Tex. |
| 44 | **Dan Quayle** | **Indianapolis, Ind.** | **1947** | **Ind.** |
| 45 | Albert Gore, Jr. | Washington, D.C. | 1948 | Tenn. |

| Inaug. | Politics | Place of death | Year | Age |
|--------|----------|----------------|------|-----|
| 1789 | Fed. | Quincy, Mass. | 1826 | 90 |
| **1797** | **Dem.-Rep.** | **Monticello, Va.** | **1826** | **83** |
| 1801 | Dem.-Rep. | Staten Island, N.Y. | 1836 | 80 |
| **1805** | **Dem.-Rep.** | **Washington, D.C.** | **1812** | **73** |
| 1813 | Dem.-Rep. | Washington, D.C. | 1814 | 70 |
| **1817** | **Dem.-Rep.** | **Staten Island, N.Y.** | **1825** | **51** |
| 1825 | Dem.-Rep. | Washington, D.C. | 1850 | 68 |
| **1833** | **Dem.** | **Kinderhook, N.Y.** | **1862** | **79** |
| 1837 | Dem. | Frankfort, Ky. | 1850 | 70 |
| **1841** | **Whig** | **Richmond, Va.** | **1862** | **71** |
| 1845 | Dem. | Philadelphia, Pa. | 1864 | 72 |
| **1849** | **Whig** | **Buffalo, N.Y.** | **1874** | **74** |
| 1853 | Dem. | Dallas Co., Ala. | 1853 | 67 |
| **1857** | **Dem.** | **Lexington, Ky.** | **1875** | **54** |
| 1861 | Rep. | Bangor, Me. | 1891 | 81 |
| **1865** | **Rep.** | **Carter Co., Tenn.** | **1875** | **66** |
| 1869 | Rep. | Mankato, Minn. | 1885 | 62 |
| **1873** | **Rep.** | **Washington, D.C.** | **1875** | **63** |
| 1877 | Rep. | Malone, N.Y. | 1887 | 68 |
| **1881** | **Rep.** | **New York, N.Y.** | **1886** | **57** |
| 1885 | Dem. | Indianapolis, Ind. | 1885 | 66 |
| **1889** | **Rep.** | **Rhinebeck, N.Y.** | **1920** | **96** |
| 1893 | Dem. | Chicago, Ill. | 1914 | 78 |
| **1897** | **Rep.** | **Paterson, N.J.** | **1899** | **55** |
| 1901 | Rep. | Oyster Bay, N.Y. | 1919 | 60 |
| **1905** | **Rep.** | **Indianapolis, Ind.** | **1918** | **66** |
| 1909 | Rep. | Utica, N.Y. | 1912 | 57 |
| **1913** | **Dem.** | **Washington, D.C.** | **1925** | **71** |
| 1921 | Rep. | Northampton, Mass. | 1933 | 60 |
| **1925** | **Rep.** | **Evanston, Ill.** | **1951** | **85** |
| 1929 | Rep. | Washington, D.C. | 1936 | 76 |
| **1933** | **Dem.** | **Uvalde, Tex.** | **1967** | **98** |
| 1941 | Dem. | Danbury, Conn. | 1965 | 77 |
| **1945** | **Dem.** | **Kansas City, Mo.** | **1972** | **88** |
| 1949 | Dem. | Lexington, Va. | 1956 | 78 |
| **1953** | **Rep.** | **New York, N.Y.** | **1994** | **81** |
| 1961 | Dem. | San Antonio, Tex. | 1973 | 64 |
| **1965** | **Dem.** | **Waverly, Minn.** | **1978** | **66** |
| 1969 | Rep. | | | |
| **1973** | **Rep.** | | | |
| 1974 | Rep. | New York, N.Y. | 1979 | 70 |
| **1977** | **Dem.** | | | |
| 1981 | Rep. | | | |
| **1989** | **Rep.** | | | |
| 1993 | Dem. | | | |

## How the States Voted, 1976-1992

## Burial Places of the Presidents

| | |
|---|---|
| Washington | Mt. Vernon, Va. |
| J. Adams. | Quincy, Mass. |
| Jefferson | Charlottesville, Va. |
| Madison | Montpelier Station, Va. |
| Monroe | Richmond, Va. |
| J.Q. Adams | Quincy, Mass. |
| Jackson | Nashville, Tenn. |
| Van Buren | Kinderhook, N.Y. |
| W.H. Harrison | North Bend, Oh. |
| Tyler | Richmond, Va. |
| Polk | Nashville, Tenn. |
| Taylor | Louisville, Ky. |
| Fillmore | Buffalo, N.Y. |
| Pierce | Concord, N.H. |
| Buchanan | Lancaster, Pa. |
| Lincoln | Springfield, Ill. |
| A. Johnson | Greeneville, Tenn. |
| Grant | New York City |
| Hayes | Fremont, Oh. |
| Garfield | Cleveland, Oh. |
| Arthur | Albany, N.Y. |
| Cleveland | Princeton, N.J. |
| B. Harrison | Indianapolis, Ind. |
| McKinley | Canton, Oh. |
| T. Roosevelt | Oyster Bay, N.Y. |
| Taft | Arlington Nat'l. Cem'y. |
| Wilson | Washington Cathedral |
| Harding | Marion, Oh. |
| Coolidge | Plymouth, Vt. |
| Hoover | West Branch, Ia. |
| F.D. Roosevelt | Hyde Park, N.Y. |
| Truman | Independence, Mo. |
| Eisenhower | Abilene, Kan. |
| Kennedy | Arlington Nat'l. Cem'y. |
| L.B. Johnson | Stonewall, Tex. |
| Nixon | Yorba Linda, Ca. |

| State | 1976 | 1980 | 1984 | 1988 | 1992 |
|---|---|---|---|---|---|
| Alabama | D | R | R | R | R |
| Alaska | R | R | R | R | R |
| Arizona | R | R | R | R | R |
| Arkansas | D | R | R | R | D |
| California | R | R | R | R | D |
| Colorado | R | R | R | R | D |
| Connecticut | R | R | R | R | D |
| Delaware | D | R | R | R | D |
| District of Columbia | D | D | D | D | D |
| Florida | D | R | R | R | R |
| Georgia | D | D | R | R | D |
| Hawaii | D | D | R | D | D |
| Idaho | R | R | R | R | R |
| Illinois | R | R | R | R | D |
| Indiana | R | R | R | R | R |
| Iowa | R | R | R | R | D |
| Kansas | R | R | R | R | R |
| Kentucky | D | R | R | R | D |
| Louisiana | D | R | R | R | D |
| Maine | R | R | R | R | D |
| Maryland | D | D | R | R | D |
| Massachusetts | D | R | R | D | D |
| Michigan | R | R | R | R | D |
| Minnesota | D | D | D | D | D |
| Mississippi | D | R | R | R | R |
| Missouri | D | R | R | R | D |
| Montana | R | R | R | R | D |
| Nebraska | R | R | R | R | R |
| Nevada | R | R | R | R | D |
| New Hampshire | R | R | R | R | D |
| New Jersey | R | R | R | R | D |
| New Mexico | R | R | R | R | D |
| New York | D | R | R | D | D |
| North Carolina | D | R | R | R | R |
| North Dakota | R | R | R | R | R |
| Ohio | D | R | R | R | D |
| Oklahoma | R | R | R | R | R |
| Oregon | R | R | R | D | D |
| Pennsylvania | D | R | R | R | D |
| Rhode Island | D | D | R | D | D |
| South Carolina | D | R | R | R | R |
| South Dakota | R | R | R | R | R |
| Tennessee | D | R | R | R | D |
| Texas | D | R | R | R | R |
| Utah | R | R | R | R | R |
| Vermont | R | R | R | R | D |
| Virginia | R | R | R | R | R |
| Washington | R | R | R | D | D |
| West Virginia | D | D | R | D | D |
| Wisconsin | D | R | R | D | D |
| Wyoming | R | R | R | R | R |

# Wives and Children of the Presidents
Listed in order of presidential administrations.

| Name | (Born–died, married) | State | Sons/daughters |
|---|---|---|---|
| Martha Dandridge Custis Washington | (1732-1802, 1759) | Va. | None |
| **Abigail Smith Adams** | **(1744-1818, 1764)** | **Mass.** | **3/2** |
| Martha Wayles Skelton Jefferson | (1748-1782, 1772) | Va. | 1/5 |
| **Dorothea "Dolley" Payne Todd Madison** | **(1768-1849, 1794)** | **N.C.** | **None** |
| Elizabeth Kortright Monroe | (1768-1830, 1786) | N.Y. | 0/2 |
| **Louisa Catherine Johnson Adams** | **(1775-1852, 1797)** | **Md.** | **3/1** |
| Rachel Donelson Robards Jackson | (1767-1828, 1791) | Va. | None |
| **Hannah Hoes Van Buren** | **(1783-1819, 1807)** | **N.Y.** | **4/0** |
| Anna Symmes Harrison | (1775-1864, 1795) | N.J. | 6/4 |
| **Letitia Christian Tyler** | **(1790-1842, 1813)** | **Va.** | **3/5** |
| Julia Gardiner Tyler | (1820-1889, 1844) | N.Y. | 5/2 |
| **Sarah Childress Polk** | **(1803-1891, 1824)** | **Tenn.** | **None** |
| Margaret Smith Taylor | (1788-1852, 1810) | Md. | 1/5 |
| **Abigail Powers Fillmore** | **(1798-1853, 1826)** | **N.Y.** | **1/1** |
| Caroline Carmichael McIntosh Fillmore | (1813-1881, 1858) | N.J. | None |
| **Jane Means Appleton Pierce** | **(1806-1863, 1834)** | **N.H.** | **3/0** |
| Mary Todd Lincoln | (1818-1882, 1842) | Ky. | 4/0 |
| **Eliza McCardle Johnson** | **(1810-1876, 1827)** | **Tenn.** | **3/2** |
| Julia Dent Grant | (1826-1902, 1848) | Mo. | 3/1 |
| **Lucy Ware Webb Hayes** | **(1831-1889, 1852)** | **Oh.** | **7/1** |
| Lucretia Rudolph Garfield | (1832-1918, 1858) | Oh. | 4/1 |
| **Ellen Lewis Herndon Arthur** | **(1837-1880, 1859)** | **Va.** | **2/1** |
| Frances Folsom Cleveland | (1864-1947, 1886) | N.Y. | 2/3 |
| **Caroline Lavinia Scott Harrison** | **(1832-1892, 1853)** | **Oh.** | **1/1** |
| Mary Scott Lord Dimmick Harrison | (1858-1948, 1896) | Pa. | 0/1 |
| **Ida Saxton McKinley** | **(1847-1907, 1871)** | **Oh.** | **0/2** |
| Alice Hathaway Lee Roosevelt | (1861-1884, 1880) | Mass. | 0/1 |
| **Edith Kermit Carow Roosevelt** | **(1861-1948, 1886)** | **Conn.** | **4/1** |
| Helen Herron Taft | (1861-1943, 1886) | Oh. | 2/1 |
| **Ellen Louise Axson Wilson** | **(1860-1914, 1885)** | **Ga.** | **0/3** |
| Edith Bolling Galt Wilson | (1872-1961, 1915) | Va. | None |
| **Florence Kling De Wolfe Harding** | **(1860-1924, 1891)** | **Oh.** | **None** |
| Grace Anna Goodhue Coolidge | (1879-1957, 1905) | Vt. | 2/0 |
| **Lou Henry Hoover** | **(1875-1944, 1899)** | **Ia.** | **2/0** |
| Anna Eleanor Roosevelt Roosevelt | (1884-1962, 1905) | N.Y. | 4/1 |
| **Bess Wallace Truman** | **(1885-1982, 1919)** | **Mo.** | **0/1** |
| Mamie Geneva Doud Eisenhower | (1896-1979, 1916) | Ia. | 1/0 |
| **Jacqueline Lee Bouvier Kennedy** | **(1929-1994, 1953)** | **N.Y.** | **1/1** |
| Claudia "Lady Bird" Alta Taylor Johnson | (b. 1912, 1934) | Tex. | 0/2 |
| **Thelma Catherine Patricia Ryan Nixon** | **(b. 1912, 1940)** | **Nev.** | **0/2** |
| Elizabeth Bloomer Warren Ford | (b. 1918, 1948) | Ill. | 3/1 |
| **Rosalynn Smith Carter** | **(b. 1927, 1946)** | **Ga.** | **3/1** |
| Anne Frances "Nancy" Davis Reagan | (b. 1921, 1952) | N.Y. | 1/1 |
| **Barbara Pierce Bush** | **(b. 1925, 1945)** | **N.Y.** | **4/2** |
| Hilary Rodham Clinton | (b. 1947, 1975) | IL | 0/1 |

**James Buchanan, 15th president, was unmarried.**

# SENATORS UP FOR RE-ELECTION IN 1996, 1998

| Senators whose terms expire in 1996 | | Senators whose terms expire in 1998 | |
|---|---|---|---|
| Senator | Service Began/Age | Senator | Service Began/Age |
| Max Baucus (D-Mont.) | 1978 53 | Robert F. Bennett (R-Utah) | 1993 61 |
| Joseph R. Biden Jr. (D-Del.) | 1973 52 | Christopher S. Bond (R-Mo.) | 1987 56 |
| Bill Bradley (D-N.J.) | 1979 51 | Barbara Boxer (D-Calif.) | 1993 54 |
| Hank Brown (R-Colo.) # | 1991 55 | John B. Breaux (D-La.) | 1987 51 |
| Thad Cochran (R-Miss.) | 1978 57 | Dale Bumpers (D-Ark.) | 1975 69 |
| William S. Cohen (R-Maine) | 1979 54 | Ben Nighthorse Campbell (R-Colo.) | 1993 62 |
| Larry E. Craig (R-Idaho) | 1991 49 | Daniel R. Coats (R-Ind.) | 1989 52 |
| Pete V. Domenici (R-N.M.) | 1973 63 | Paul Coverdell (R-Ga.) | 1993 56 |
| Jim Exon (D-Neb.) # | 1979 73 | Alfonse M. D'Amato (R-N.Y.) | 1981 57 |
| Phil Gramm (R-Texas) | 1985 52 | Tom Daschle (D-S.D.) | 1987 47 |
| Tom Harkin (D-Iowa) | 1985 55 | Christopher J. Dodd (D-Conn.) | 1981 51 |
| Mark O. Hatfield (R-Ore.) | 1967 72 | Bob Dole (R-Kan.) | 1969 71 |
| Howell Heflin (D-Ala.) # | 1979 74 | Byron L. Dorgan (D-N.D.) | 1992 53 |
| Jesse Helms (R-N.C.) | 1973 73 | Lauch Faircloth (R-N.C.) | 1993 67 |
| James M. Inhofe (R-Okla.) | 1994 60 | Russell D. Feingold (D-Wis.) | 1993 42 |
| J. Bennett Johnston (D-La.) # | 1972 63 | Wendell H. Ford (D-Ky.) | 1974 70 |
| Nancy L. Kassebaum (R-Kan.) | 1978 62 | John Glenn (D-Ohio) | 1974 73 |
| John Kerry (D-Mass.) | 1985 51 | Bob Graham (D-Fla.) | 1987 58 |
| Carl Levin (D-Mich.) | 1979 60 | Charles E. Grassley (R-Iowa) | 1981 61 |
| Mitch McConnell (R-Ky.) | 1985 53 | Judd Gregg (R-N.H.) | 1993 48 |
| Sam Nunn (D-Ga.) | 1972 56 | Ernest F. Hollings (D-S.C.) | 1966 73 |
| Claiborne Pell (D-R.I.) | 1961 76 | Daniel K. Inouye (D-Hawaii) | 1963 70 |
| Larry Pressler (R-S.D.) | 1979 53 | Dirk Kempthorne (R-Idaho) | 1993 43 |
| David Pryor (D-Ark.) # | 1979 60 | Patrick J. Leahy (D-Vt.) | 1975 55 |
| John D. Rockefeller IV (D-W.Va.) | 1985 58 | John McCain (R-Ariz.) | 1987 58 |
| Paul Simon (D-Ill.) # | 1985 66 | Barbara A. Mikulski (D-Md.) | 1987 58 |
| Alan K. Simpson (R-Wyo.) | 1979 63 | Carol Moseley-Braun (D-Ill.) | 1993 47 |
| Robert C. Smith (R-N.H.) | 1990 54 | Frank H. Murkowski (R-Alaska) | 1981 62 |
| Ted Stevens (R-Alaska) | 1968 71 | Patty Murray (D-Wash.) | 1993 44 |
| Fred Thompson (R-Tenn.) | 1994 52 | Don Nickles (R-Okla.) | 1981 46 |
| Strom Thurmond (R-S.C.) | 1956 92 | Bob Packwood (R-Ore.) | 1969 62 |
| John W. Warner (R-Va.) | 1979 68 | Harry Reid (D-Nev.) | 1987 55 |
| Paul Wellstone (D-Minn.) | 1991 50 | Richard C. Shelby (R-Ala.) | 1987 61 |
| | | Arlen Specter (R-Pa.) | 1981 65 |

# Not seeking re-election.
+ Barred from seeking re-election.

# SENATORS UP FOR RE-ELECTION IN 2000

## Senators whose terms expire in 2000

| Senator | Service Began | Age |
|---|---|---|
| Robert F. Bennett (R-Utah) | 1993 | 61 |
| Spencer Abraham (R-Mich.) | 1995 | 43 |
| Daniel K. Akaka (D-Hawaii) | 1990 | 70 |
| John Ashcroft (R-Mo.) | 1995 | 53 |
| Jeff Bingaman (D-N.M.) | 1983 | 51 |
| Richard H. Bryan (D-Nev.) | 1989 | 57 |
| Conrad Burns (R-Mont.) | 1989 | 60 |
| Robert C. Byrd (D-W.Va.) | 1959 | 77 |
| John H. Chafee (R-R.I.) | 1976 | 72 |
| Kent Conrad (D-N.D.) | 1987 | 47 |
| Mike DeWine (R-Ohio) | 1995 | 48 |
| Dianne Feinstein (D-Calif.) | 1992 | 62 |
| Bill Frist (R-Tenn.) | 1995 | 43 |
| Slade Gorton (R-Wash.) | 1989 | 67 |
| Rod Grams (R-Minn.) | 1995 | 47 |
| Orrin G. Hatch (R-Utah) | 1977 | 61 |
| Kay Bailey Hutchison (R-Texas) | 1993 | 51 |
| James M. Jeffords (R-Vt.) | 1989 | 61 |
| Edward M. Kennedy (D-Mass.) | 1962 | 63 |
| Bob Kerrey (D-Neb.) | 1989 | 51 |
| Herb Kohl (D-Wis.) | 1989 | 60 |
| Jon Kyl (R-Ariz.) | 1995 | 53 |
| Frank R. Lautenberg (D-N.J.) | 1982 | 71 |
| Joseph I. Lieberman (D-Conn.) | 1989 | 53 |
| Trent Lott (R-Miss.) | 1989 | 53 |
| Richard G. Lugar (R-Ind.) | 1977 | 63 |
| Connie Mack (R-Fla.) | 1989 | 54 |
| Daniel Patrick Moynihan (D-N.Y.) | 1977 | 68 |
| Charles S. Robb (D-Va.) | 1989 | 56 |
| William V. Roth Jr. (R-Del.) | 1971 | 73 |
| Rick Santorum (R-Pa.) | 1995 | 37 |
| Paul S. Sarbanes (D-Md.) | 1977 | 62 |
| Olympia J. Snowe (R-Maine) | 1995 | 48 |
| Craig Thomas (R-Wyo.) | 1995 | 62 |

# Governor Election Years

## Governors up for Re-election in 1996

| State | Governor | Service Began/Age | |
|---|---|---|---|
| Delaware | Thomas R. Carper (D) | 1993 | 48 |
| Indiana | Evan Bayh (D) | 1989 | 39 |
| Missouri | Mel Carnahan (D) | 1993 | 60 |
| Montana | Marc Racicot (R) | 1993 | 46 |
| North Carolina | James B. Hunt Jr. (D) | 1993 | 57 |
| North Dakota | Edward T. Schafer (R) | 1992 | 48 |
| Utah | Michael O. Leavitt (R) | 1993 | 43 |
| Vermont | Howard Dean (D) | 1991 | 46 |
| West Virginia | +Gaston Caperton (D) | 1989 | 54 |
| Washington | Mike Lowry (D) | 1993 | 55 |

## Governors up for Re-election in 1997

| State | Governor | Service Began/Age | |
|---|---|---|---|
| New Jersey | Christine Whitman (R) | 1994 | 48 |
| Virginia | George F. Allen (R) | 1994 | 42 |

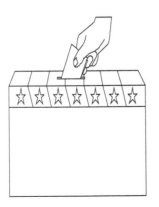

## Governors up for Re-election in 1998

| State | Governor | Service Began/Age | |
|---|---|---|---|
| Montana | Marc Racicot (R) | 1993 | 46 |
| Delaware | Thomas R. Carper (D) | 1993 | 48 |
| Alabama | Fob James Jr. (R) | 1995 | 60 |
| Alaska | Tony Knowles (D) | 1994 | 52 |
| Arizona | Fife Symington (R) | 1991 | 49 |
| Arkansas | Jim Guy Tucker (D) | 1992 | 51 |
| California | Pete Wilson (R) | 1991 | 61 |
| Colorado | Roy Romer (D) | 1987 | 66 |
| Connecticut | John G. Rowland (R) | 1995 | 37 |
| Florida | Lawton Chiles (D) | 1991 | 64 |
| Georgia | Zell Miller (D) | 1991 | 62 |
| Hawaii | Benjamin Cayetano (D) | 1995 | 55 |
| Idaho | Phil Batt (R) | 1995 | 67 |
| Illinois | Jim Edgar (R) | 1991 | 48 |
| Iowa | Terry E. Branstad (R) | 1983 | 48 |
| Kansas | Bill Graves (R) | 1995 | 42 |
| Maine | Angus King (I) | 1995 | 50 |
| Massachusetts | William F. Weld (R) | 1991 | 49 |
| Maryland | Parris Glendening (D) | 1995 | 52 |
| Michigan | John Engler (R) | 1991 | 46 |
| Minnesota | Arne Carlson (R) | 1991 | 60 |
| New Hampshire | Stephen Merrill (R) | 1993 | 48 |
| New Mexico | Gary E. Johnson (R) | 1995 | 42 |
| New York | George E. Pataki (R) | 1995 | 49 |
| Nebraska | Ben Nelson (D) | 1991 | 53 |
| Nevada | Bob Miller (D) | 1989 | 49 |
| Ohio | George Voinovich (R) | 1991 | 58 |
| Oklahoma | Frank Keating (R) | 1995 | 50 |
| Oregon | John Kitzhaber (D) | 1995 | 47 |
| Pennsylvania | Tom Ridge (R) | 1995 | 49 |
| Rhode Island | Lincoln C. Almond (R) | 1995 | 58 |
| South Carolina | David Beasley (R) | 1995 | 37 |
| South Dakota | William J. Janklow (R) | 1995 | 55 |
| Tennessee | Don Sundquist (R) | 1995 | 58 |
| Texas | George W. Bush (R) | 1995 | 48 |
| Wisconsin | Tommy Thompson (R) | 1987 | 53 |
| Wyoming | Jim Geringer (R) | 1995 | 50 |

\# Not seeking re-election.
+ Barred from seeking re-election.

PRESIDENTIAL ELECTION 52

# 1992

## BILL CLINTON

George Bush's approval rating soared to 89 percent in February, 1991, at the conclusion of the Persian Gulf War. Yet a year later the President was in deep political trouble because of a lack of confidence in his domestic leadership. At the beginning of the 1988 campaign, Bush had dramatically stated, "Read my lips—no new taxes." But as President, faced with a huge and growing deficit he had inherited from Ronald Reagan, Bush agreed to a package of tax increases, alienating many of his supporters. Bush also suffered from the massive savings and loan crisis and new revelations about his possible role in the Iran Contra scandal. Finally, numerous gaffes by Dan Quayle raised questions about Bush's ability to evaluate people. Bush, however, easily won renomination at the Republican convention, and over the objections of many advisers once again chose Quayle as his running mate.

Early in the Democratic campaign, the front-runner had been Arkansas Governor Bill Clinton. A Rhodes scholar and a graduate of Yale Law School, the thirty-two year-old Clinton had become the nation's youngest governor when he captured his state's highest office in 1979. Clinton's candidacy seemed doomed in late 1991 amid charges of adultery, but Clinton and his wife quickly attacked the charges by appearing together on national television, and the Arkansas governor regained his momentum in the primaries. He was nominated on the first ballot and the convention added Tennessee Senator Al Gore to the ticket.

The race was made more interesting by the entrance of a rare third-party candidate who had no ties to either major party. H. Ross Perot, a flamboyant Texas billionaire, used his coffers to establish a national organization and get on the ballot in all fifty states. His major theme was that both major party candidates were economic amateurs and that what the country needed was a hard-headed, experienced businessman at the helm.

Bush's campaign strategy was to emphasize Clinton's inexperience in foreign affairs and to hammer home the recurrent Republican theme that all Democrats wanted to do was tax and spend. However, as a moderate who had supervised something of an economic revival in his home state, the label didn't fit Clinton as well as it had the previous Democratic candidates. And Clinton turned the issue against Bush, pounding away at the theme that twelve years of Republican rule had made the rich richer while the middle-class and the poor suffered from a prolonged recession.

On Election Day, H. Ross Perot captured nearly 20 million votes, many of which would have gone to Bush in a two-man race. Although he only received 42 percent of the popular vote, Bill Clinton became the forty-second President of the United States.

| Electoral votes: | | Popular vote: | |
|---|---|---|---|
| Clinton | 370 | Clinton | 44,909,889 |
| Bush | 168 | Bush | 39,104,545 |
| | | Perot | 19,742,267 |

# PRESIDENTIAL ELECTION
# NIGHT SCORECARD

Half the fun of watching any contest is keeping score, and presidential elections are no exception. You can keep track of the returns as they come in below. Remember: the magic number to win the race is 270 electoral votes.

| STATE | ELECTORAL VOTES | DEMOCRATIC ELECTORAL VOTES | REPUBLICAN ELECTORAL VOTES |
|---|---|---|---|
| Alabama | 9 | | |
| Alaska | 3 | | |
| Arizona | 8 | | |
| Arkansas | 6 | | |
| California | 54 | | |
| Colorado | 8 | | |
| Connecticut | 8 | | |
| Delaware | 3 | | |
| District of Columbia | 3 | | |
| Florida | 5 | | |
| Georgia | 13 ✓ | | |
| Hawaii | 4 | | |
| Idaho | 4 | | |
| Illinois | 22 | | |
| Indiana | 12 | | |
| Iowa | 7 | | |
| Kansas | 6 | | |
| Kentucky | 8 ✓ | | |
| Louisiana | 9 | | |
| Maine | 4 | | |
| Maryland | 10 | | |
| Massachusetts | 12 | | |
| Michigan | 18 | | |

| STATE | ELECTORAL VOTES | DEMOCRATIC ELECTORAL VOTES | REPUBLICAN ELECTORAL VOTES |
|---|---|---|---|
| Minnesota | 10 | | |
| Mississippi | 7 | | |
| Missouri | 11 | | |
| Montana | 3 | | |
| Nebraska | 5 | | |
| Nevada | 4 | | |
| New Hampshire · | 4 | | |
| New Jersey | 15 | | |
| New Mexico | 5 | | |
| New York | 33 | | |
| North Carolina | 14 | | |
| North Dakota | 3 | | |
| Ohio ✓ | 21 | | |
| Oklahoma | 8 | | |
| Oregon | 7 | | |
| Pennsylvania | 23 | | |
| Rhode Island | 4 | | |
| South Carolina | 8 | | |
| South Dakota | 3 | | |
| Tennessee | 11 | | |
| Texas | 32 | | |
| Utah | 5 | | |
| Vermont | 3 | | |
| Virginia | 13 | | |
| Washington | 11 | | |
| West Virginia ✓ | 5 | | |
| Wisconsin | 11 | | |
| Wyoming | 3 | | |
| TOTAL | 538 | | |

269

# STATE
# POLITICAL PROFILES

## ALABAMA
Population  4,040,587  (22)
Per capita income $15,557 (41)
73%  White
28%  Black
1%  Hispanic
1%  Asian/Pacific Islander
**60% urban 40% rural**

ELECTORAL VOTES 9
PRESIDENTIAL VOTING

| 1992 | CLINTON | 41% |
| | BUSH | 43% |
| | PEROT | 11% |
| 1988 | DUKAKIS | 40% |
| | BUSH | 59% |
| 1984 | MONDALE | 38% |
| | REAGAN | 61% |

CONGRESS (1994)

| SENATE | 1D | 1R |
| HOUSE | 4D | 3R |

**Governor: Republican**

STATE LEGISLATURE (1994)

| SENATE | 23D | 12R |
| | 34 MEN | 1 WOMEN |
| HOUSE | 74D | 31R |
| | 100 MEN | 5 WOMEN |

## ALASKA
Population  550,982  (49)
Per capita income $21,982  (6)
76%  White
4%  Black
3%  Hispanic
17%  Asian/Pacific Islander
**67% urban 33% rural**

ELECTORAL VOTES 3
PRESIDENTIAL VOTING

| 1992 | CLINTON | 30% |
| | BUSH | 39% |
| | PEROT | 28% |
| 1988 | DUKAKIS | 38% |
| | BUSH | 60% |
| 1984 | MONDALE | 30% |
| | REAGAN | 67% |

CONGRESS (1994)

| SENATE | 2R |
| HOUSE | 1R |

**Governor: Democrat**

STATE LEGISLATURE (1994)

| SENATE | 8D | 12R |
| | 16 MEN | 4 WOMEN |
| HOUSE | 17D | 22R |
| | 30 MEN | 10 WOMEN |

## ARIZONA
Population  3,655,226  (24)
Per capita income $16,401 (35)
81%  White
3%  Black
19%  Hispanic
2%  Asian/Pacific Islander
**88% urban 12% rural**

ELECTORAL VOTES 8
PRESIDENTIAL VOTING

| 1992 | CLINTON | 37% |
| | BUSH | 39% |
| | PEROT | 24% |
| 1988 | DUKAKIS | 39% |
| | BUSH | 60% |
| 1984 | MONDALE | 33% |
| | REAGAN | 65% |

CONGRESS (1994)

| SENATE | 2 R |
| HOUSE | 1 D | 5R |

**Governor: Republican**

STATE LEGISLATURE (1994)

| SENATE | 19 D | 11R |
| | 22 MEN | 8 WOMEN |
| HOUSE | 22 D | 38R |
| | 41 MEN | 19 WOMEN |

## ARKANSAS
Population  2,350,725  (33)
Per capita income $14,763 (47)
83%  White
16%  Black
1%  Hispanic
1%  Asian/Pacific Islander
**54% urban 46% rural**

ELECTORAL VOTES 6
PRESIDENTIAL VOTING

| 1992 | CLINTON | 53% |
| | BUSH | 35% |
| | PEROT | 10% |
| 1988 | DUKAKIS | 42% |
| | BUSH | 55% |
| 1984 | MONDALE | 38% |
| | REAGAN | 60% |

CONGRESS (1994)

| SENATE | 2D |
| HOUSE | 2D | 2R |

**Governor: Democrat**

STATE LEGISLATURE (1994)

| SENATE | 28 D | 7R |
| | 34 MEN | 1 WOMEN |
| HOUSE | 88 D | 12R |
| | 84 MEN | 12 WOMEN |

## CALIFORNIA
Population  29,760,021  (1)
Per capita income $20,952  (8)
69%  White
7%  Black
26%  Hispanic
10%  Asian/Pacific Islander
**93% urban 7% rural**

ELECTORAL VOTES 54
PRESIDENTIAL VOTING

| 1992 | CLINTON | 45% |
| | BUSH | 33% |
| | PEROT | 21% |
| 1988 | DUKAKIS | 49% |
| | BUSH | 51% |
| 1984 | MONDALE | 41% |
| | REAGAN | 58% |

CONGRESS (1994)

| SENATE | 2D |
| HOUSE | 27D | 25R |

**Governor: Republican**

STATE LEGISLATURE (1994)

| SENATE | 21 D | 17R |
| | 34 MEN | 6 WOMEN |
| HOUSE | 39 D | 40R |
| | 60 MEN | 20 WOMEN |

## COLORADO
Population  3,294,394  (20)

Per capita income $19,440 (14)
88% White
4% Black
13% Hispanic
2% Asian/Pacific Islander
**82% urban 18% rural**

ELECTORAL VOTES 8
PRESIDENTIAL VOTING

| 1992 | CLINTON | 43% |
| | BUSH | 35% |
| | PEROT | 23% |
| 1988 | DUKAKIS | 45% |
| | BUSH | 53% |
| 1984 | MONDALE | 35% |
| | REAGAN | 63% |

CONGRESS (1994)
SENATE 2R
HOUSE 2D 4R

**Governor: Democrat**

STATE LEGISLATURE (1994)

| SENATE | 16D | 19R |
| | 25 MEN | 10 WOMEN |
| HOUSE | 24D | 41R |
| | 43 MEN | 22 WOMEN |

## CONNECTICUT

Population 3,287,116 (28)
Per capita income $25,881 (1)
87% White
8% Black
6% Hispanic
2% Asian/Pacific Islander
**79% urban 21% rural**

ELECTORAL VOTES 8
PRESIDENTIAL VOTING

| 1992 | CLINTON | 42% |
| | BUSH | 36% |
| | PEROT | 22% |
| 1988 | DUKAKIS | 47% |
| | BUSH | 52% |
| 1984 | MONDALE | 39% |
| | REAGAN | 61% |

CONGRESS (1994)
SENATE 2D
HOUSE 3D 3R

**Governor: Republican**

STATE LEGISLATURE (1994)

| SENATE | 17D | 19R |
| | 28 MEN | 8 WOMEN |
| HOUSE | 90D | 61R |
| | 109 MEN | 42 WOMEN |

## DELAWARE

Population 656.168 (46)
Per capita income $20,349 (11)
80% White
17% Black
2% Hispanic
1% Asian/Pacific Islander
**73% urban 27% rural**

ELECTORAL VOTES 3
PRESIDENTIAL VOTING

| 1992 | CLINTON | 44% |
| | BUSH | 35% |
| | PEROT | 20% |
| 1988 | DUKAKIS | 43% |
| | BUSH | 56% |
| 1984 | MONDALE | 40% |
| | REAGAN | 60% |

CONGRESS (1994)
SENATE 1D 1R
HOUSE 1R

**Governor: Democrat**

STATE LEGISLATURE (1994)

| SENATE | 12D | 9R |
| | 15 MEN | 6 WOMEN |
| HOUSE | 14D | 27R |
| | 34 MEN | 7 WOMEN |

## FLORIDA

Population 12,987,925 (4)
Per capita income $18,880 (18)
73% White
14% Black
12% Hispanic
1% Asian/Pacific Islander
**85% urban 15% rural**

ELECTORAL VOTES 25
PRESIDENTIAL VOTING

| 1992 | CLINTON | 39% |
| | BUSH | 41% |
| | PEROT | 20% |
| 1988 | DUKAKIS | 39% |
| | BUSH | 61% |
| 1984 | MONDALE | 35% |
| | REAGAN | 65% |

CONGRESS (1994)
SENATE 1D 1R
HOUSE 8D 15R

**Governor: Democrat**

STATE LEGISLATURE (1994)

| SENATE | 19D | 21R |
| | 34 MEN | 6 WOMEN |
| HOUSE | 63D | 57R |
| | 95 MEN | 25 WOMEN |

## GEORGIA

Population 6,478,216 (11)
Per capita income $17,354 (29)
71% White
27% Black
2% Hispanic
1% Asian
**63% urban 37% rural**

ELECTORAL VOTES 13
PRESIDENTIAL VOTING

| 1992 | CLINTON | 43% |
| | BUSH | 43% |
| | PEROT | 13% |
| 1988 | DUKAKIS | 39% |
| | BUSH | 60% |
| 1984 | MONDALE | 40% |
| | REAGAN | 60% |

CONGRESS (1994)
SENATE 1D 1R
HOUSE 4D 7R

**Governor: Democrat**

STATE LEGISLATURE (1994)

| SENATE | 35D | 21R |
| | 48 MEN | 8 WOMEN |
| HOUSE | 114D | 65R |
| | 145 MEN | 35 WOMEN |

## HAWAII

Population 1,106,229 (40)
Per capita income $21,306 (7)
33% White
2% Black
7% Hispanic
62% Asian/Pacific Islander
**89% urban 11% rural**

ELECTORAL VOTES 4
PRESIDENTIAL VOTING

| 1992 | CLINTON | 48% |
| | BUSH | 37% |
| | PEROT | 14% |
| 1988 | DUKAKIS | 54% |
| | BUSH | 45% |
| 1984 | MONDALE | 55% |
| | REAGAN | 45% |

CONGRESS (1994)
SENATE 2D

**Page 208 — ELECTING OUR GOVERNMENT**


House 2D
Governor: Democrat
STATE LEGISLATURE (1994)
SENATE 23D 2R
19 MEN 6 WOMEN
HOUSE 44D 7R
41 MEN 10 WOMEN

**IDAHO**
Population 1,006,749 (42)
Per capita income $15,431 (44)
94% White
1% Black
5% Hispanic
1% Asian/Pacific Islander
57% urban 43% rural
ELECTORAL VOTES 4
PRESIDENTIAL VOTING
1992 CLINTON 28%
BUSH 42%
PEROT 27%
1988 DUKAKIS 36%
BUSH 62%
1984 MONDALE 25%
REAGAN 72%
CONGRESS (1994)
SENATE 2R
HOUSE 2R
Governor: Republican
STATE LEGISLATURE (1994)
SENATE 8D 27R
27 MEN 8 WOMEN
HOUSE 13D 57R
48 MEN 22 WOMEN

**ILLINOIS**
Population 11,430,502 (6)
Per capita income $20,824 (10)
79% White
15% Black
8% Hispanic
2% Asian/Pacific Islander
85% urban 15% rural
ELECTORAL VOTES 22
PRESIDENTIAL VOTING
1992 CLINTON 49%
BUSH 34%
PEROT 17%
1988 DUKAKIS 49%
BUSH 51%
1984 MONDALE 43%


REAGAN 55%
CONGRESS (1994)
SENATE 2D
HOUSE 10D 10R
Governor: Republican
STATE LEGISLATURE (1994)
SENATE 26D 33R
48 MEN 11 WOMEN
HOUSE 54D 64R
87 MEN 31 WOMEN

**INDIANA**
Population 5,544,159 (14)
Per capita income $17,217 (32)
91% White
8% Black
2% Hispanic
1% Asian/Pacific Islander
65% urban 35% rural
ELECTORAL VOTES 12
PRESIDENTIAL VOTING
1992 CLINTON 37%
BUSH 43%
PEROT 20%
1988 DUKAKIS 40%
BUSH 60%
1984 MONDALE 38%
REAGAN 61%
CONGRESS (1994)
SENATE 2R
HOUSE 4D 6R
Governor: Democrat
STATE LEGISLATURE (1994)
SENATE 30D 30R
37 MEN 13 WOMEN
HOUSE 44D 56R
81 MEN 19 WOMEN

**IOWA**
Population 3,776,733 (30)
Per capita income $17,505 (28)
96% White
2% Black
1% Hispanic
1% Asian/Pacific Islander
61% urban 39% rural
ELECTORAL VOTES 7
PRESIDENTIAL VOTING
1992 CLINTON 43%
BUSH 37%
PEROT 19%


1988 DUKAKIS 55%
BUSH 44%
1984 MONDALE 46%
REAGAN 53%
CONGRESS (1994)
SENATE 1D 1R
HOUSE 5R
Governor: Republican
STATE LEGISLATURE (1994)
SENATE 27D 23R
41 MEN 9 WOMEN
HOUSE 36D 64R
83 MEN 17 WOMEN

**KANSAS**
Population 2,477,574 (32)
Per capita income $18,511 (21)
90% White
6% Black
4% Hispanic
1% Asian/Pacific Islander
69% urban 31% rural
ELECTORAL VOTES 6
PRESIDENTIAL VOTING
1992 CLINTON 34%
BUSH 39%
PEROT 27%
1988 DUKAKIS 43%
BUSH 56%
1984 MONDALE 33%
REAGAN 66%
CONGRESS (1994)
SENATE 2R
HOUSE 4R
Governor: Republican
STATE LEGISLATURE (1994)
SENATE 13D 27R
27 MEN 13 WOMEN
HOUSE 45D 80R
93 MEN 32 WOMEN

**KENTUCKY**
Population 3,665,296 (23)
Per capita income $15,539 (42)
92% White
7% Black
1% Hispanic
1% Asian/Pacific Islander
52% urban 48% rural
ELECTORAL VOTES 8
PRESIDENTIAL VOTING

| 1992 | CLINTON | 45% |
| | BUSH | 41% |
| | PEROT | 14% |
| 1988 | DUKAKIS | 44% |
| | BUSH | 55% |
| 1984 | MONDALE | 39% |
| | REAGAN | 60% |

CONGRESS (1994)

| SENATE | 1D | 1R |
| HOUSE | 2D | 4R |

Governor: Democrat

STATE LEGISLATURE (1994)

| SENATE | 21D | 17R |
| | 36 MEN | 2 WOMEN |
| HOUSE | 64D | 36R |
| | 91 MEN | 9 WOMEN |

## LOUISIANA

Population 4,219,973 (21)
Per capita income $15,143 (45)
67% White
31% Black
2% Hispanic
1% Asian/Pacific Islander
**68% urban 32% rural**

ELECTORAL VOTES 9
PRESIDENTIAL VOTING

| 1992 | CLINTON | 46% |
| | BUSH | 41% |
| | PEROT | 12% |
| 1988 | DUKAKIS | 44% |
| | BUSH | 54% |
| 1984 | MONDALE | 61% |
| | REAGAN | 39% |

CONGRESS (1994)

| SENATE | 2D | |
| HOUSE | 4D | 3R |

Governor: Democrat

STATE LEGISLATURE (1994)

| SENATE | 33D | 6R |
| | 37 MEN | 2 WOMEN |
| HOUSE | 86D | 17R |
| | 92 MEN | 12 WOMEN |

## MAINE

Population 1,227,928 (38)
Per capita income $17,306 (30)
98% White
>1% Black
1% Hispanic
1% Asian/Pacific Islander

**45% urban 55% rural**

ELECTORAL VOTES 4
PRESIDENTIAL VOTING

| 1992 | CLINTON | 39% |
| | BUSH | 30% |
| | PEROT | 30% |
| 1988 | DUKAKIS | 44% |
| | BUSH | 55% |
| 1984 | MONDALE | 39% |
| | REAGAN | 61% |

CONGRESS (1994)

| SENATE | 2R | |
| HOUSE | 1D | 1R |

Governor: Independent

STATE LEGISLATURE (1994)

| SENATE | 16D | 18R |
| | 24 MEN | 11 WOMEN |
| HOUSE | 77D | 74R |
| | 111 MEN | 40 WOMEN |

## MARYLAND

Population 4,781,468 (19)
Per capita income $22,080 (5)
71% White
23% Black
3% Hispanic
3% Asian/Pacific Islander
**81% urban 19% rural**

ELECTORAL VOTES 10
PRESIDENTIAL VOTING

| 1992 | CLINTON | 50% |
| | BUSH | 36% |
| | PEROT | 14% |
| 1988 | DUKAKIS | 49% |
| | BUSH | 51% |
| 1984 | MONDALE | 47% |
| | REAGAN | 53% |

CONGRESS (1994)

| SENATE | 2D | |
| HOUSE | 4D | 4R |

Governor: Democrat

STATE LEGISLATURE (1994)

| SENATE | 32D | 15R |
| | 40 MEN | 7 WOMEN |
| HOUSE | 100D | 41R |
| | 94 MEN | 47 WOMEN |

## MASSACHUSETTS

Population 6,016,425 (13)
Per capita income $22,897 (3)
90% White

5% Black
5% Hispanic
2% Asian/Pacific Islander
**84% urban 16% rural**

ELECTORAL VOTES 13
PRESIDENTIAL VOTING

| 1992 | CLINTON | 48% |
| | BUSH | 29% |
| | PEROT | 23% |
| 1988 | DUKAKIS | 53% |
| | BUSH | 45% |
| 1984 | MONDALE | 49% |
| | REAGAN | 51% |

CONGRESS (1994)

| SENATE | 2D | |
| HOUSE | 9D | 2R |

Governor: Republican

STATE LEGISLATURE (1994)

| SENATE | 30D | 10R |
| | 32 MEN | 8 WOMEN |
| HOUSE | 125 | 34R |
| | 120 MEN | 40 WOMEN |

## MICHIGAN

Population 9,697,297 (8)
Per capita income $18,697 (20)
83% White
14% Black
2% Hispanic
1% Asian/Pacific Islander
**71% urban 29% rural**

ELECTORAL VOTES 18
PRESIDENTIAL VOTING

| 1992 | CLINTON | 44% |
| | BUSH | 35% |
| | PEROT | 19% |
| 1988 | DUKAKIS | 46% |
| | BUSH | 54% |
| 1984 | MONDALE | 40% |
| | REAGAN | 59% |

CONGRESS (1994)

| SENATE | 1D | 1R |
| HOUSE | 9D | 7R |

Governor: Republican

STATE LEGISLATURE (1994)

| SENATE | 16D | 22R |
| | 35 MEN | 3 WOMEN |
| HOUSE | 53D | 56R |
| | 78 MEN | 31 WOMEN |

## MINNESOTA

Population 4,375,099 (20)
Per capita income $19,107 (19)
94% White
2% Black
1% Hispanic
2% Asian/Pacific Islander
**70% urban 30% rural**
ELECTORAL VOTES 10
PRESIDENTIAL VOTING

| 1992 | CLINTON | 43% |
| | BUSH | 32% |
| | PEROT | 24% |
| 1988 | DUKAKIS | 53% |
| | BUSH | 45% |
| 1984 | MONDALE | 50% |
| | REAGAN | 50% |

CONGRESS (1994)

| SENATE | 1D | 1R |
| HOUSE | 6D | 2R |

**Governor: Republican**
STATE LEGISLATURE (1994)

| SENATE | 43D | 23R |
| | 48 MEN | 18 WOMEN |
| HOUSE | 71D | 63R |
| | 102 MEN | 32 WOMEN |

## MISSISSIPPI

Population 2,073,216 (31)
Per capita income $13,343 (50)
64% White
35% Black
1% Hispanic
1% Asian/Pacific Islander
**47% urban 53% rural**
ELECTORAL VOTES 7
PRESIDENTIAL VOTING

| 1992 | CLINTON | 41% |
| | BUSH | 50% |
| | PEROT | 9% |
| 1988 | DUKAKIS | 39% |
| | BUSH | 60% |
| 1984 | MONDALE | 37% |
| | REAGAN | 62% |

CONGRESS (1994)

| SENATE | 2R |
| HOUSE | 4D | 1R |

**Governor: Republican**
STATE LEGISLATURE (1994)

| SENATE | 37D | 15R |
| | 48 MEN | 4 WOMEN |

| HOUSE | 89D | 31R |
| | 106 MEN | 16 WOMEN |

## MISSOURI

Population 5,117,073 (15)
Per capita income $17,842 (25)
88% White
11% Black
1% Hispanic
1% Asian/Pacific Islander
**69% urban 31% rural**
ELECTORAL VOTES 11
PRESIDENTIAL VOTING

| 1992 | CLINTON | 44% |
| | BUSH | 34% |
| | PEROT | 22% |
| 1988 | DUKAKIS | 48% |
| | BUSH | 52% |
| 1984 | MONDALE | 40% |
| | REAGAN | 60% |

CONGRESS (1994)

| SENATE | 2R |
| HOUSE | 6D | 3R |

**Governor: Democrat**
STATE LEGISLATURE (1994)

| SENATE | 19D | 10R |
| | 31 MEN | 3 WOMEN |
| HOUSE | 87D | 76R |
| | 127 MEN | 36 WOMEN |

## MONTANA

Population 799,065 (44)
Per capita income $16,043 (39)
98% White
>1% Black
1% Hispanic
1% Asian/Pacific Islander
**53% urban 47% rural**
ELECTORAL VOTES 3
PRESIDENTIAL VOTING

| 1992 | CLINTON | 38% |
| | BUSH | 35% |
| | PEROT | 25% |
| 1988 | DUKAKIS | 45% |
| | BUSH | 53% |
| 1984 | MONDALE | 38% |
| | REAGAN | 60% |

CONGRESS (1994)

| SENATE | 1D | 1R |
| HOUSE | 1D |

**Governor: Republican**

STATE LEGISLATURE (1994)

| SENATE | 19D | 31R |
| | 41 MEN | 9 WOMEN |
| HOUSE | 33D | 67R |
| | 73 MEN | 27 WOMEN |

## NEBRASKA

Population 1,578,365 (36)
Per capita income $17,852 (24)
94% White
4% Black
2% Hispanic
1% Asian/Pacific Islander
**66% urban 34% rural**
ELECTORAL VOTES 5
PRESIDENTIAL VOTING

| 1992 | CLINTON | 29% |
| | BUSH | 47% |
| | PEROT | 24% |
| 1988 | DUKAKIS | 39% |
| | BUSH | 60% |
| 1984 | MONDALE | 29% |
| | REAGAN | 71% |

CONGRESS (1994)

| SENATE | 2D |
| HOUSE | 3R |

**Governor: Democrat**
STATE LEGISLATURE (1994)
ONE HOUSE, NON-PARTISAN
LEGISLATURE
37 MEN 12 WOMEN

## NEVADA

Population 1,201,833 (39)
Per capita income $19,175 (18)
84% White
7% Black
10% Hispanic
3% Asian/Pacific Islander
**88% urban 12% rural**
ELECTORAL VOTES 4
PRESIDENTIAL VOTING

| 1992 | CLINTON | 37% |
| | BUSH | 36% |
| | PEROT | 26% |
| 1988 | DUKAKIS | 38% |
| | BUSH | 59% |
| 1984 | MONDALE | 32% |
| | REAGAN | 66% |

CONGRESS (1994)

| SENATE | 2D |

HOUSE 1D 1R
**Governor: Democrat**
STATE LEGISLATURE (1994)
SENATE 8D 13R
16 MEN 5 WOMEN
HOUSE 21D 21R
25 MEN 17 WOMEN

## NEW HAMPSHIRE
Population 1,109,252 (40)
Per capita income $20,961 (9)
98% White
1% Black
1% Hispanic
1% Asian/Pacific Islander
**51% urban 49% rural**
ELECTORAL VOTES 4
PRESIDENTIAL VOTING
1992 CLINTON 39%
BUSH 38%
PEROT 23%
1988 DUKAKIS 38%
BUSH 62%
1984 MONDALE 31%
REAGAN 69%
CONGRESS (1994)
SENATE 2R
HOUSE 2R
**Governor: Republican**
STATE LEGISLATURE (1994)
SENATE 6D 18R
18 MEN 6 WOMEN
HOUSE 112D 286R
278 MEN 122 WOMEN

## NEW JERSEY
Population 7,730,186 (9)
Per capita income $25,372 (2)
79% White
13% Black
10% Hispanic
4% Asian/Pacific Islander
**89% urban 11% rural**
ELECTORAL VOTES 15
PRESIDENTIAL VOTING
1992 CLINTON 43%
BUSH 41%
PEROT 16%
1988 DUKAKIS 43%
BUSH 58%
1984 MONDALE 39%

REAGAN 60%
CONGRESS (1994)
SENATE 2D
HOUSE 5D 8R
**Governor: Republican**
STATE LEGISLATURE (1994)
SENATE 16D 24R
39 MEN 1 WOMAN
HOUSE 26D 52R
67 MEN 13 WOMEN

## NEW MEXICO
Population 1,515,869 (37)
Per capita income $14,844 (45)
76% White
2% Black
38% Hispanic
1% Asian/Pacific Islander
**73% urban 27% rural**
ELECTORAL VOTES 5
PRESIDENTIAL VOTING
1992 CLINTON 46%
BUSH 37%
PEROT 16%
1988 DUKAKIS 47%
BUSH 53%
1984 MONDALE 39%
REAGAN 60%
CONGRESS (1994)
SENATE 1D 1R
HOUSE 1D 2R
**Governor: Republican**
STATE LEGISLATURE (1994)
SENATE 27D 15R
34 MEN 8 WOMEN
HOUSE 46D 24R
55 MEN 15 WOMEN

## NEW YORK
Population 17,990,455 (2)
Per capita income $22,456 (4)
94% White
2% Black
1% Hispanic
2% Asian/Pacific Islander
**84% urban 16% rural**
ELECTORAL VOTES 33
PRESIDENTIAL VOTING
1992 CLINTON 50%
BUSH 34%
PEROT 16%

1988 DUKAKIS 52%
BUSH 48%
1984 MONDALE 46%
REAGAN 54%
CONGRESS (1994)
SENATE 1D 1R
HOUSE 17D 14R
**Governor: Republican**
STATE LEGISLATURE (1994)
SENATE 25D 36R
52 MEN 9 WOMEN
HOUSE 94D 56R
120 MEN 30 WOMEN

## NORTH CAROLINA
Population 6,628,637 (10)
Per capita income $16,642 (34)
76% White
22% Black
1% Hispanic
1% Asian/Pacific Islander
**50% urban 50% rural**
ELECTORAL VOTES 14
PRESIDENTIAL VOTING
1992 CLINTON 43%
BUSH 43%
PEROT 14%
1988 DUKAKIS 42%
BUSH 58%
1984 MONDALE 38%
REAGAN 62%
CONGRESS (1994)
SENATE 2R
HOUSE 4D 8R
**Governor: Democrat**
STATE LEGISLATURE (1994)
SENATE 26D 24R
44 MEN 6 WOMEN
HOUSE 52D 68R
99 MEN 21 WOMEN

## NORTH DAKOTA
Population 638,800 (47)
Per capita income $16,088 (38)
96% White
1% Black
1% Hispanic
1% Asian/Pacific Islander
**53% urban 47% rural**
ELECTORAL VOTES 3
PRESIDENT VOTING

| 1992 | CLINTON | 32% |
|------|---------|-----|
|      | BUSH    | 44% |
|      | PEROT   | 23% |
| 1988 | DUKAKIS | 43% |
|      | BUSH    | 56% |
| 1984 | MONDALE | 34% |
|      | REAGAN  | 66% |

CONGRESS (1994)

| SENATE | 2D |
|--------|----|
| HOUSE  | 1D |

**Governor: Republican**

STATE LEGISLATURE (1994)

| SENATE | 20D | 29R |
|--------|-----|-----|
|        | 40 MEN | 19 WOMEN |
| HOUSE  | 23D | 75R |
|        | 85 MEN | 13 WOMEN |

## OHIO

Population 10,847,115 (7)
Per capita income $17,916 (23)
88% White
11% Black
1% Hispanic
1% Asian/Pacific Islander
**74% urban 26% rural**
ELECTORAL VOTES 21
PRESIDENTIAL VOTING

| 1992 | CLINTON | 40% |
|------|---------|-----|
|      | BUSH    | 38% |
|      | PEROT   | 21% |
| 1988 | DUKAKIS | 44% |
|      | BUSH    | 55% |
| 1984 | MONDALE | 40% |
|      | REAGAN  | 59% |

CONGRESS (1994)

| SENATE | 1D | 1R |
|--------|----|----|
| HOUSE  | 6D | 13R |

**Governor: Republican**

STATE LEGISLATURE (1994)

| SENATE | 13D | 20R |
|--------|-----|-----|
|        | 25 MEN | 8 WOMEN |
| HOUSE  | 43D | 56R |
|        | 75 MEN | 24 WOMEN |

## OKLAHOMA

Population 3,145,585 (28)
Per capita income $15,827 (40)
87% White
7% Black
3% Hispanic
1% Asian/Pacific Islander

**68% urban 32% rural**
ELECTORAL VOTES 8
PRESIDENTIAL VOTING

| 1992 | CLINTON | 34% |
|------|---------|-----|
|      | BUSH    | 43% |
|      | PEROT   | 23% |
| 1988 | DUKAKIS | 41% |
|      | BUSH    | 58% |
| 1984 | MONDALE | 31% |
|      | REAGAN  | 69% |

CONGRESS (1994)

| SENATE | 2R |    |
|--------|----|----|
| HOUSE  | 1D | 5R |

**Governor: Republican**

STATE LEGISLATURE (1994)

| SENATE | 35D | 13R |
|--------|-----|-----|
|        | 41 MEN | 7 WOMEN |
| HOUSE  | 65D | 36R |
|        | 92 MEN | 9 WOMEN |

## OREGON

Population 2,842,321 (29)
Per capita income $17,592 (27)
90% White
2% Black
4% Hispanic
2% Asian/Pacific Islander
**70% urban 30% rural**
ELECTORAL VOTES 7
PRESIDENTIAL VOTING

| 1992 | CLINTON | 42% |
|------|---------|-----|
|      | BUSH    | 33% |
|      | PEROT   | 24% |
| 1988 | DUKAKIS | 51% |
|      | BUSH    | 47% |
| 1984 | MONDALE | 44% |
|      | REAGAN  | 55% |

CONGRESS (1994)

| SENATE | 2R |    |
|--------|----|----|
| HOUSE  | 3D | 2R |

**Governor: Democrat**

STATE LEGISLATURE (1994)

| SENATE | 11D | 19R |
|--------|-----|-----|
|        | 25 MEN | 5 WOMEN |
| HOUSE  | 26D | 34R |
|        | 41 MEN | 19 WOMEN |

## PENNSYLVANIA

Population 11,881,643 (5)
Per capita income $19,128 (16)
89% White

9% Black
2% Hispanic
1% Asian/Pacific Islander
**69% urban 31% rural**
ELECTORAL VOTES 23
PRESIDENTIAL VOTING

| 1992 | CLINTON | 45% |
|------|---------|-----|
|      | BUSH    | 36% |
|      | PEROT   | 18% |
| 1988 | DUKAKIS | 49% |
|      | BUSH    | 51% |
| 1984 | MONDALE | 46% |
|      | REAGAN  | 53% |

CONGRESS (1994)

| SENATE | 2R |    |
|--------|----|----|
| HOUSE  | 11D | 10R |

**Governor: Republican**

STATE LEGISLATURE (1994)

| SENATE | 21D | 29R |
|--------|-----|-----|
|        | 46 MEN | 4 WOMEN |
| HOUSE  | 101D | 102R |
|        | 177 MEN | 26 WOMEN |

## RHODE ISLAND

Population 1,003,464 (43)
Per capita income $18,840 (19)
91% White
4% Black
5% Hispanic
2% Asian/Pacific Islander
**86% urban 14% rural**
ELECTORAL VOTES 4
PRESIDENTIAL VOTING

| 1992 | CLINTON | 47% |
|------|---------|-----|
|      | BUSH    | 29% |
|      | PEROT   | 23% |
| 1988 | DUKAKIS | 56% |
|      | BUSH    | 44% |
| 1984 | MONDALE | 48% |
|      | REAGAN  | 52% |

CONGRESS (1994)

| SENATE | 1D | 1R |
|--------|----|----|
| HOUSE  | 2D |    |

**Governor: Republican**

STATE LEGISLATURE (1994)

| SENATE | 40D | 10R |
|--------|-----|-----|
|        | 40 MEN | 10 WOMEN |
| HOUSE  | 84D | 16R |
|        | 74 MEN | 26 WOMEN |

## SOUTH CAROLINA

Population  3,486,703  (25)
Per capita income $15,420 (43)
- 69%  White
- 30%  Black
- 1%  Hispanic
- 1%  Asian/Pacific Islander

**55% urban 45% rural**

ELECTORAL VOTES 8

PRESIDENTIAL VOTING

| 1992 | CLINTON | 48% |
| | BUSH | 40% |
| | PEROT | 12% |
| 1988 | DUKAKIS | 38% |
| | BUSH | 62% |
| 1984 | MONDALE | 35% |
| | REAGAN | 64% |

CONGRESS (1994)

| SENATE | 1D | 1R |
| HOUSE | 2D | 4R |

**Governor: Republican**

STATE LEGISLATURE (1994)

| SENATE | 29D | 17R |
| | 43 MEN | 3 WOMEN |
| HOUSE | 58D | 62R |
| | 105 MEN | 19 WOMEN |

## SOUTH DAKOTA

Population  696,004  (45)
Per capita income $16,392 (35)
- 98%  White
- >1%  Black
- 1%  Hispanic
- >1%  Asian/Pacific Islander

**50% urban 50% rural**

ELECTORAL VOTES 3

PRESIDENTIAL VOTING

| 1992 | CLINTON | 41% |
| | BUSH | 37% |
| | PEROT | 22% |
| 1988 | DUKAKIS | 47% |
| | BUSH | 53% |
| 1984 | MONDALE | 37% |
| | REAGAN | 63% |

CONGRESS (1994)

| SENATE | 1D | 1R |
| HOUSE | 1D | |

**Governor: Republican**

STATE LEGISLATURE (1994)

| SENATE | 16D | 19R |
| | 30 MEN | 5 WOMEN |

| HOUSE | 24D | 46R |
| | 56 MEN | 14 WOMEN |

## TENNESSEE

Population  4,877,185  (17)
Per capita income $16,325 (37)
- 83%  White
- 16%  Black
- 1%  Hispanic
- 1%  Asian/Pacific Islander

**61% urban 39% rural**

ELECTORAL VOTES 11

PRESIDENTIAL VOTING

| 1992 | CLINTON | 47% |
| | BUSH | 42% |
| | PEROT | 10% |
| 1988 | DUKAKIS | 42% |
| | BUSH | 58% |
| 1984 | MONDALE | 42% |
| | REAGAN | 58% |

CONGRESS (1994)

| SENATE | 2R | |
| HOUSE | 4D | 5R |

**Governor: Republican**

STATE LEGISLATURE (1994)

| SENATE | 18D | 15R |
| | 30 MEN | 3 WOMEN |
| HOUSE | 59D | 40R |
| | 84 MEN | 15 WOMEN |

## TEXAS

Population  16,986,510  (3)
Per capita income $17,305 (31)
- 75%  White
- 12%  Black
- 26%  Hispanic
- 2%  Asian/Pacific Islander

**91% urban 9% rural**

ELECTORAL VOTES 32

PRESIDENTIAL VOTING

| 1992 | CLINTON | 37% |
| | BUSH | 41% |
| | PEROT | 22% |
| 1988 | DUKAKIS | 43% |
| | BUSH | 56% |
| 1984 | MONDALE | 35% |
| | REAGAN | 64% |

CONGRESS (1994)

| SENATE | 2R | |
| HOUSE | 19D | 11R |

**Governor: Republican**

STATE LEGISLATURE (1994)

| SENATE | 17D | 14R |
| | 26 MEN | 5 WOMEN |
| HOUSE | 89D | 61R |
| | 121 MEN | 29 WOMEN |

## UTAH

Population  1,722,850  (35)
Per capita income $14,529 (48)
- 94%  White
- 1%  Black
- 5%  Hispanic
- 2%  Asian/Pacific Islander

**87% urban 13% rural**

ELECTORAL VOTES 5

PRESIDENTIAL VOTING

| 1992 | CLINTON | 25% |
| | BUSH | 43% |
| | PEROT | 27% |
| 1988 | DUKAKIS | 32% |
| | BUSH | 66% |
| 1984 | MONDALE | 25% |
| | REAGAN | 75% |

CONGRESS (1994)

| SENATE | 2R | |
| HOUSE | 1D | 2R |

**Governor: Republican**

STATE LEGISLATURE (1994)

| SENATE | 10D | 19R |
| | 26 MEN | 1 WOMEN |
| HOUSE | 20D | 55R |
| | 61 MEN | 14 WOMEN |

## VERMONT

Population  562,758  (48)
Per capita income $17,747 (26)
- 98%  White
- >1%  Black
- 1%  Hispanic
- 1%  Asian/Pacific Islander

**32% urban 68% rural**

ELECTORAL VOTES 3

PRESIDENTIAL VOTING

| 1992 | CLINTON | 46% |
| | BUSH | 30% |
| | PEROT | 23% |
| 1988 | DUKAKIS | 48% |
| | BUSH | 51% |
| 1984 | MONDALE | 41% |
| | REAGAN | 59% |

CONGRESS (1994)

SENATE 1D 1R
HOUSE 1IND.

**Governor: Democrat**

STATE LEGISLATURE (1994)

SENATE 12D 18R
20 MEN 10 WOMEN
HOUSE 86D 61R
107 MEN 43 WOMEN

## VIRGINIA

Population 6,187,358 (12)
Per capita income $19,976 (12)
77% White
19% Black
3% Hispanic
3% Asian/Pacific Islander
**69% urban 31% rural**

ELECTORAL VOTES 13
PRESIDENTIAL VOTING

| 1992 | CLINTON | 41% |
| | BUSH | 46% |
| | PEROT | 14% |
| 1988 | DUKAKIS | 39% |
| | BUSH | 60% |
| 1984 | MONDALE | 37% |
| | REAGAN | 62% |

CONGRESS (1994)

SENATE 1D 1R
HOUSE 6D 5R

**Governor: Republican**

STATE LEGISLATURE (1994)

SENATE 22D 18R
36 MEN 4 WOMEN
HOUSE 52D 47R
88 MEN 12 WOMEN

## WASHINGTON

Population 4,866,692 (18)
Per capita income $19,442 (13)
89% White
3% Black
4% Hispanic
4% Asian/Pacific Islander
**76% urban 24% rural**

ELECTORAL VOTES 11
PRESIDENTIAL VOTING

| 1992 | CLINTON | 43% |
| | BUSH | 32% |
| | PEROT | 24% |
| 1988 | DUKAKIS | 48% |
| | BUSH | 50% |

| 1984 | MONDALE | 43% |
| | REAGAN | 55% |

CONGRESS (1994)

SENATE 1D 1R
HOUSE 2D 7R

**Governor: Democrat**

STATE LEGISLATURE (1994)

SENATE 25D 24R
29 MEN 20 WOMEN
HOUSE 38D 60R
60 MEN 38 WOMEN

## WEST VIRGINIA

Population 1,793,477 (34)
Per capita income $14,174 (49)
96% White
3% Black
>1% Hispanic
>1% Asian/Pacific Islander
**36% urban 64% rural**

ELECTORAL VOTES 5
PRESIDENTIAL VOTING

| 1992 | CLINTON | 48% |
| | BUSH | 35% |
| | PEROT | 16% |
| 1988 | DUKAKIS | 52% |
| | BUSH | 47% |
| 1984 | MONDALE | 45% |
| | REAGAN | 55% |

CONGRESS (1994)

SENATE 2D
HOUSE 3D

**Governor: Democrat**

STATE LEGISLATURE (1994)

SENATE 26D 8R
29 MEN 5 WOMEN
HOUSE 69D 30R
84 MEN 15 WOMEN

## WISCONSIN

Population 4,891,769 (16)
Per capita income $18,046 (22)
92% White
5% Black
2% Hispanic
1% Asian/Pacific Islander
**66% urban 34% rural**

ELECTORAL VOTES 11
PRESIDENTIAL VOTING

| 1992 | CLINTON | 41% |
| | BUSH | 37% |

| | PEROT | 22% |
| 1988 | DUKAKIS | 51% |
| | BUSH | 48% |
| 1984 | MONDALE | 45% |
| | REAGAN | 54% |

CONGRESS (1994)

SENATE 2D
HOUSE 13D 6R

**Governor: Republican**

STATE LEGISLATURE (1994)

SENATE 16D 11R
25 MEN 8 WOMEN
HOUSE 48D 51R
75 MEN 24 WOMEN

## WYOMING

Population 463,588 (50)
Per capita income $17,188 (33)
94% White
1% Black
6% Hispanic
1% Asian/Pacific Islander
**65% urban 35% rural**

ELECTORAL VOTES 3
PRESIDENTIAL VOTING

| 1992 | CLINTON | 40% |
| | BUSH | 34% |
| | PEROT | 25% |
| 1988 | DUKAKIS | 39% |
| | BUSH | 61% |
| 1984 | MONDALE | 29% |
| | REAGAN | 71% |

CONGRESS (1994)

SENATE 2R
HOUSE 1R

**Governor: Republican**

STATE LEGISLATURE (1994)

SENATE 10D 20R
29 MEN 1 WOMEN
HOUSE 13D 47R
42 MEN 18 WOMEN

# THE CONSTITUTION
# OF THE UNITED STATES

## Preamble

We the People of the United States, in Order to form a more perfect Union, establish Justice, insure domestic Tranquility, provide for the common defence, promote the general Welfare, and secure the Blessings of Liberty to ourselves and our Posterity, do ordain and establish this Constitution for the United States of America.

## Article I

### Section 1.

All legislative Powers herein granted shall be vested in a Congress of the United States, which shall consist of a Senate and House of Representatives.

### Section 2.

The House of Representatives shall be composed of Members chosen every second Year by the People of the several States, and the Electors in each State shall have the Qualifications requisite for Electors of the most numerous Branch of the State Legislature.

No Person shall be a Representative who shall not have attained to the Age of twenty five Years, and been seven Years a Citizen of the United States, and who shall not, when elected, be an Inhabitant of that State in which he shall be chosen.

Representatives and direct Taxes shall be apportioned among the several States which may be included within this Union, according to their respective Numbers, which shall be determined by adding to the whole Number of free Persons, including those bound to Service for a Term of Years, and excluding Indians not taxed, three fifths of all other Persons. The actual Enumeration shall be made within three Years after the first Meeting of the Congress of the United States, and within every subsequent Term of ten Years, in such Manner as they shall by Law direct. The Number of Representatives shall not exceed one for every thirty Thousand, but each State shall have at Least one Representative; and until such enumeration shall be made, the State of New Hampshire shall be entitled to choose three, Massachusetts eight, Rhode-Island and Providence Plantations one, Connecticut five, New York six, New Jersey four, Pennsylvania eight, Delaware one, Maryland six, Virginia ten, North Carolina five, South Carolina five, and Georgia three.

When vacancies happen in the Representation from any State, the Executive Authority thereof shall issue Writs of Election to fill such Vacancies.

The House of Representatives shall choose their speaker and other Officers; and shall have the sole Power of Impeachment.

## Section 3.

The Senate of the United States shall be composed of two Senators from each State, chosen by the Legislature thereof, for six Years; and each Senator shall have one Vote.

Immediately after they shall be assembled in Consequence of the first Election, they shall be divided as equally as may be into three Classes. The Seats of the Senators of the first Class shall be vacated at the Expiration of the second Year, of the second Class at the Expiration of the fourth Year, and of the third Class at the Expiration of the sixth Year, so that one third may be chosen every second Year; and if Vacancies happen by Resignation, or otherwise, during the Recess of the Legislature of any State, the Executive thereof may make temporary Appointments until the next Meeting of the Legislature, which shall then fill such Vacancies.

No Person shall be a Senator who shall not have attained to the Age of thirty Years, and been nine Years a citizen of the United States, and who shall not, when elected, be an Inhabitant of that State for which he shall be chosen.

The Vice President of the United States shall be President of the Senate, but shall have no Vote, unless they be equally divided.

The Senate shall choose their other Officers, and also a President pro tempore, in the Absence of the Vice President, or when he shall exercise the Office of President of the United States.

The Senate shall have the sole Power to try all Impeachments. When sitting for that Purpose, they shall be on Oath or Affirmation. When the President of the United States is tried, the Chief Justice shall preside: And no Person shall be convicted without the Concurrence of two thirds of the Members present.

Judgment in Cases of Impeachment shall not extend further than to removal from Office, and disqualification to hold and enjoy any Office of honor, Trust or Profit under the United States: but the Party convicted shall nevertheless be liable and subject to Indictment, Trial, Judgment and Punishment, according to law.

## Section 4.

The Times, Places, and Manner of holding Elections for Senators and Representatives, shall be prescribed in each State by the Legislature thereof; but the Congress may at any time by Law make or alter such Regulations, except as to the Places of choosing Senators.

The Congress shall assemble at least once in every Year, and such Meeting shall be on the first Monday in December, unless they shall by Law appoint a different Day.

## Section 5.

Each House shall be the Judge of the Elections, Returns, and Qualifications of its own Members, and a Majority of each shall constitute a Quorum to do Business; but a smaller Number may adjourn from day to day, and may be authorized to compel the Attendance of absent Members, in such Manner, and under such Penalties as each

House may provide.

Each House may determine the Rules of its Proceedings, punish its Members for disorderly Behaviour, and, with the Concurrence of two thirds, expel a Member.

Each House shall keep a journal of its Proceedings, and from time to time publish the same, excepting such Parts as may in their Judgment require Secrecy; and the Yeas and Nays of the Members of either House on any question shall, at the Desire of one fifth of those Present, be entered on the journal.

Neither House, during the Session of Congress, shall, without the Consent of the other, adjourn for more than three days, nor to any other Place than that in which the two Houses shall be sitting.

## Section 6.

The Senators and Representatives shall receive a Compensation for their Services, to be ascertained by Law, and paid out of the Treasury of the United States. They shall in all Cases, except Treason, Felony and Breach of the Peace, be privileged from Arrest during their Attendance at the Session of their respective Houses, and in going to and returning from the same; and for any Speech or Debate in either House, they shall not be questioned in any other Place.

No Senator or Representative shall, during the Time for which he was elected, be appointed to any civil Office under the Authority of the United States, which shall have been created, or the Emoluments whereof shall have been increased during such time; and no Person holding any Office under the United States, shall be a Member of either House during his Continuance in Office.

## Section 7.

All Bills for raising Revenue shall originate in the House of Representatives; but the Senate may propose or concur with Amendments as on other Bills.

Every Bill which shall have passed the House of Representatives and the Senate, shall, before it become a Law, be presented to the President of the United States; If he approve he shall sign it, but if not he shall return it, with his Objections to that House in which it shall have originated, who shall enter the Objections at large on their Journal, and proceed to reconsider it. If after such Reconsideration two thirds of that House shall agree to pass the Bill, it shall be sent, together with the Objections, to the other House, by which it shall likewise be reconsidered, and if approved by two thirds of that House, it shall become a Law. But in all such Cases the Votes of both Houses shall be determined by Yeas and Nays, and the Names of the Persons voting for and against the Bill shall be entered on the Journal of each House respectively. If any Bill shall not be returned by the President within ten Days (Sundays excepted) after it shall have been presented to him, the Same shall be a Law, in like Manner as if he had signed it, unless the Congress by their Adjournment prevent its Return, in which Case it shall not be a Law.

Every Order, Resolution, or Vote to which the Concurrence of the Senate and House of Representatives may be necessary (except on a question of Adjournment) shall be presented to the President of the United States; and before the Same shall take Effect, shall be approved by him, or being disapproved by him, shall be repassed by two thirds of the Senate and House of Representatives, according to the Rules and Limitations prescribed in the Case of a Bill.

**Section 8.**

The Congress shall have Power To lay and collect Taxes, Duties, Imposts and Excises, to pay the Debts and provide for the common Defence and general Welfare of the United States; but all Duties, Imposts and Excises shall be uniform throughout the United States;

To borrow Money on the Credit of the United States;

To regulate Commerce with foreign Nations, and among the several States, and with the Indian Tribes;

To establish an uniform Rule of Naturalization, and uniform Laws on the subject of Bankruptcies throughout the United States;

To coin Money, regulate the Value thereof, and of foreign Coin, and fix the Standard of Weights and Measures;

To provide for the Punishment of counterfeiting the securities and current Coin of the United States;

To establish Post Offices and post Roads;

To promote the Progress of Science and useful Arts, by securing for limited Times to Authors and Inventors the exclusive Right to their respective Writings and Discoveries;

To constitute Tribunals inferior to the supreme Court;

To define and punish Piracies and Felonies committed on the high Seas, and Offences against the Law of Nations;

To declare War, grant Letters of Marque and Reprisal, and make Rules concerning Captures on Land and Water;

To raise and support Armies, but no Appropriation of Money to that Use shall be for a longer Term than two Years;

To provide and maintain a Navy;

To make Rules for the Government and Regulation of the land and naval Forces;

To provide for calling forth the Militia to execute the Laws of the Union, suppress Insurrections and repel Invasions;

To provide for organizing, arming, and disciplining the Militia, and for governing such Part of them as may be employed in the Service of the United States, reserving to the States respectively, the Appointment of the Officers, and the Authority of training the Militia according to the discipline prescribed by Congress;

To exercise exclusive Legislation in all Cases whatsoever, over such District (not exceeding ten Miles square) as may, by Cession of particular States, and the Acceptance of Congress, become the Seat of the Government of the United States, and to exercise like Authority over all Places purchased by the Consent of the Legislature of the State in which the Same shall be for the Erection of Forts, Magazines, Arsenals, dock-Yards, and other needful Buildings; And To make all Laws which shall be necessary and proper for carrying into Execution the foregoing Powers, and all other Powers vested by this Constitution in the Government of the United States, or in any Department or Officer thereof.

**Section 9.**

The Migration of Importation of such Persons as any of the States now existing shall think proper to admit, shall not be prohibited by the Congress prior to the Year one thousand eight hundred and eight, but a Tax or duty may be imposed on such Importation, not exceeding ten dollars for each Person.

The Privilege of the Writ of Habeas Corpus shall not be suspended, unless when in Cases of Rebellion or Invasion the public Safety may require it.

No Bill of Attainder or ex post facto Law shall be passed.

No Capitation, or other direct, Tax shall be laid, unless in Proportion to the Census or Enumeration herein before directed to be taken.

No Tax or Duty shall be laid on Articles exported from any State.

No preference shall be given by any Regulation of Commerce or Revenue to the Ports of one State over those of another: nor shall Vessels bound to, or from, one State, be obliged to enter, clear, or pay Duties in another.

No money shall be drawn from the Treasury, but in Consequence of Appropriations made by Law; and a regular Statement and Account of the Receipts and Expenditures of all public Money shall be published from time to time.

No Title of Nobility shall be granted by the United States: And no Person holding any Office of Profit or Trust under them, shall, without the Consent of the Congress, accept of any present, Emolument, Office, or Title, of any kind whatever, from any King, Prince, or foreign State.

**Section 10.**

No State shall enter into any Treaty, Alliance, or Confederation; grant Letters of Marque and Reprisal; coin Money; emits Bills of Credit; make any Thing but gold and silver Coin a Tender in Payment of Debts; pass any Bill of Attainder, ex post facto Law, or Law impairing the Obligation of Contracts, or grant any Title of Nobility.

No State shall, without the Consent of the Congress, lay any Imposts or Duties on Imports or Exports, except what may be absolutely necessary for executing it's inspection Laws: and the net Produce of all Duties and Imposts, laid by any State on Imports or Exports, shall be for the Use of the Treasury of the United States; and all

such Laws shall be subject to the Revision and Control of the Congress.

No State shall, without the Consent of the Congress, lay any Duty of Tonnage, keep Troops, or Ships of War in time of Peace, enter into any Agreement or Compact with another State, or with a foreign Power, or engage in War, unless actually invaded, or in such imminent Danger as will not admit of delay.

## Article II

### Section 1.

The executive Power shall be vested in a President of the United States of America. He shall hold his Office during the Term of four Years, and, together with the Vice President, chosen for the same term, be elected, as follows

Each State shall appoint, in such Manner as the Legislature thereof may direct, a Number of Electors, equal to the whole Number of Senators and Representatives to which the State may be entitled in the Congress: but no Senator or Representative, or Person holding an Office of Trust or Profit under the United States, shall be appointed an Elector.

The Electors shall meet in their respective States, and vote by Ballot for two Persons, of whom one at least shall not be an Inhabitant of the same State with themselves. And they shall make a List of all the Persons voted for, and of the Number of Votes for each; which List they shall sign and certify, and transmit sealed to the Seat of the Government of the United States, directed to the President of the Senate. The President of the Senate shall, in the Presence of the Senate and House of Representatives, open all the Certificates, and the Votes shall then be counted. The Person having the greatest Number of Votes shall be the President, if such Number be a majority of the whole Number of Electors appointed; and if there be no more than one who have such Majority, and have an equal Number of Votes, then the House of Representatives shall immediately choose by Ballot one of them for President: and if no Person have a Majority, then from the five highest on the List the said House shall in like Manner choose the President. But in choosing the President, the Votes shall be taken by the states, the Representation from each State having one Vote; A quorum for this Purpose shall consist of a Member or Members from two thirds of the States, and a Majority of all the States shall be necessary to a Choice. In every Case, after the Choice of the President, the Person having the greatest Number of Votes of the Electors shall be the Vice President. But if there should remain two or more who have equal Votes, the Senate shall choose from them by Ballot the Vice President.

The Congress may determine the Time of choosing the Electors, and the Day on which they shall give their Votes; which Day shall be the same throughout the United States.

No Person except a natural born Citizen, or a Citizen of the United States, at the

time of the Adoption of this Constitution, shall be eligible to the Office of President; neither shall any Person be eligible to that Office who shall not have attained to the Age of thirty five Years, and been fourteen Years a Resident within the United States.

In Case of the Removal of the President from Office, or of his Death, Resignation, or Inability to discharge the Powers and Duties of the said Office, the Same shall devolve on the Vice President, and the Congress may by Law provide for the Case of Removal, Death, Resignation or Inability, both of the President and Vice President, declaring what Officer shall then act as President, and such Officer shall act accordingly, until the Disability be removed, or a President shall be elected.

The President shall, at stated Times, receive for his Services, a Compensation, which shall neither be increased nor diminished during the Period for which he shall have been elected, and he shall not receive within that Period any other Emolument from the United States, or any of them.

Before he enter on the Execution of his Office, he shall take the following Oath or Affirmation: ÕI do solemnly swear (or affirm) that I will faithfully execute the Office of President of the United States, and will to the best of my Ability, preserve, protect and defend the Constitution of the United States. Œ

## Section 2.

The President shall be Commander in Chief of the Army and Navy of the United States, and of the Militia of the several States, when called into the actual Service of the United States; he may require the Opinion, in writing, of the principal Officer in each of the executive Departments, upon any Subject relating to the Duties of their respective Offices, and he shall have Power to grant Reprieves and Pardons for Offences against the United States, except in Cases of Impeachment.

He shall have Power, by and with the Advice and Consent of the Senate, to make Treaties, provided two thirds of the Senators present concur; and he shall nominate, and by and with the Advice and Consent of the Senate, shall appoint Ambassadors, other public Ministers and Consuls, Judges of the supreme Court, and all other Officers of the United States, whose Appointments are not herein otherwise provided for, and which shall be established by Law: but the Congress may by Law vest the Appointment of such inferior Officers, as they think proper, in the President alone, in the Courts of Law, or in the Heads of Departments.

The President shall have Power to fill up all Vacancies that may happen during the Recess of the Senate, by granting Commissions which shall expire at the End of their next Session.

## Section 3.

He shall from time to time give to the Congress Information of the State of the Union, and recommend to their Consideration such Measures as he shall judge necessary and

expedient; he may, on extraordinary Occasions, convene both Houses, or either of them, and in Case of Disagreement between them, with Respect to the Time of Adjournment, he may adjourn them to such Time as he shall think proper; he shall receive Ambassadors and other public Ministers; he shall take Care that the Laws be faithfully executed, and shall Commission all the Officers of the United States.

**Section 4.**

The President, Vice President, and all civil Officers of the United States, shall be removed from Office on Impeachment for, and Conviction of, Treason, Bribery, or other High Crimes and Misdemeanors.

## Article III

**Section 1.**

The judicial Power of the United States, shall be vested in one supreme Court, and in such inferior Courts as the Congress may from time to time ordain and establish. The Judges, both of the supreme and inferior Courts, shall hold their Offices during good Behaviour, and shall, at stated Times, receive for their Services, a Compensation, which shall not be diminished during their Continuance in Office.

**Section 2.**

The judicial Power shall extend to all Cases, in Law and Equity, arising under this Constitution, the Laws of the United States, and Treaties made, or which shall be made, under their Authority; to all Cases affecting Ambassadors, other public Ministers and Consuls; to all Cases of admiralty and maritime Jurisdiction; to Controversies to which the United States shall be a Party; to Controversies between two or more States; between a State and Citizens of another state; between Citizens of different States; between Citizens of the same State claiming Lands under Grants of different States, and between a State, or the Citizens thereof, and foreign States, Citizens or Subjects.

In all Cases affecting Ambassadors, other public Ministers and Consuls, and those in which a State shall be Party, the supreme Court shall have original Jurisdiction. In all the other Cases before mentioned, the supreme Court shall have appellate Jurisdiction, both as to Law and Fact, with such Exceptions, and under such Regulations as the Congress shall make.

The Trial of all Crimes, except in Cases of Impeachment, shall be by Jury; and such Trial shall be held in the State where the said Crimes shall have been committed; but when not committed within any State, the Trial shall be at such Place or Places as the Congress may by Law have directed.

**Section 3.**

Treason against the United States, shall consist only in levying War against them, or in adhering to their Enemies, giving them Aid and Comfort. No Person shall be convict-

ed of Treason unless on the Testimony of two Witnesses to the same overt Act, or on Confession in open Court.

The Congress shall have Power to declare the Punishment of Treason, but no Attainder of Treason shall work Corruption of Blood, or Forfeiture except during the Life of the Person attainted.

## Article IV

### Section 1.

Full Faith and Credit shall be given in each State to the public Acts, Records, and judicial Proceedings of every other State. And the Congress may be general Laws prescribe the Manner in which such Acts, Records and Proceedings shall be proved, and the Effect thereof.

### Section 2.

The Citizens of each State shall be entitled to all Privileges and Immunities of Citizens in the several States.

A Person charged in any State with Treason, Felony, or other Crime, who shall flee from Justice, and be found in another State, shall on Demand of the executive Authority of the State from which he fled, be delivered up, to be removed to the State having Jurisdiction of the Crime.

No Person held to Service or Labour in one State, under the Laws thereof, escaping into another, shall, in Consequence of any Law or Regulation therein, be discharged from such Service or Labour, but shall be delivered up on Claim of the Party to whom such Service or Labour may be due.

### Section 3.

New States may be admitted by the Congress into this Union; but no new State shall be formed or erected within the Jurisdiction of any other State; nor any State be formed by the Junction of two or more States, or Parts of States, without the Consent of the Legislatures of the States concerned as well as of the Congress.

The Congress shall have Power to dispose of and make all needful Rules and Regulations respecting the Territory or other Property belonging to the United States; and nothing in this Constitution shall be so construed as to Prejudice any Claims of the United States, or of any particular State.

### Section 4.

The United States shall guarantee to every State in this Union a Republican Form of Government, and shall protect each of them against Invasion; and on Application of the Legislature, or of the Executive (when the Legislature cannot be convened) against domestic Violence.

## Article V

The Congress, whenever two thirds of both Houses shall deem it necessary, shall

propose Amendments to this Constitution, or, on the Application of the Legislatures of two thirds of the several States, shall call a Convention for proposing Amendments, which, in either Case, shall be valid to all Intents and Purposes, as Part of this Constitution, when ratified by the Legislatures of three fourths of the several States, or by Conventions in three fourths thereof, as the one or the other Mode of Ratification may be proposed by the Congress; Provided that no Amendment which may be made prior to the Year One Thousand eight hundred and eight shall in any Manner affect the first and fourth Clauses in the Ninth Section of the first Article; and that no State, without its Consent, shall be deprived of its equal Suffrage in the Senate.

## Article VI

All Debts contracted and Engagements entered into, before the Adoption of this Constitution, shall be as valid against the United States under this Constitution, as under the Confederation.

This Constitution, and the Laws of the United States which shall be made in Pursuance thereof; and all Treaties made, or which shall be made, under the Authority of the United States, shall be the supreme Law of the Land; and the Judges in every State shall be bound thereby, any Thing in the Constitution or Laws of any State to the Contrary notwithstanding.

The Senators and Representatives before mentioned, and the Members of the several State Legislatures, and all executive and judicial Officers, both of the United States and of the several States, shall be bound by Oath or Affirmation, to support this Constitution; but no religious Test shall ever be required as a Qualification to any Office or public Trust under the United States.

## Article VII

The Ratification of the Conventions of nine States, shall be sufficient for the Establishment of this Constitution between the States so ratifying the Same.

## Amendments to the Constitution

(The first ten Amendments were ratified Dec. 15, 1791, and form what is known as the Bill of Rights.)

## Amendment 1

Congress shall make no law respecting an establishment of religion, or prohibiting the free exercise thereof; or abridging the freedom of speech, or of the press, or the right of the people peaceably to assemble, and to petition the Government for a redress of grievances.

## Amendment 2
A well regulated Militia, being necessary to the security of a free State, the right of the people to keep and bear Arms, shall not be infringed.
## Amendment 3
No Soldier shall, in time of peace be quartered in any house, without the consent of the Owner, nor in time of war, but in a manner to be prescribed by law.
## Amendment 4
The right of the people to be secure in their persons, houses, papers, and effects, against unreasonable searches and seizures, shall not be violated, and no Warrants shall issue, but upon probable cause, supported by Oath or affirmation, and particularly describing the place to be searched, and the persons or things to be seized.
## Amendment 5
No person shall be held to answer for a capital, or otherwise infamous crime, unless on a presentment or indictment of a Grand Jury, except in cases arising in the land or naval forces, or in the Militia, when in actual service in time of War or public danger; nor shall any person be subject for the same offence to be twice put in jeopardy of life or limb; nor shall be compelled in any criminal case to be a witness against himself, nor be deprived of life, liberty, or property, without due process of law; nor shall private property be taken for public use, without just compensation.
## Amendment 6
In all criminal prosecutions, the accused shall enjoy the right to a speedy and public trial, by an impartial jury of the State and district wherein the crime shall have been committed, which district shall have been previously ascertained by law, and to be informed of the nature and cause of the accusation; to be confronted with the witnesses against him; to have compulsory process for obtaining witnesses in his favor, and to have the Assistance of Counsel for his defence.
## Amendment 7
In Suits at common law, where the value in controversy shall exceed twenty dollars, the right of trial by jury shall be preserved, and no fact tried by a jury, shall be otherwise re-examined in any Court of the United States, than according to the rules of the common law.
## Amendment 8
Excessive bail shall not be required, nor excessive fines imposed, nor cruel and unusual punishments inflicted.
## Amendment 9
The enumeration in the Constitution, of certain rights, shall not be construed to deny or disparage others retained by the people.
## Amendment 10
The powers not delegated to the United States by the Constitution, nor prohibited by

it to the States, are reserved to the States respectively, or to the people.

## Amendment 11

(Ratified Feb. 7, 1795)

The Judicial power of the United States shall not be construed to extend to any suit in law or equity, commenced or prosecuted against one of the United States by Citizens of another State, or by Citizens or Subjects of any Foreign State.

## Amendment 12

(Ratified July 27, 1804)

The Electors shall meet in their respective States and vote by ballot for President and Vice President, one of whom, at least, shall not be an inhabitant of the same State with themselves; they shall name in their ballots the person voted for as President, and in distinct ballots the person voted for as Vice President, and they shall make distinct lists of all persons voted for as President, and of all persons voted for as Vice President, and of the number of votes for each, which lists they shall sign and certify, and transmit sealed to the seat of the government of the United States, directed to the President of the Senate; The President of the Senate shall, in the presence of the Senate and House of Representatives, open all the certificates and the votes shall then be counted; The person having the greatest number of votes for President, shall be the President, if such number be a majority of the whole number of Electors appointed; and if no person have such majority, then from the persons having the highest numbers not exceeding three on the list of those voted for as President, the House of Representatives shall choose immediately, by ballot, the President. But in choosing the President, the votes shall be taken by states, the representation from each state having one vote; a quorum for this purpose shall consist of a member or members from two-thirds of the states, and a majority of all the states shall be necessary to a choice. And if the House of Representatives shall not choose a President whenever the right of choice shall devolve upon them, before the fourth day of March next following, then the Vice President shall act as President, as in the case of the death or other constitutional disability of the President. The person having the greatest number of votes as Vice President, shall be the Vice President, if such number be a majority of the whole number of Electors appointed, and if no person have a majority, then from the two highest numbers on the list, the Senate shall choose the Vice President; a quorum for the purpose shall consist of two-thirds of the whole number of Senators, and a majority of the whole number shall be necessary to a choice. But no person constitutionally ineligible to the office of President shall be eligible to that of Vice President of the United States.

## Amendment 13

(Ratified Dec. 6, 1865)

## Section 1.

Neither Slavery, nor involuntary servitude, except as a punishment for crime whereof the party shall have been duly convicted, shall exist within the United States, or any place subject to their jurisdiction.

## Section 2.

Congress shall have power to enforce this article by appropriate legislation.

## Amendment 14

(Ratified July 9, 1868)

## Section 1.

All persons born or naturalized in the United States, and subject to the jurisdiction thereof, are citizens of the United States and of the State wherein they reside. No State shall make or enforce any law which shall abridge the privileges or immunities of citizens of the United States; nor shall any State deprive any person of life, liberty, or property, without due process of law; nor deny to any person within its jurisdiction the equal protection of the laws.

## Section 2.

Representatives shall be apportioned among the several States according to their respective numbers, counting the whole number of persons in each State, excluding Indians not taxed. But when the right to vote at any election for the choice of electors for President and Vice President of the United States, Representatives in Congress, the Executive and Judicial officers of a State, or the members of the Legislature thereof, is denied to any of the male inhabitants of such State, being twenty-one years of age, and citizens of the United States, or in any way abridged, except for participation in rebellion, or other crime, the basis of representation therein shall be reduced in the proportion which the number of such male citizens shall bear to the whole number of male citizens twenty-one years of age in such State.

## Section 3.

No person shall be a Senator or Representative in Congress, or elector of President and Vice President, or hold any office, civil or military, under the United States, or under any State, who, having previously taken an oath, as a member of Congress, or as an officer of the United States, or as a member of any State legislature, or as an executive or judicial officer of any State, to support the Constitution of the United States, shall have engaged in insurrection or rebellion against the same, or given aid or comfort to the enemies thereof. But Congress may by a vote of two-thirds of each House, remove such disability.

## Section 4.

The validity of the public debt of the United States, authorized by law, including debts incurred for payment of pensions and bounties for services in suppressing

insurrection or rebellion, shall not be questioned. But neither the United States nor any State shall assume or pay any debt or obligation incurred in aid of insurrection or rebellion against the United States, or any claim for the loss or emancipation of any slave; but all such debts, obligations and claims shall be held illegal and void.

**Section 5.**

The Congress shall have power to enforce, by appropriate legislation, the provision of this article.

**Amendment 15**

(Ratified Feb. 3, 1870)

**Section 1.**

The right of citizens of the United States to vote shall not be denied or abridged by the United States or by any State on account of race, color or previous condition of servitude.

**Section 2.**

The Congress shall have power to enforce this article by appropriate legislation.

**Amendment 16**

(Ratified Feb. 3, 1913)

The Congress shall have power to lay and collect taxes on incomes, from whatever source derived, without apportionment among the several States, and without regard to any census or enumeration.

**Amendment 17**

(Ratified April 8, 1913)

The Senate of the United States shall be composed of two Senators from each State, elected by the people thereof for six years; and each Senator shall have one vote. The electors in each State shall have the qualifications requisite for electors of the most numerous branch of the State legislatures.

When vacancies happen in the representation of any State in the Senate, the executive authority of such State shall issue writs of election to fill such vacancies: Provided, That the legislature of any State may empower the executive thereof to make temporary appointments until the people fill the vacancies by election as the legislature may direct.

This amendment shall not be so construed as to affect the election or term of any Senator chosen before it becomes valid as part of the Constitution.

**Amendment 18**

(Ratified Jan. 16, 1919)

**Section 1.**

After one year from the ratification of this article the manufacture, sale, or transportation of intoxicating liquors within, the importation thereof into, or the expor-

tation thereof from the United States and all territory subject to the jurisdiction thereof for beverage purposes is hereby prohibited.

**Section 2.**

The Congress and the several States shall have concurrent power to enforce this article by appropriate legislation.

**Section 3.**

This article shall be inoperative unless it shall have been ratified as an amendment to the Constitution by the legislatures of the several States, as provided in the Constitution, within seven years from the date of the submission hereof to the States by the Congress.

**Amendment 19**

(Ratified Aug. 26, 1920)

The right of citizens of the United States to vote shall not be denied or abridged by the United States or by any State on account of sex.

Congress shall have power to enforce this article by appropriate legislation.

**Amendment 20**

(Ratified Jan. 23, 1933)

**Section 1.**

The terms of the President and Vice President shall end at noon on the 20th day of January, and the terms of Senators and Representatives at noon on the third day of January, of the years in which such terms would have ended if this article had not been ratified; and the terms of their successors shall then begin.

**Section 2.**

The Congress shall assemble at least once in every year, and such meeting shall begin at noon on the third day of January, unless they shall by law appoint a different day.

**Section 3.**

If, at the time fixed for the beginning of the term of the President, the President elect shall have died, the Vice President elect shall become President. If a President shall not have been chosen before the time fixed for the beginning of his term, or if the President elect shall have failed to qualify, then the Vice President elect shall act as President until a President shall have qualified; and the Congress may by law provide for the case wherein neither a President elect nor a Vice President elect shall have qualified, declaring who shall then act as President, or the manner in which one who is to act shall be selected, and such person shall act accordingly until a President or Vice President shall have qualified.

**Section 4.**

The Congress may by law provide for the case of the death of any of the persons from whom the House of Representatives may choose a President whenever the right of

choice shall have devolved upon them, and for the case of the death of any of the persons from whom the Senate may choose a Vice President whenever the right of choice shall have devolved upon them.

**Section 5.**

Sections 1 and 2 shall take effect on the 15th day of October following the ratification of this article.

**Section 6.**

This article shall be inoperative unless it shall have been ratified as an amendment to the Constitution by the legislatures of three-fourths of the several States within seven years from the date of its submission.

**Amendment 21**

(Ratified Dec. 5, 1933)

**Section 1.**

The eighteenth article of amendment to the Constitution of the United States is hereby repealed.

**Section 2.**

The transportation or importation into any State, Territory, or possession of the United States for delivery or use therein of intoxicating liquors, in violation of the laws thereof, is hereby prohibited.

**Section 3.**

This article shall be inoperative unless it shall have been ratified as an amendment to the Constitution by conventions in the several States, as provided in the Constitution, within seven years from the date of the submission hereof to the States by the Congress.

**Amendment 22**

(Ratified Feb. 27, 1951)

**Section 1.**

No person shall be elected to the office of the President more than twice, and no person who has held the office of President, or acted as President, for more than two years of a term to which some other person was elected President shall be elected to the office of the President more than once. But this Article shall not apply to any person holding the office of President when this Article was proposed by the Congress, and shall not prevent any person who may be holding the office of President, or acting as President, during the term within which this Article becomes operative from holding the office of President or acting as President during the remainder of such term.

**Section 2.**

This article shall be inoperative unless it shall have been ratified as an amendment

to the Constitution by the legislatures of three-fourths of the several States within seven years from the date of its submission to the States by the Congress.

## Amendment 23

(Ratified March 29, 1961)

### Section 1.

The District constituting the seat of Government of the United States shall appoint in such manner as the Congress may direct:

A number of electors of President and Vice President equal to the whole number of Senators and Representatives in Congress to which the District would be entitled if it were a State, but in no event more than the least populous State; they shall be in addition to those appointed by the States, but they shall be considered, for the purposes of the election of President and Vice President, to be electors appointed by a State; and they shall meet in the District and perform such duties as provided by the twelfth article of amendment.

### Section 2.

The Congress shall have power to enforce this article by appropriate legislation.

## Amendment 24

(Ratified Jan. 23, 1964)

### Section 1.

The right of citizens of the United States to vote in any primary or other election for President or Vice President, for electors for President or Vice President, or for Senator or Representative in Congress, shall not be denied or abridged by the United States or any State by reason of failure to pay any poll tax or other tax.

### Section 2.

The Congress shall have power to enforce this article by appropriate legislation.

## Amendment 25

(Ratified Feb. 10, 1967)

### Section 1.

In case of the removal of the President from office or of his death or resignation, the Vice President shall become President.

### Section 2.

Whenever there is a vacancy in the office of the Vice President, the President shall nominate a Vice President who shall take office upon confirmation by a majority vote of both Houses of Congress.

### Section 3.

Whenever the President transmits to the President pro tempore of the Senate and the Speaker of the House of Representatives his written declaration that he is unable to discharge the powers and duties of his office, and until he transmits to them a written declaration to the contrary, such powers and duties shall be discharged by the Vice President as Acting President.

**Section 4.**

Whenever the Vice President and a majority of either the principal officers of the executive departments or of such other body as Congress may by law provide, transmit to the President pro tempore of the Senate and the Speaker of the House of Representatives their written declaration that the President is unable to discharge the powers and duties of his office, the Vice President shall immediately assume the powers and duties of the office as Acting President.

Thereafter, when the President transmits to the President pro tempore of the Senate and the Speaker of the House of Representatives his written declaration that no inability exists, he shall resume the powers and duties of his office unless the Vice President and a majority of either the principal officers of the executive department or of such other body as Congress may by law provide, transmit within four days to the President pro tempore of the Senate and the Speaker of the House of Representatives their written declaration that the President is unable to discharge the powers and duties of his office. Thereupon Congress shall decide the issue, assembling within forty-eight hours for that purpose if not in session. If the Congress, within twenty-one days after receipt of the latter written declaration, or, if Congress is not in session, within twenty-one days after Congress is required to assemble, determines by two-thirds vote of both Houses that the President is unable to discharge the powers and duties of his office, the Vice President shall continue to discharge the same as Acting President; otherwise, the President shall resume the powers and duties of his office.

**Amendment 26**

(Ratified June 30, 1971)

**Section 1.**

The right of citizens of the United States, who are 18 years of age or older, to vote shall not be denied or abridged by the United States or by any State on account of age.

**Section 2.**

The Congress shall have power to enforce this article by appropriate legislation.

# GLOSSARY

**Administration**: The period of time in which a president is in office; also, the collective group of officials who serve during a president's term in office. For example, the Persian Gulf War occurred during the Bush administration.

**Affirmative action:** Government and private policies aimed at compensating for previous pattern of discrimination against minorities, such as blacks or women.

**Amendment:** A change in a bill. Also, a revision in the U. S. Constitution.

**Anti-Federalists:** A political party, lead by Thomas Jefferson in the late 1700s, that was firmly opposed to a strong federal government

**Apportionment:**The distribution of congressional districts among the states.

**Apprenticeship:** A folkway of Congress suggesting that newcomers should learn their way around and carefully study senior members before plunging into their duties.

**Appropriation:** A law that authorizes money to be spent by the federal treasury.

**Balancing the ticket:** A tactic used by presidential candidates in selecting a vice-presidential nominee with contrasting political and personal traits to maximize the ticket's appeal to as many votes as possible.

**Bandwagon:** A political campaign that is far in front of the opposition. Thus, *jumping on the bandwagon*, is to join the campaign of the candidate who seems to be the likely winner. Derives from the old practice of candidates to stage colorful parades: leading the parade was a musical band, perched on a large wagon. As a show of support for the candidate, local politicians would leap on to the bandwagon.

**Bicameral:** A legislature with two houses, such as the House and Senate. The American Congress is a bicameral legislature, consisting of the Senate and the House of Representatives.

**Bill:** A proposed law. There are two types of bills, public and private. A private bill is designed to help a private citizen. A public bill is designed to make broad changes which affect many people, and sometimes the entire country.

**Bill of Rights:** The first ten amendments to the Constitution, which guarantee a variety of personal liberties.

**Bureaucracy:** A large, hierarchical administrative organization with complex rules and regulations.

**Cabinet:** An unofficial group of advisors to a president which consists of the heads of the fourteen major executive departments of government and other important presidential advisors.

**Campaign:** The process by which a candidate attempts to persuade the electorate to vote for him or her.

**Candidate:** A person seeking public office.

**Capitol Hill:** The home of our Congress; a small hill in Washington, D.C., where the Capitol Building is situated. Called *the hill* for short.

**Casework:** The errands that Congressmen and their staffs perform for the people from their district or state. Examples of casework are when a congressmen tracks down a voter's social security check, or arranges for emergency leave for someone in the Armed Forces.

**Caucus/Conference:** A meeting of all members of one party in one House of Congress. Democrats use the term caucus; Republican prefer conference. .

**Checks and Balances:** The built-in structure of our federal government that distributes power so that no one branch or person can become too dominant.

**Civil liberties:** The rights guaranteed to individuals by the Constitution, most specifically the Bill of Rights.

**Civil rights:** The right of citizens not to be discriminated against due to their race, gender, religion, national origin, or physical disability.

**Civil service:** The term used for the system of hiring and discharging government employees solely on the basis of merit.

**Cloture:** A vote in order to end debate; sixty senators must support the motion for cloture to be successful.

**Coalition:** A group of supporters that a candidate must assemble to help whom win the election. A coalition might contribute money, endorsements, and workers to the campaign effort.

**Coattail Effect:** The voting pattern that results when an overwhelmingly popular presidential candidate enables other members of his party, such as are presentatives and senators, to coast into office with him by *hanging on to his coattails.*

**Commander-in chief:** The presidential role which places the nation's chief executive as supreme commander of the armed forces.

**Committee on Committees:** A group of members set up by each party in each house of congress to make committee assignments.

**Confederation:** A political system in which the states have the ultimate power and the central government is weak.

**Conference Committee:** A temporary panel consisting of representatives and senators who iron out differences in bills which have passed through each house of Congress. Once the conference committee forges the two versions into one, the bill goes back to each house for final approval, and then to the president.

**Congress:** The collective term for the U.S. House of Representatives and the Senate; also, used to identify a specific two year period, such as the 102nd Congress.

**Dealignment:** The process by which the loyalty and attachment of voters to the major political parties is weakened.

**Delegate:** An official representative to a convention, such as a national political convention.

**Delegated powers:** Powers specifically listed in the Constitution as belonging to Congress, such as the power to declare war or to borrow money.

**Democracy:** A government in which the supreme power is vested in the people and exercised by them directly or indirectly through a system of representation based on free elections. The American government is a representative democracy.

**Direct democracy:** A type of democracy in which all the citizens participate in political decision making, such as the New England town meetings.

**Direct lobbying:** Lobbying directed at elected or appointed government officials.

**Due-process:** The Constitutional guarantee that the government will not deprive any person of life, liberty, or property by any unfair, arbitrary, or unreasonable action.

**Electoral College:** The 538 electors who actually elect the President and Vice-President of the United States after the popular votes have been cast. When we vote for candidates for these offices, we actually are voting for electors, who in turn cast their ballots for the candidate who wins the majority of votes in the state. Each state has a number of electors equal to

it's representation in Congress; thus, if a state has four Representatives and two Senators, it would have six electors—and six electoral votes. All of a states electors are expected to cast their electoral votes for the candidate who received the most votes in their state.

**Electors:** Members of the electoral college.

**Electorate:** The body of people eligible to vote.

**Endorsement:** A statement of support for a candidate. It can come from an individual, an organization, a newspaper, or a radio or television station.

**Equal time provision:** The FCC requirement that radio or television states make air time available to all candidates running for political office.

**Executive agreement:** A presidential agreement with another head of state that has the power of law but does not require Senate approval.

**Executive Branch:** The part of the federal government headed by the president. It includes a host of departments and agencies, all of which fall under the president's control.

**Federal deficit:** An economic condition in which the government spending exceeds collected revenues.

**Federalism:** A cooperative relationship in which the states and the federal government have overlapping powers and responsibilities.

**Federalists:** A political party in the early  years of the nation that supported a powerful national government. Led by Alexander Hamilton, this group was wary of giving the people too much say in government, preferring to keep power in the hands of a select group of leaders or elected officials.

**Formal party organization:** Party leaders who organize and operate party structures on the local, state, and federal level.

**Gerrymander:** The political art of drawing the boundaries of a congressional district to suit the needs of one political party, at the expense of the other. Republican gerrymanders, thus, would yield the maximum number of Congressional seats for its party, and as few as possible for the Democrats.

**Government:** The institution and processes which are responsible for developing rules and decisions for all of society.

**Impeachment:** The procedure by which a president or any federal official may be removed for misconduct in office. The House brings formal charges against the accused and the Senate acts as the jury. A two-thirds vote of the Senate is necessary for conviction.

**Implied powers:** Powers which are logically deduced through court interpretation or presidential or congressional action and stem from delegated powers granted Congress and/or the president.

**Incumbent:** A candidate for office who already holds the office. Thus, a senator or representative running for reelection is an incumbent. The opponent is known as the challenger.

**Independent voter:** A voter whose allegiance to the two major political parties is weak or non-existent.

**Indirect lobbying:** Lobbying directed at public opinion or grass-roots membership of an interest group.

**Interest group:** A group of individuals who share common attitudes and try to influence government for specific policy goals.

**Judicial Branch:** The branch of government that judges legal disputes and interprets the United States Constitution.

**Keynote address:** The first major speech at a national nominating convention which serves to rally the party faithful for the upcoming election.

**Landslide:** An election won by a large margin.

**Law:** A binding rule that is enforced by the government .

**Legislative Branch:** The lawmaking branch of the government. Congress, comprised of the Senate and the House of Representatives , is the legislative branch of the United States.

**Lobbying:** The process of trying to influence the policy decisions and views of an elected or appointed government official.

**Lobbyist:** A representative from an organization who tries to get various pieces of legislation passed or defeated. For example, a lobbyist from an environmental group will try to influence Congress to make laws limiting pollution, and try to block laws that might increase pollution. The names comes from the place where these people used to talk to legislators in the lobby, right outside the chamber.

**Midterm elections:** Congressional elections held midway through a president's term of office. Thus, 1996 is a presidential election year; 1998 will be a midterm election year.

**Negative campaigning:** Campaigning designed to raise questions about a candidate's opponent by focusing on character deficiencies, especially through political commercials.

**Nominee:** A candidate who wins his party's primary; the winner of the party's nomination.

**Ombudsman:** An official who helps citizens resolve their problems with government agencies.

**One-party district:** A congressional district in which one party is clearly dominant—and always wins the elections.

**Oversight function:** The power of Congress to investigate the performance of executive agencies or to hold hearings on major problems facing American society.

**Platform:** A national party's stands on important public issues.

**Party identification:** The degree to which citizens view themselves as loyal to the Republican or Democratic parties.

**Party in government:** The appointed or elected office holders who are members of a political party.

**Party platform:** A written document, approved at the national conventions, which delineates where the party stands on important issues.

**Plank:** One specific issue in a party platform.

**Political action committee:** Committee established by corporations, labor unions, or interest groups which distribute funds to election campaigns.

**Political party:** A group of people who voluntarily band together for the purpose of winning political offices and making public policy.

**Politics:** The allocation of values, or "who gets what, when, and how."

**Precinct:** The smallest voting district. Each precinct has well-defined boundaries, and all the people living within them vote at the same polling place. There are more than 150,000 precincts in the country.

**Presidential primary:** A nominating election in which voters can directly express their preference for a nominee and/or delegates to the national convention.

**Primary:** An election in which the voters of a specific party select a candidate to compete in the general election.

**Public policy:** What a government does or does not do about a social problem.

**Reapportionment:** The changing allotment of congressional districts to states, as dictated by the census taken every ten years. Under reapportionment, states that have gained sub-

stantially in population will pick up one or more districts, while those that have declined in population stand to lose one or more seats.

**Recruit:** A candidate for office who was sought out and and encouraged to run by local and/or party leaders.

**Redistricting:** The redrawing of boundaries of congressional districts. It is done every ten years, after the state knows from reapportionment, how many districts it will have.

**Registration:** The process, intended to prevent voter fraud, by which a voters name, address, place of residence, etc. are verified at a local registrar's office before a person can vote in an election.

**Representative:** A member of the United States House of Representatives. A representative is also called a congressman, congresswoman or congressperson.

**Representative democracy:** A democracy in which the people elect representatives who in turn make public policy and decisions.

**Self-starter:** A candidate for office who decides on his own to run for office, without special encouragement from local leaders. He may get their support later, but he takes the first step by himself.

**Senate:** One of the two houses of Congress. It consists of two persons elected from each state, one hundred members in all.

**Senator:** A member of the Senate. Senators also are congressmen, though in practice, many people restrict the use of "congressman" to representatives.

**Seniority:** The length of service on a given House or Senate committee.

**Single member district system:** The type of electoral system in the United States whereby there can only be one winner per office, the individual who receives a plurality of the votes.

**Social contract:** The concept that the rulers and the ruled have mutual obligations.

**Spoils system:** The policy of filling government positions with party supporters or friends regardless of their qualifications for the job.

**Stump:** The campaign trail. When a candidate goes on the stump, he is traveling around at a hectic pace, meeting and talking to voters. The phrase "taking the stump" means delivering a speech on the trail. It derives from the old method of campaigning on the frontier, when a candidate would get up on a tree stump to talk to the people.

**Suffrage:** The right to vote.

**Two-party district:** A congressional district in which the Republicans and Democrats both have a chance of winning the election. A two-party state exhibits the same sort of party balance.

**Unicameral legislature:** A lawmaking branch of government with only one chamber. Under the Articles of Confederation, Congress was a unicameral legislature. Some state legislatures, such as Nebraska, are unicameral legislatures.

**Veto:** The presidential power which is used to reject a bill passed by Congress.

**Watchdog role:** The role of the media in protecting the public from political excesses by exposing those officials responsible for misconduct.

**Whips:** Party officers in each house of Congress who are the communication links between party members and party leaders. It is the job of the whips to round up support for the party policies, and make sure its members are on hand for important votes.

# INDEX